THE GREAT EXPOSITION OF SECRET MANTRA

VOLUME TWO

The Great Exposition of Secret Mantra

VOLUME ONE
Tantra in Tibet

VOLUME TWO
Deity Yoga

VOLUME THREE
Yoga Tantra

The Great Exposition of Secret Mantra

VOLUME TWO

Deity Yoga

TSONGKHAPA

WITH A COMMENTARY BY THE

Dalai Lama

TRANSLATION, EDITING, AND EXPLANATORY MATERIAL BY

Jeffrey Hopkins

ASSOCIATE EDITORS FOR TSONGKHAPA'S TEXT

Lati Rinpoche and Danma Lochö Rinpoche

CO-EDITOR

Elizabeth Napper

SNOW LION
BOULDER
2017

Snow Lion
An imprint of Shambhala Publications, Inc.
2129 13th Street
Boulder, Colorado 80302
www.shambhala.com

First published as *The Yoga of Tibet* by George Allen & Unwin Ltd., London, England, 1981, and previously published as *Deity Yoga* by arrangement with Unwin & Hyman Ltd., 1987. Some spellings and portions of the translation have been updated.

Revised edition

Snow Lion is distributed worldwide by Penguin Random House, Inc., and its subsidiaries.

Library of Congress Cataloging-in-Publication Data
Names: Bstan-'dzin-rgya-mtsho, Dalai Lama XIV, 1935– author. | Tsong-kha-pa Blo-bzang-grags-pa, 1357–1419, author. | Hopkins, Jeffrey, translator, editor.
Title: The Great Exposition of Secret Mantra / The Dalai Laṃa, Tsongkhapa; translated and edited by Jeffrey Hopkins.
Description: Boulder, Colorado: Snow Lion, 2016–2017. | Includes bibliographical references and index. Contents: volume 1. Tantra in Tibet — volume 2. Deity Yoga — volume 3. Yoga Tantra. | Includes translations from Tibetan.
Identifiers: LCCN 2016000757| ISBN 9781611803594 (v. 1) | ISBN 9781611803587 (v. 2) | ISBN 9781611803600 (v. 3)
Subjects: LCSH: Tantric Buddhism. | Buddhist mantras. | BISAC: RELIGION / Buddhism / Tibetan. | RELIGION / Buddhism / Rituals & Practice.
Classification: LCC BQ7935.B774 G74 2016 | DDC 294.3/444—dc23
LC record available at https://lccn.loc.gov/2016000757

The authorized representative in the EU for product safety and compliance is eucomply OÜ, Pärnu mnt 139b-14, 11317 Tallinn, Estonia, hello@eucompliancepartner.com.

157594684

Contents

Preface

Homage to Vajradhara.

This book is a continuation of *Tantra in Tibet.* Centered on the second and third parts of Tsongkhapa's *The Great Exposition of Secret Mantra,* it presents the profound process of meditation in Action and Performance Tantra. Tsongkhapa lays out the procedure of practice in Action Tantra, mainly combining the expositions in two tantras—the *Susiddhi Tantra*[1] and the *Concentration Continuation Tantra*[2]—and their respective expositions by Varabodhi[3] and Buddhaguhya.[4] The *Susiddhi Tantra* and Varabodhi's formulation of it into a practice rite called a Means of Achievement,[5] also detail the preliminary rites, the pledges, and so forth. Almost all of Tsongkhapa's presentation can be found in these four texts; his creative innovation is to interweave them into a complete system of practice of this class of tantra.

Tsongkhapa's brief exposition of Performance Tantra, which is drawn only from the *Vairochanābhisambodhi Tantra* and Buddhaguhya's two commentaries on it,[6] present the yoga with signs, which has both external and internal versions of the four-branched repetition, and then the yoga without signs. The brevity is likely due to the length and complexity of the exposition of Action Tantra, whose meditation has many similarities. These explanations of the extraordinary features of the Action Tantra path and of an outline of Performance Tantra system illustrate the immense psychological complexity of the tantric path and also lay the groundwork for those who wish to cultivate these tantras upon receiving initiation from a qualified lama.

Part I is an introduction by His Holiness the Dalai Lama, whose commentary on Tsongkhapa's text I received in 1974 and subsequently translated and edited. His lucid exposition of the complex meditative rites of deity yoga—the distinctly tantric process in which a yogi cultivates imaginative appearance in a Buddha's divine body—affords an accessibility to Part II, Tsongkhapa's text itself. Part III is a supplement primarily on the structure of the path in Action Tantra. In addition to the first two parts of this book, it is drawn from:

- Butön's *Extensive General Presentation of the Tantra Sets*
- Khaydrub Geleg Palsang's *Extensive Explanation of the Format of the General Tantra Sets*
- Duldzin Dragpa Gyaltshan's *Presentation of the General Rites of Action and Performance Tantra and Their Application to the Three Lineages, Set Down by Duldzin According to the Foremost [Tsongkhapa's] Practice*
- Bodong Choglay Namgyal's *General Presentation of Action Tantra*
- Paṇchen Sönam Dragpa's *General Presentation of the Tantra Sets: Captivating the Minds of the Fortunate*
- Yeshay Gyaltshan's *Illumination of the Meaning of Action Tantra*
- Ngagwang Paldan's *Presentation of the Grounds and Paths of Mantra*
- the oral teachings of Lati Jangchub Tshultrim Rinpoche, philosophy master and tantric lama who served as abbot of the Shartse College of Gandan Monastery in Mundgod, Karnataka State, India
- the oral teachings of Danma Lochö Rinpoche, philosophy master and tantric lama who served as abbot of the Tibetan Monastery at Kulu and later as the abbot of Namgyal Monastery in Dharmsala, India

Based on Tsongkhapa's remark at end of the chapter on Action Tantra:

> If one propounds to know the meaning of Action and
> Performance Tantras

> By knowing a portion of their meditations and repetitions
> Such as rites of fasting, bathing, and so forth, it is a source of laughter.
> Therefore, cherish arrangement of the tantra meanings into paths.

it is easily seen that Tsongkhapa's chief aim is go beyond the often reduction of Action Tantra to mere rituals for fasting, bathing, and the like and present the entire scope of the general Action Tantra meditation beginning with the preparatory rituals and extending through the elaborate and very rich meditative practices that culminate with the achievement of yogic feats and the progress along the spiritual path. Since he does this with careful citation of sources of tantras and Indian commentaries, I have sought in this edition of the book to put more focus on the practical implementation of his ingenious amalgamation of sources by putting these practical instructions in a *Means of Achievement* (*sgrub thabs, sādhana*). It is found after an introduction about the structure of the path in the second chapter of the Supplement.[7]

I orally retranslated Tsongkhapa's text into Tibetan for the late Lati Jangchub Tshultrim Rinpoche, who knew almost no English, for the sake of correction and verification, and I received a complete commentary of Tsongkhapa's text from the late Danma Lochö Rinpoche. Dr. Elizabeth Napper, then a doctoral candidate in Buddhist Studies at the University of Virginia, provided crucial help in editing the entire manuscript. A guide to Tsongkhapa's text, following his own mode of division of the contents, is given in tabular form in an appendix.

The chapter divisions and their titles in the Dalai Lama's commentary and in Tsongkhapa's text were added to facilitate understanding. The transliteration scheme for Sanskrit names and titles is aimed at easy pronunciation, using *sh, ṣh,* and *ch* rather than *ś*, *ṣ*, and *c*. With the first occurrence of each Indian title, the Sanskrit is given, if available. Often Tsongkhapa refers only to the title or the author of a work, whereas both are given in translation to obviate the need for checking back and forth. The full Sanskrit and Tibetan titles are to be found in the bibliography, which is arranged alphabetically according to the authors of other works. The Tibetan originals of the key terms are given in a glossary at the end. Photographs of the thirty-eight seals (hand configurations, *mudrā*) are given throughout Tsongkhapa's text; the formation of several of these is speculative since a full-fledged transmission of their practice has not been found among the refugee lamas in India.

Jeffrey Hopkins
President and Founder, UMA Institute for Tibetan Studies
Emeritus Professor of Tibetan Studies
University of Virginia

Seals or Hand-Configurations (*Mudrā*)

The names of the seals are taken either from Tsongkhapa's text or from Varabodhi's *Clear Realization of Susiddhi,* except for those that are bracketed, these being inferred from the context. All but numbers 29 and 37 appear in Varabodhi's text, Tsongkhapa's source. Several are similar to those given for the *Susiddhi Tantra* in the Chinese cannon (*Taishō daizōkyō, Zuzō* 8, [3164, 3165]: 1–58).

I

Heart of Mantra

The Dalai Lama

TRANSLATED AND EDITED BY

Jeffrey Hopkins

CO-EDITED BY

Elizabeth Napper

Techniques for Improvement

All of us have attained a human life; we are, in a sense, incomparable among the various types of sentient beings as we are able to think about many topics with a subtler mind and are endowed with vaster capabilities. Dogs, birds, and so forth do communicate, but only humans can settle and ascertain deep topics on the basis of words; it is obvious that there are no other sentient beings capable of as many thoughts and techniques. Nowadays, humans are engaging in many activities that were not even objects of thought a century or two ago. The metaphors of the poets of the past, such as "the wonderful house of the moon," are becoming actualities.

Still, it is definite that we must die and prior to death must all suffer inadequacies, whether in terms of resources or our own bodies. Our sources of happiness and welfare are essentially our body, companions, and the use of resources—gaining happiness in dependence on good food, clothing, companions, and conversation. These are said to be sources of happiness and comfort, but are in fact sources of suffering.

After our conception, a body that is a basis of suffering is formed. When we gather relatives, friends, and companions, we form the basis for the suffering of losing them. We make effort over our whole lifetime, thinking "May I be happy and comfortable," hoping for the arising of happiness and comfort, and temporarily we achieve a little superficial pleasure. However, in terms of their own inner nature all these means serve as bases of suffering. In essence, we must all spend our lives suffering either physically or mentally. The mass of people suffer in terms of food, shelter, and clothing and even those who have these suffer mentally.

In general, the countries of the East have had less material progress and thus have great suffering from poverty. In the West, though poverty is not severe except in certain areas, there is the suffering of worry and not knowing satisfaction. In both East and West, many persons spend their lives in jealousy and competition; some think only of money, and when they meet with conditions unfavorable to their wish develop a dislike or enmity for these unfavorable circumstances from the very orb of their heart. Within and between countries people are disturbed, not trusting and believing each other, having to spend their lives in continual lies and deceit. Since the most we can live is a hundred years, what point is there in spending our lives in jealousy, deceit, and competition?

People have made great effort right up to this century, thinking to become free from suffering, but we cannot point to even one person in the world, no matter how rich he or she is, who has no worry—except for those who have the inner happiness of renouncing the material way of life. Without internal renunciation it is difficult to achieve happiness and comfort.

Seeing that the people of the world could not achieve happiness solely in terms of food and clothing, many teachers including Buddha—whether they were capable or not of presenting the final mode of existence of phenomena—set forth teachings for the achievement of happiness and comfort in terms of the mind, inner happiness. Among these the best is the doctrine of dependent-arising of Buddha, the Monarch of Sages, who taught it to others exactly as he knew it, in accordance with their dispositions, interests, and beliefs. Born in the Shākya clan over 2,500 years ago in India, the country of Superiors, he established limitless sentient beings in the path of liberation through the sport of his speech. Among the many religious systems of the world the doctrine that he taught is without parallel.

Although it may seem, when we superficially look at it, that happiness and comfort can be achieved in dependence on external factors, in fact if one's mind is tamed, there is happiness and comfort even as a householder. If one's mind is not tamed, there is no happiness and comfort even as a monk or a scholar learned in doctrine.

The essence of the 84,000 bundles of doctrine is just to tame this wild mind, not letting it go under the influence of the afflictions—desire, hatred, and ignorance. When the mind is no longer polluted by afflictions or their latent predispositions, then its taming is complete. The aged should engage in a method suited for old age; the young, in one suited for youth; the learned, in a method suited for the learned, and those not so learned, in one suited to their abilities.

Religion does not mean just precepts, a temple, monastery, or other external signs, for these as well as hearing and thinking are subsidiary factors in taming the mind. When the mind becomes the practices, one is a practitioner of religion, and when the mind does not become the practices, one is not.

Do we not see among our acquaintances that their happiness is proportionate to the extent to which they have tamed their minds? Also, considering ourselves, is it not the case that as much as we tame our minds, so much do we have happiness and comfort? We have happiness of mind and freedom from anxiety to just the degree that our minds are tamed. To that same degree are unsalutary deeds of body and speech lessened; as much as they are lessened, so much is lessened the accumulation of bad karma. As much as that diminishes, so much does hope of ending cyclic existence arise.

At this time, when we have a physical life-support of a human such that we are capable of many techniques and thoughts, it is very important to engage in religious practice. It is our own choice to have no belief, faith, interest, or wish to practice. Buddha did not forcibly say, "You must practice." The great commentators will not bring guns and swords. We must ascertain the need for religion with reasoning. Once we want happiness and do not want suffering, we should engage in the means to achieve happiness and eliminate suffering. Practice is based on reasoning, not force; it is up to oneself.

Indeed, if we think about it, happiness of mind comes with religious practice. No matter how much goes wrong, one reflects that this is the nature of cyclic existence, that these are irreversible effects of actions accumulated in the past, that even if the

Supramundane Buddha were here himself, he could not stop the unfolding of these effects. One reflects on the cause and effect of actions and the nature of cyclic existence, and if capable of more thought, one engages in meditation, giving away whatever happiness one has and assuming the sufferings of other sentient beings, having thought about the faults of cherishing oneself and the advantages of cherishing others. It is confirmed by our experience that as much as one can engage in such thoughts, so much is there peace of mind; therefore, methods for taming the mind are extremely valuable.

The time for engaging in these techniques is now. Some feel, "I did not succeed in this lifetime; I will ask a lama for help in my future life." To think that we will practice in the future is only a hope. It is foolish to feel that the next life will be as suitable as this. No matter how bad our condition is now, since we have a human brain, we can think; since we have a mouth, we can recite mantra. No matter how old one may be, there is time for practice. However, when we die and are reborn, we are unable even to recite *"oṃ maṇi padme hūṃ."* Thus, it is important to make all effort possible at this time when we have obtained the precious physical life-support of a human.

Religious activities involve mixing the mind with the practices—causing the mind to become the practices. Among these the lowest is to turn away from the marvels of this lifetime and seek to provide for the next lifetime. One should also turn away from the marvels of future lifetimes and seek to become liberated from cyclic existence entirely, thinking from the depths of the heart. "How nice it would be if I did not have to take rebirth by the power of contaminated actions and afflictive emotions!" Then one identifies ignorance as the root of cyclic existence and seeks by overcoming ignorance to attain a state of liberation. This is a middling mode of the mind's becoming religious practice; it is very good—the internal motivation is steady and decided.

Then, not just thinking of oneself, one realizes that all sentient beings, self and others, equally want happiness and do not want suffering. Oneself is just one; others are vast as space and, therefore, should be cherished more than oneself. Based on this, one generates a mind wishing to free all sentient beings from suffering and the causes of suffering and, motivated by that aspiration, seeks from the depths of the heart to attain Buddhahood for the sake of all sentient beings. This is the highest mode of the mind's becoming religious practice.

At the least, one must have turned away from this lifetime; there is no way without reversing attachment to this life. Death is definite, but the time of death indefinite. We make many plans for the future, but there is no certainty that we can carry them out. Even monks and nuns plan this and that, to go here or there, to meet acquaintances, and so forth; yet there is no certainty that before carrying out these plans we will not see the time of death.

Since the choice is in our own hands, we should make sure, using our past experience as an example, that the months ahead are not wasted. There is no way to return the years that have already passed. We cannot say, "I have erred," and exchange those years. Wasted time is gone. If we ourselves do not take care, then, even if those at our side attempt to force us, they cannot help at all.

We may not wish to engage in religious practice or we may wish to but because of our own fault postpone it, but we are not bereft of a religion to practice. Within Buddhism, the most profound is the Great Vehicle; within the Great Vehicle the most profound is Secret Mantra; and common to all four tantras is deity yoga, which contains within it the important essentials of the entire path. Transmitted from Vajradhara, deity yoga was formulated in India on the basis of much profound thought. Being the simultaneous unification of method and wisdom in one consciousness—the appearance of oneself as a deity, such as Vairochana, coupled with realization of emptiness—it is the essence of tantra. Merely ascertaining the significance of deity yoga aids the mental continuum, not to speak of the immeasurable improvement that occurs through incorporating it into daily practice.

Purpose of Deity Yoga

In all four tantras—Action, Performance, Yoga, and Highest Yoga—it is established that a practitioner must view his or her body as a divine one. However, some persons are frightened by viewing their body this way. Discriminating their own body as unclean—composed of lumps of flesh, blood, and bone—and themselves as possessing all types of fetters, they feel that it would not be suitable to meditate on themselves as deities. For the same reason they also consider that it would not be right for an actual deity—meditated in front of them—to dissolve into and become undifferentiable in entity from themselves. Unable to fit the higher paths into their minds, they are outside the sphere of such practice.

The *Wisdom Vajra Compendium* (*jñānavajrasamuccaya*), a Highest Yoga Tantra, says that such trainees abide in Action Tantra. Taken literally, it would seem to be saying that such persons—given that they have the other qualifications of a tantrist—would practice Action Tantra. Thus it seems that according to this text, in Action Tantra there would be no generation of oneself as a deity or consideration of the pledge-being [oneself imagined as a deity] and the wisdom-being [the actual deity] as one undifferentiable entity.

Indeed, many texts of the Action class do not clearly explain meditation on oneself as a deity; rather, they describe a process of imagining a deity in front of oneself and receiving a feat, or capacity for a special activity, from that deity. However, Buddhaguhya and Varabodhi, both great scholars of Action Tantra, point out that it is not that self-generation is not taught in Action Tantra. For example, the *Concentration Continuation Tantra* and other Action Tantras describe repetition of mantra after (1) generating oneself as a deity, (2) generating a deity in front of oneself, (3) imagining a moon at the heart of the deity in front, and (4) imagining the letters of the mantra to be repeated around the edge of that moon. These are the four branches—self-base, other-base, mind (the wisdom realizing emptiness appearing as a moon), and sounds, specifically the letters of the mantra. Thus, it is clear that this Action Tantra explicitly teaches self-generation, imagination of oneself as a deity.

When through the force of continued practice mantrikas [tantric practitioners] naturally have the pride of being a deity, they come to possess the capacity to achieve quickly feats of secret mantra. They meditate until their own body appears as a divine one as if in direct perception, with adornments and so forth swaying. They clearly see the deity and hear its exalted speech, whereby they are blessed into magnificence, resulting in a longer lifespan, unusual increase in wisdom, and so forth, all of which promote progress in the path.

Since Action Tantras prescribe such meditation necessarily involving self-generation, it is clear that there is deity meditation in Action Tantra. Thus, the *Wisdom Vajra Compendium* is referring not to all Action Tantra trainees but to those unable to do deity yoga.

The word "yoga" means in general to join one's mind to an actual fact, but here it can also refer to a joining or nonduality of the profound—realization of emptiness—and the manifest—appearance as a deity. In order to achieve the feats of pacification, increase, and so forth, it is absolutely necessary to have emptiness yoga and deity yoga. Hence it is clear that there is deity meditation in Action Tantra.

There is no doubt about deity yoga in Performance Tantra since the *Vairochanābhisambodhi Tantra* (*vairocanābhisaṃbodhi*) and *Vajrapāṇi Initiation Tantra* (*vajrapāṇyabhiṣeka*) clearly describe it. Moreover, that both Action and Performance Tantras have such is confirmed by statements in Highest Yoga Tantra explaining that in Action and Performance Tantras the desires involved in the god's and goddess's respectively gazing and smiling at each other are used in the path. Since these refer to meditated deities, there is no way for these tantras not to have deity yoga. Within clarification of oneself as a deity, the attributes of the desire realm are used in the path; there is no way to perform this practice within conceiving oneself to be ordinary.

However, this is not merely a case of taking the thought of Highest Yoga Tantra and superimposing it on the lower tantras. For the *Vajroṣhṇīṣha Tantra* (*vajroṣṇīṣa*), an Action Tantra, clearly describes deity yoga; its continuation or supplement, called the *Concentration Continuation Tantra,* refers to a description of deity yoga when it says, "Flow to the bases, mind, and sound," alluding to the four branches mentioned above. A similar description is also found in the *Vairochanābhisambodhi,* a Performance Tantra, where the term "bases" is clearly explained as the bases for the placement of the mantra letters—the deity whom oneself is imagined to be and the deity generated in front.

Another source is the *Extensive Tantra of Vajravidāraṇā* (*vajravidāraṇāvaipūlya* [?]), where meditation on the six deities involved in self-generation is explained. These show that Action Tantra in its own right has meditation on oneself as a deity—that it is not just brought over from descriptions in Highest Yoga Tantra. Thus, the *main* trainees of Action Tantra must cultivate self-generation; however, because those who cannot do so but are nevertheless trainees of Action Tantra outnumber them, the majority of Action Tantras do not clearly present deity yoga.

The most important and difficult of the Mantra disciplines is to meditate at all times on one's body as a divine body and to view whatever appears as a deity's sport. Whether one is going about, lying down, or staying still, one must be able to maintain the continuous pride of being a deity. Similarly, whatever forms are seen, sounds heard, odors smelled, tastes tasted, or tangible objects touched must be viewed as manifestations of the wisdom realizing emptiness. When this occurs in a nonartificial way, one possesses the ethics of a Mantra Bodhisattva. One must remain free from conceptions of ordinariness and of inherent existence.

The clear appearance of the divine body is a subsidiary branch of a process whose main factor is the pride of being the deity; however, in order for divine pride to become firm there must be clear appearance as that deity, whereupon the pride of being that deity is naturally generated. The process is this: For one's mind ordinary appearances must be stopped, and with the disappearance of the ordinary body and mind, there is no longer a sense of an ordinary I. In place of that impure body and mind, the mind that earlier realized emptiness is used as the basis of emanation, and itself manifests as a divine form with a face, arms, and so forth. When the pure mental and physical aggregates of a deity appear clearly to the mind, the place of the designation I has become these pure appearances of mind and body. At that point one develops divine pride, a sense of an I that is designated in dependence upon the divine body and mind that are appearing to one's mind. Since this pride is merely a sense of an imputedly existent I, it is capable of acting as an antidote to the conception of self—the conception of the inherent existence of persons and other phenomena.

Once the main practitioners of Action Tantra must have this type of self-generation, there is no reason why they could not engage in the practice of causing an actual deity meditated in front of them to dissolve into themselves. Thus, Action Tantra has both self-generation and entry of a wisdom-being.

With respect to deity yoga the *Vajrapāṇi Initiation Tantra* [a Performance Tantra] says (see p. 59) "Mind itself is speech; speech itself is also divine form." This is like the teaching of the union of illusory body and clear light in the *Guhyasamāja Tantra* [a Highest Yoga Tantra], which says, "View body as mind; view mind as body; view speech as mind; view mind as speech." Though the *Vajrapāṇi Initiation,* being a Performance Tantra, cannot explicitly set forth such a union, which is found only in Highest Yoga Tantra, it can be said that what it is getting at is the union of illusory body and clear light. For instance, Chandrakīrti in his *Brilliant Lamp* (*pradīpoddyotana*) quotes the *Vairochanābhisambodhi,* a Performance Tantra (see p. 186), within the context of presenting the divine bodies of the stages of generation and completion. Since in the Yoga Tantras and below the topics of the stage of completion in Highest Yoga Tantra are not explained, there is no way that the *Vairochanābhisambodhi* can explicitly indicate such. However, it can be said that the doctrine of the bodies of the two stages is hidden in the *Vairochanābhisambodhi,* not in the sense of being taught nonmanifestly but in the sense of being hidden without in the least being taught. Since from between the two types of hidden meanings it is this latter, the words of the *Vairochanābhisambodhi* do not either explicitly or implicitly indicate these topics, but it still can be said that they are getting at the bodies of the two stages.

In the same way, here it is not suitable to say that the *Vajrapāṇi Initiation* indicates, either explicitly or implicitly, the union of illusory body and clear light, but it can be said that what it is getting at is such a union. In their coarse form the body, speech, and mind that we have had since beginningless cyclic existence are different entities, but in terms of the very subtle clear light and the very subtle wind that is its mount, these are not different entities. Since such subtle minds and winds are topics of Highest Yoga Tantra, here in Performance Tantra this passage is teaching on the literal level that if one considers one's own body, speech, and mind to be a deity's, they will be the undifferentiable three vajras of a deity's exalted body, speech, and mind—"undifferentiable" in the sense of having the same taste of the emptiness of inherent existence.

In essence, when yogis view all physical movement, all verbal expression, and all thoughts and realizations as the seals, mantras, and wisdom of a deity, then they accumulate vast merit, establishing the capacity to manifest at Buddhahood in numerous Form Bodies in order to help sentient beings.

Initiations and Vows

For the achievement of Mantra it is appropriate to use the systems of Action and Performance Tantra, and not pretend that one can achieve something one cannot. For most people the attempt to practice Highest Yoga Tantra is a case of pretending such. Action and Performance Tantra, on the other hand, are very practical for many people.

In these tantras the body of the path for achieving the supreme feat of Buddhahood and the common feats of activities of pacification, increase, and ferocity is included within ten causal branches (see pp. 61–62). Of these the four-branched repetition and the concentrations of abiding in fire and in sound are called yoga with signs. This is because although they involve meditation on emptiness and on a deity, they are yogas in which the mind realizing emptiness itself does not manifest as a deity. The meditator is mainly concerned here with achieving clarity of appearance of a divine body, mantra letters, and so forth, and thus cannot *mainly* meditate on emptiness. In contradistinction to this, the concentration bestowing liberation at the end of sound is called yoga without signs because in it deity yoga is actually conjoined with meditation on emptiness. In Action and Performance as well as in Yoga Tantra, the body of the path is divided into these two yogas, with and without signs, whereas in Highest Yoga the path is divided into the stages of generation and completion.

In order to make trainees suitable vessels for cultivating these paths initiation is conferred. In Action Tantra it is permissible to confer the five knowledge initiations—water, crown, vajra, bell, and name initiations. However, in general it is said that Action Tantra has the water and crown initiations as well as subsequent rites granting permission to meditate on a specific deity whereas Performance Tantra has all five initiations. The tantric vows are taken only in Yoga and Highest Yoga Tantra since the vajra master initiation occurs only in them.

The initiation of a particular deity is granted in accordance with one's lineage. In Action and Performance there are two basic lineages, mundane and supramundane. Within the latter there are three—One-Gone-Thus, lotus, and vajra in order of superiority. When initiation is attained in a higher lineage, one is allowed to listen to and explain to others teachings of the other lineages as well as to engage in their meditations and approximations, but to confer initiation it is necessary to receive the initiation of that particular deity and do the necessary preliminary rites. Although the *Kālachakra Tantra* (*kālacakra*) [a Highest Yoga text] says that if the Kālachakra initiation is attained, one can act as a vajra master for all tantras, according to the explanation by Kelsang Gyatsho (*bskal bzang rgya mtsho,* the Seventh Dalai Lama) this is an expression of the greatness of the *Kālachakra Tantra* and is not to be taken literally. The specific initiations of the other deities are needed in order for oneself, as a vajra master, to grant initiation to others.

Since Action and Performance Tantras do not have the vajra master initiation, the vows to be maintained more dearly than one's own life are the Bodhisattva vows, not the tantric. These are the eighteen root vows as well as the maintenance of the aspirational mind of enlightenment. In addition, there are many tantric pledges to be kept.

Though many of these pledges are concerned with maintaining cleanliness, there are teachings in Action Tantra not to conceive of dirtiness and cleanliness; hence, Ratnākarashānti (see p. 74) says that it is suitable for practitioners even of Highest Yoga Tantra to observe the pledges of the lower tantras. Nevertheless, external *activities* of cleanliness are stressed in Action Tantras, which is why they are called by that name. There is a story of a yogi trying to achieve an Action Tantra deity who, though he practiced a long time, could not generate even an auspicious dream. He went to see his lama, who inquired how he was doing. Upon investigation the lama found that there was nothing wrong with the way the yogi was performing the rite except that he had not bathed. The lama advised him to do so, and thereafter signs of success emerged.

Although bathing or not makes no difference to the deity, there is a difference in how the deity appears to trainees. For instance, although Mañjushrī is one, for those who are practicing in accordance with the procedure of Action Tantra there comes to be a Mañjushrī associated with that tantra set, whereas for someone who is practicing in the manner of Highest Yoga Tantra there is another one associated with Highest Yoga. A person whose meditative stabilization and so forth are improved through maintaining cleanliness and so forth should use an Action Tantra rite whereas someone of very sharp faculties can achieve a deity faster with a Highest Yoga rite. The difference in deities is established in relation to the individual trainees.

With respect to the bathing rite, since the general dictum is to bathe until one becomes free of grime, our usual mode of bathing with soap and water and the wearing of clean clothes—not necessarily new—are sufficient. Beyond that, one's food must be clean; meat cannot be eaten, and smelly foods such as garlic and onion are not allowed.

Those who are seriously engaged in meditation also sometimes have to take precautions against contamination that can occur when they eat food given by another. Some meditators here and in Tibet have said that ill effects can be immediate and that the mind is much clearer when living from what one oneself can acquire, even if it is not of good quality, without using any offerings from others. It has been said that even eating a bowl of yogurt given by another can adversely affect the mind.

Divine Approximation

Through the practice of tantra one is seeking to achieve the supreme feat of Buddhahood in order to become a source of help and happiness for all beings. Along the way common feats are also sought for the sake of enhancing the accumulation of merit necessary for attaining Buddhahood. For both supreme and common feats deity yoga is necessary, the initial process being called "approximation" because through imagining the deity one is approaching closer to it. Without preliminary approximation the feats of lengthening the lifespan, becoming youthful, gaining the five clairvoyances, and so forth cannot be achieved. It is to achieve such feats that prior approximation is performed, called "prior" because it necessarily precedes actualizing a specific feat and using it for the welfare of others.

With regard to how to do prior approximation there are concentrations with repetition and concentrations not relying on repetition. Concerning the concentrations with repetition, one first invites a deity in front as a field, or basis, for the accumulation of merit through making offerings, praises, and so forth; then one meditates on oneself as a deity. These are called generation in front and self-generation.

For the first, if you have a painting or statue of a deity, you can use that as a basis of imagination by placing it in front of you. Meditate on its emptiness and then from within that emptiness imagine the many features of the place to which the deity will be invited—the ground, mountain, and lotus seat on which is an inestimable mansion of light. This is called generation of the residence—the abode of the deity.

Then, invite the deity—the resident—ask him or her to sit, display seals (hand configurations), and make offerings and praises.

Actually, since Form Bodies appear instantaneously to a person of faith from within the sphere of the Truth Body of great bliss, there is no need to invite a deity to come here from some specific place. However, since we are bound by our conceptions of true existence, it is helpful to imagine inviting the likes of a Complete Enjoyment Body from a pure land to the place where one is meditating and thereupon to make offerings in accordance with ordinary customs. The offerings prescribed are distinctly Indian, being geared to receiving a guest in a hot country—cool water for the feet, a cool drink, a garland for the head, fragrant perfume for the feet, sprinkling of water, and so forth. These are followed by disclosure, refuge, admiration of one's own and others' virtues, entreaty, supplication, and prayer-wishes. The final step is cultivation of the four immeasurables—love, compassion, joy, and equanimity—called immeasurable because one is observing an immeasurable number of sentient beings and accumulating an immeasurable amount of merit through the practice.

Then, you are ready to do self-generation. Set your body in the cross-legged posture of Vairochana, for when the body is straightened, the channels in which the winds (energies) course will be straightened, thereby balancing the mind. Withdraw your sense consciousnesses from observing their respective objects—visible forms, sounds, odors, tastes, and tangible objects—and set your mind inside. Raise the back of your head and bend it slightly down like a swan's; breathe naturally and gently without either panting or grasping. Open your eyes a little since, although there seems to be an immediate benefit in lesser disturbance from closing them, in time it harms by causing unclarity. Similarly, if the eyes are left wide open, they will smart later on. Aim them at the point of the nose, or if that is uncomfortable, farther away. Generally, one leaves the teeth as usual, but here (p. 100) Buddhaguhya says to "press teeth with teeth," most likely meaning to leave them touching. Put the tongue to the roof of the mouth for the sake of reducing the flow of saliva and yet keeping the mouth moist.

Thereupon, the altruistic mind of enlightenment is to be cultivated. This good mind of cherishing others rather than oneself should be generated if you have not yet done so and should be enhanced if you have. When you are able to have such a good mind continuously and steadily, Buddhahood is easily attained, and while you are still in cyclic existence, happiness is brought to yourself and others.

Then, you may begin the process of self-generation by way of the six deities: ultimate, sound, letter, form, seal, and sign deities.

Ultimate Deity

Only non-Buddhists assert that there is a self, or I, that is a separate entity from mind and body. If there were such a separate entity, it would have to be apprehensible totally separate from mind and body, but it is not. Therefore, the I is designated only in dependence on the mental and physical aggregates.

Here in the first of the six deities you are to realize the suchness, or final nature, of the imputedly existent I. Tsongkhapa makes a similar presentation in his *The Essence of Eloquence:* first he sets forth many assertions on how various systems posit the I—such as asserting consciousness as I, the continuum of the mental and physical aggregates as I, and the continuum of consciousness as I. Then he says that in our own Middle Way Consequentialist system there is nothing among the five mental and physical aggregates—forms, feelings, discriminations, compositional factors, or consciousnesses—which can be put as I, and thus the I is only imputed in dependence on the aggregates. He adds that when the Middle Way view of emptiness is found in relation to such an imputedly existent person rather than the person in general, there is a great difference. In this Action Tantra, the *Concentration Continuation,* one is directed to realize the suchness, or emptiness, of such an imputedly existent I.

The self that is merely imputed in dependence upon mind and body has two natures, conventional and ultimate; its final nature is the ultimate one—the suchness of self, which is free from all signs of dualistic proliferations. A mind that knows one's own nature to be beyond the limits of dualistic proliferations in accordance with its actual mode of abiding ascertains suchness. Emptiness is called suchness because the nature of phenomena is exhausted as just such, as nothing else. The contemplation of suchness as equally the nature of yourself and the deity being meditated is called the ultimate deity.

Just as one's own nature, or mode of being, is ultimately free from all proliferations of the conception of inherent existence and is essentially at peace since the self is only nominally existent, so is the status of the deity being meditated. Though the bases of this emptiness of inherent existence, oneself and the deity, are different, their mode of abiding—their mere absence of inherent existence, their suchness—are the same and should be viewed as undifferentiable like a mixture of water and milk. All phenomena are the same taste in their final nature, emptiness.

Sound Deity

Stay within meditative equipoise on suchness as long as you can and then within the sphere of emptiness use this mind realizing emptiness as the basis of emanation and manifest a flat clear white moon disc at the place where, in the later steps, you will manifest as a deity. Above the moon disc the sounds of the mantra of the deity, as whom you the meditator will later appear, reverberate in space.

Letter Deity

First one meditated on emptiness; then, one imagined that the wisdom mind manifested as a moon disc and as the sounds of the mantra. After setting in equipoise for a little time while contemplating these, the sounds of the mantra appear in the form of letters set in order around the edge of the moon. This is the letter deity, a manifestation of the pristine wisdom realizing emptiness.

Imagine that from the moon and the mantra letters light rays are emitted, from the points of which emerge forms of the deity to be meditated. These deities emanate clouds of offerings to the

Buddhas, Bodhisattvas, and so forth, as well as clouds with a rain of nectar. It falls on the beings in cyclic existence and purifies them, giving a good body to those who need it, coolness to those suffering from heat, the warmth of the sun to those suffering from cold, food and drink to the hungry and thirsty—emanating to each just what he or she needs, affording beings the basis for practicing the path as well as teachers to instruct them in the essential paths of the four truths, the two truths, and so forth. They are caused to ascend the paths and attain the final happiness of Buddhahood.

Form Deity

Then, the emanated deities and the beams of light are withdrawn back into the moon and mantra letters that turn into the form of the deity being meditated. The deity has now been generated.

The meditator is not separate from the deity, but appears *as* the deity. Earlier all appearances were withdrawn and emptiness contemplated; now the only appearances are of pure mind and body. The impure are not considered to be nonexistent, but their appearance has been purposely withdrawn. The basis giving rise to the thought "I" is now just this pure mind and body.

Seal Deity

The next step is to bless into magnificence various important places in your divine body through touching them with hand configurations, called seals.

Sign Deity

At this point you can invite the wisdom-being [the actual being] who dissolves into the pledge-being [yourself imagined as the deity]. This completion of deity generation, involving a combination of clear appearance and the pride of being that deity, is called the sign deity.

Meditation on, or cultivation of, the six deities is like faith and love meditation in that the mind is being generated into the entity of the object meditated. When faith or love are meditated, those two are not the object observed but the entity into which the consciousness is being generated. Meditation on impermanence or emptiness, on the other hand, means to take these as the object and meditate on them. Thus, there are two types of meditation—*of* a subjective aspect and *on* an objective aspect. Meditation on the six deities is the former, for first one generates wisdom knowing the sameness in suchness of oneself and the deity—the ultimate—and then causes it to appear as the sounds, letters, and finally the form of the deity.

Within this yoga there are two modes of meditatively cultivating the six deities—by way of concentration and by way of meditative stabilization. In the first, one contemplates the six deities in series and then, inspecting the color of the deity, the hand symbol, and so forth, corrects their appearance—adjusting clarity and so forth. In the mode of meditative stabilization, however, one observes a single object, the general body or the deity's face, for instance, and without any adjustment remains one-pointedly on that object.

First, in cultivation by way of concentration one visualizes the divine form in stages by way of the six deities, making adjustments for clarity and so forth. Then, engaging in cultivation by way of meditative stabilization one remains in one-pointed meditation, stopping breath and distraction for the sake of keeping the mind from coming under the influence of scattering and excitement. This stopping of breath and distraction is called "stopping vitality and exertion" (*prāṇāyāma*); one binds "vitality," that is to say, wind—the breath that is inhaled and exhaled through the nose as well as the winds that course through the hair-pores of the head and body, the male or female organs, eyes, and so forth—and stops "exertion," which here means "mindfulness" not in the usual sense of keeping a virtuous object in mind but in the sense of taking an object other than that of the meditation to mind—in other words, distraction.

Since wind acts as the basis, or mount, for consciousness, the scattering of the mind is caused by wind; hence, if the winds are restrained, the mind's scattering is stopped. We can confirm with our own experience that wind serves as the mount for consciousness by the fact that when the mind becomes somewhat one-pointed, the movement of the breath in the nostrils lessens. Even with a little stability of mind, the breath becomes more relaxed and less obvious.

Though meditation by way of concentration—in which the divine body is contemplated in series—involves preventing distraction to other objects, the mind is not kept one-pointedly on a single object. Rather, one is reviewing in stages the face, arms, and so forth of the divine body, and thus a series of minds is being generated. However, in meditation by way of meditative stabilization, one stops the movement of the mind and holds it on one object. Thus, the stopping of "vitality and exertion," or breath and distraction, is explained at the point of meditative stabilization and not for the earlier serial meditation by way of concentration.

Here in Action Tantra the stopping of vitality and exertion is done for the sake of keeping the mind from being distracted to other objects, whereas in Highest Yoga Tantra another practice of holding the winds is done to stop the movement of the winds in the right and left channels and cause them to enter the central channel. There it is not just for the sake of stopping distraction.

To review the process: you first gain a clear appearance of yourself as a deity whereupon arises the "pride," which is a sense of being that I designated in dependence on the clearly appearing divine body. Then, within that clear appearance and pride you one-pointedly observe the mental appearance of the general divine body or a particular part—the face, for instance—holding the breath as long as possible and keeping the mind from straying to other objects. Then when exhaling, loosen the mode of observation and more relaxedly view the general divine body, loosening mindfulness and introspection a little.

When you get tired, it is appropriate to repeat mantra. However, for a beginner the main part of the meditation revolves around the six deities, which should be cultivated carefully and leisurely. This is because clear appearance of oneself as a deity must be achieved for the sake of amassing the two collections of merit and wisdom, achieving firm meditative stabilization, and transforming all physical and verbal actions into powerful aids for others' welfare. Hence, before repeating mantra, the yoga of nondual profundity (realization of emptiness) and manifestation (appearance as a deity) should be sustained, developing clarity within observing the divine form and ascertaining its lack of inherent existence. When, having done this one-pointedly, you become tired, then for the sake of resting begin repeating mantra.

There was an Am-do lama, Jetsun Jamyang Tshultrim Chökyi Nyima (*rje btsun 'jam dbyangs tshul khrims chos kyi nyi ma*), who said that since we usually recite the instructions for a rite of deity generation quickly and then immediately repeat mantra, we are taking mantra repetition rather than meditation as the main part of the session. He joked that once the technique for resting is used for the basic session, there is no way to rest when tired except to leave the session! His point was well taken, for the Indians meditated in the main session and then when tired moved on to repetition as a second level of practice for the sake of resting. Tsongkhapa also says that in the approximation phase meditation is chief, mantra repetition is secondary. It is not sufficient to recite the memorized rite and then count mantra.

Concerning the three types of repetition that are part of the actual meditation [and not the resting type of repetition just mentioned], the first involves repeating a mantra within the context of observing the form of the letters of the mantra on a flat moon disc at the heart of the deity visualized in front of yourself. The moon is a manifestation of the mind realizing emptiness and thus is called "mind." The letters of the mantra, set around the edge of the moon with the seed syllable of the deity in the middle, are called "sound." The "base" where these are set is the deity meditated in front of yourself; the second "base" is yourself clarified as a deity. These are the four branches of repetition—mind, sound, and two bases—to be maintained while repeating mantra. As if reading the letters of the mantra at the heart of the deity in front, repeat the mantra.

When the mind becomes one-pointed, cease reciting the mantra orally and begin mental repetition—holding the breath during the recitation and then when exhaling, viewing your own divine body. Finally, when you are tired, undo the process of visualization in reverse order, passing from observing the forms of the letters to the moon, then the body of the deity in front, and then your own divine body. This, in turn, is left through passing backwards through the process of self-generation—observing the forms of the letters on the moon at your own heart, then the sounds, moon disc, sameness in nature of yourself and the deity, and your own suchness—finally setting in meditative equipoise on emptiness. Then, even when leaving the session, you should rise within a sense of divine pride, maintaining it throughout all activities.

The second type of repetition is done within the context of observing the form of the mantra letters at your own heart. From within the former meditation, the moon and letters at the heart of the deity in front are transferred with an inhalation of breath to your own heart, whereupon repetition is performed. With exhalation, stop the repetition and observe the divine body in front to which the moon and letters again move with the outgoing breath. Then with inhalation repeat the process. As before, this can be done with both whispered and mental repetition—the latter being more subtle.

Then, pass to an even subtler object by mainly observing the sounds of the letters, though not entirely leaving off observing your own divine body with moon and mantra letters at the heart. Later on in the concentrations of abiding in fire and in sound, one concentrates on the mantra sounds as if listening to someone else recite them, but here one is as if listening to one's own recitation. Again, this can be done with whispered or mental repetition, the latter being necessary when the breath is held since oral recitation would be impossible.

These are the three types of repetition—observing the forms of the mantra letters (1) in the heart of the deity in front, (2) in your own heart, and (3) observing the sounds of the mantra. Each of these in turn has two forms, whispered and mental repetition. For each of the three types, whispered repetition is done first and then mental while the breath is held. The process becomes subtler and subtler and should be done in order. If one knows how to meditate, the meditations of Action Tantra are very profound, its progression of stages accomplishing a withdrawal of winds that enhances meditative stabilization.

The first type is said to have three objects of observation—the deity in front, moon at its heart, and mantra letters; the second type, two—moon and mantra letters at one's own heart; and the third, one—the mantra sounds. These refer to the *main* objects of observation on which the mind focuses and should not be taken as meaning that the other factors do not remain vividly appearing to the mind. You must remain undistractedly on whatever the object is at that point.

When facility is gained with those concentrations, you pass on to the concentrations not relying on repetition—abiding in fire, abiding in sound, and bestowing liberation at the end of sound. The concentration of abiding in fire bestows feats in the sense of empowering and stabilizing the mind. The concentration of abiding in sound is the time of achieving a fully qualified calm abiding (*śamatha*)—an exertionless and spontaneous meditative stabilization induced by physical and mental pliancy. The yoga of concentration on the end of sound is a cultivation of a union of calm abiding and special insight (*vipaśyanā*) observing suchness, whereby the liberation of Buddhahood is eventually attained. These three concentrations are all performed within vivid and continuous visualization of oneself as a deity.

With regard to the concentration of abiding in fire, you must cease the conception of inherent existence in the sense of not giving it a chance to be produced. Still, it is necessary to maintain conception of a conventional deity, that is to say, one with a face, arms, and so forth. Previously, during the repetition of mantra while observing the sound of the letters, it was as if you were listening to the reverberation of the sounds of your own recitation, whether whispered or mental. However, here you are to listen to the mantra sounds as if someone else were reciting them. Therefore, that the concentration of abiding in fire is said not to rely on mantra repetition means that it is free from the aspect of *one's own* repetition, not that it is free from mantra sounds altogether.

These sounds are "heard" from within a tongue of flame imagined at the heart—all this within the clear appearance of your own body as a deity's. Your own mind is as if inside the tongue of flame, appearing in the form of the mantra sounds resounding as if by their own power. This is like the practice on other occasions of the mind's taking the mind as its object of observation—a factor of the mind taking the general mind as its object. Here the mind is appearing as the sounds of someone else's repetition and is simultaneously listening to those sounds.

In the previous meditations all forms and sounds were appearances of the mind realizing suchness; thus, all forms seen and sounds heard were appearances of the mind. Within that, one was as if listening to the mantra repeated by oneself; hence, there still was a sense of a listener and the listened. However, here in the concentration of abiding in fire one's own basis of imputation is as if dwelling inside the tongue of flame, and it itself is appearing as the sounds being listened to in that same place. The external sign of proficiency with the concentration of abiding in fire is to become free from hunger and thirst—meditative stabilization itself having become your sustenance.

Then, you should pass on to the concentration of abiding in sound. Here you imagine a *subtle* moon at the heart of your divine body. This is because the smaller the object is, the easier it is to eliminate scattering and excitement, and the brighter the object is, the easier it is to eliminate laxity. If the object observed is too large, it is difficult to eliminate conceptions; therefore a small object of observation is required. Earlier, in the concentration of abiding in fire, you imagined a tongue of flame at the heart in which the sounds of the mantra resounded. Now, in that flame on the moon place a small divine figure with a tongue of flame at its heart in which the mantra sounds reverberate. Then, leave off one-pointed concentration on that—without leaving it altogether—and focus on the mantra sounds. As before, you are as if listening to the mantra recited by someone else. When exhaling, view the outer divine body.

These unusual objects of observation in the concentrations of abiding in fire and in sound are for the sake of achieving clear appearance and thereby avoiding laxity. For, even if the earlier meditations involved the appearance of bright mantra letters and so forth, here one imagines fire itself, even the name of which evokes a bright appearance, thereby helping in relieving the mind of laxity—any looseness in the mode of apprehension of the object. The uncommon purpose of the concentrations of abiding in fire and in sound is not concerned with ascertaining the meaning of the absence of inherent existence but with withdrawing the mind and achieving a fully qualified calm abiding that is conjoined with a bliss of physical and mental pliancy.

As was explained earlier [in *Tantra in Tibet*] the three lower tantras—Action, Performance, and Yoga—have unusual techniques for achieving the special insight realizing emptiness. Since, to do this, calm abiding must first be achieved, the three lower tantras have methods superior to those of the Perfection Vehicle for inducing calm abiding. These are techniques such as the stopping of the breath and the observation of a divine body, as well as subtler internal objects such as fire and sound. These generate the capacity quickly to achieve calm abiding—a state in which the mind can remain one-pointedly on its object of observation as long as one wants, free from even subtle laxity and excitement, and conjoined with physical and mental pliancy.

Since with its attainment you have a fully qualified meditative stabilization (*samādhi*), you can then switch the object of observation to emptiness in accordance with the concentration bestowing liberation at the end of sound. It is now possible to analyze the nature of phenomena with the powerful, penetrating, steady, serviceable, and undistracted mind of calm abiding. However, if you analyze too much, it will harm the stability factor of the mind, and similarly if you stabilize too much it will harm the analytical factor. Therefore, you need skillfully to alternate analytical and stabilizing meditation, through which a state arisen from meditation with emptiness as the object is generated. This is a union of calm abiding and special insight realizing emptiness, the yoga of signlessness, and the beginning of the path of preparation.

The mode of procedure in the three lower tantras is to attain calm abiding first and then alternate analytical and stabilizing meditation whereby special insight is achieved. However, in the stage of generation of Highest Yoga Tantra even during the period of achieving calm abiding one can engage in more and more intensive analysis without harming the stability factor. This is due to special objects of observation—such as an entire maṇḍala within a tiny drop—and due to special places of meditation within the body—essential channel points. During the stage of completion in Highest Yoga Tantra, however, one mainly uses stabilizing meditation during the session for the sake of drawing the winds into the central channel; nevertheless, between sessions analysis on emptiness is still done. It seems that some persons have misapplied this predominance of stabilizing meditation during the stage of completion—the highest level of the path—to the beginning stages, recommending nonanalysis and thereby confusing the process of the path.

In Action and Performance Tantra analytical and stabilizing meditation—with emptiness as the object—must be *alternated* after achieving calm abiding. Gradually, analysis itself comes to induce even greater stability, whereupon alternation is no longer needed and a union of calm abiding and special insight is attained. Through using the above-mentioned special objects of observation and so forth the four levels of the path of preparation—heat, peak, forbearance, and supreme mundane quality—proceed faster than in sūtra, whereupon the path of seeing, the initial direct realization of emptiness, and the first of the ten grounds are simultaneously attained. However, the three lower tantras do not set forth any techniques for proceeding more quickly than in the Perfection Vehicle with regard to the abandoning of obstructions and advancing over the ten grounds. Thus, from among the five paths—accumulation, preparation, seeing, meditation, and no more learning—the profound distinguishing features of the three lower tantras are concerned with the first two. Whereas in the Perfection Vehicle the paths of accumulation and preparation take one period of countless great eons, in the three lower tantras it can be done in one lifetime or even in a few years. Yoga Tantra has the further profundity of subtler objects of observation much like the *Guhyasamāja* [a Highest Yoga Tantra].

In the concentration bestowing liberation at the end of sound one leaves even sound and focuses on emptiness, free from the two extremes of inherent existence and no nominal existence. One is no longer mainly concerned with developing clear appearance but is mainly meditating on emptiness. Still, this does not mean that the divine body, sounds, and so forth necessarily no longer appear. Rather, to the *ascertainment factor* of the concentration on the end of sound only emptiness—a negative of inherent existence—appears. However, sounds and so forth may still appear to what is called the appearance factor of that consciousness. This means that although the sounds and so forth may appear, the mind is ascertaining or realizing only emptiness. This is the union of the two truths in Mantra—one consciousness appearing in the form of divine body or speech and simultaneously realizing emptiness.

These meditations depend on initially developing clear appearance of a divine body—clarity being developed through familiarizing, or taking to mind again and again, the features of the object. For instance, if one takes to mind again and again the features of a person whom one desires, that person will eventually appear as if before one's own eyes. Thus, an object of meditation does not have to be true for clear appearance to emerge; rather, the sole factor is familiarization. This is established in Dharmakīrti's *Commentary on (Dignāga's) "Compilation of Valid Cognition"* (*pramāṇavarttika*).

When clear appearance of the object—divine form or speech—is achieved, one's consciousness is nonconceptual with respect to that even if it is conceptually realizing emptiness, as is the case with the early forms of the concentration on the end of sound. To realize emptiness conceptually means to know it through a generic image of it, not directly or nakedly as is done at the beginning of the path of seeing. Thus it seems that the one consciousness would have to be nonconceptual with respect to the divine body and conceptual with respect to the suchness—emptiness—of that body.

Clear appearance of the object and within this an intense subjective clarity are important. Many people nowadays seem to be confusing subtle laxity with meditation. In subtle laxity the mind is stable but without an intense mode of apprehension. Tsongkhapa explains at length in his *Stages of the Path Common to the Vehicles* that mere stability of the mind—an ability to stay on the object—is not sufficient. Here in Mantra also clarity of the object—the divine form—as well as subjective stability and clarity, free from even subtle laxity, are needed. In Action Tantra such vivid and steady meditative stabilization is achieved through the concentration of abiding in sound, which though it is blissful, clear, and nonconceptual as well as being conjoined with the force of realizing emptiness is not sufficient. It is still necessary to cultivate the concentration bestowing liberation at the end of sound; unlike the former, it is capable of cutting the root of cyclic existence because it takes only emptiness as its object of apprehension. In this way the concentrations with repetition and not relying on repetition provide profound means for speedy progress on the path.

Performance Tantra

Like Action Tantra, Performance Tantra has three supramundane lineages—One-Gone-Thus, lotus, and vajra. According to Butön, the *Vairochanābhisambodhi Tantra* is a tantra of the One-Gone-Thus lineage; the *Extensive Tantra of Hayagrīva,* which was not translated into Tibetan, is of the lotus lineage; and the *Vajrapāṇi Initiation Tantra* is of the vajra lineage.

Initially one's continuum is ripened through initiation—the means of ripening—whereupon one works at keeping the vows and pledges in pure form. Specifically, one must properly maintain the correct view of emptiness and the altruistic mind of enlightenment, not losing these even for the sake of one's life. These are again and again said to be the root of the vows and pledges. Tsongkhapa's description of the Bodhisattva vows and the reasons why the tantric ones do not apply in Performance Tantra are found in his *Explanation of the Ethics Chapter* and *Explanation of the Root Infractions,* which thereby become subsidiaries of the *Great Exposition of Secret Mantra* and should be studied in detail.

With respect to the yoga of Performance Tantra, the *Vairochanābhisambodhi Tantra* speaks of thoroughly pure and impure divine bodies and yogas with and without signs. Thoroughly pure divine bodies are mainly entities of the realization of emptiness, having the aspect of the ultimate, whereas the "impure" mainly have the aspect of the conventional, a deity with face, arms, and so forth. A path without signs has the full qualifications of an undifferentiability of method and wisdom, due to which the Truth and Form Bodies of a Buddha are achieved in dependence on it. A path or yoga with signs, even though involving emptiness and deity yoga, is unlike yoga without signs in that it is not *mainly* concerned with meditation on emptiness. Thus, the yoga without signs occurs when the capacity for meditation in which a divine circle is observed and its absence of inherent existence is ascertained has developed to a high degree; emptiness yoga is then predominant.

In Action Tantra, yoga without signs begins with the concentration bestowing liberation at the end of sound and thus with the attainment of a union of calm abiding and special insight observing emptiness. There, yoga without signs is deity yoga that has reached the level of a state arisen from meditation, such being gained simultaneously with the attainment of a union of calm abiding and special insight. Here in Performance Tantra it seems that yoga without signs refers to yogas on the occasion of mainly cultivating the view of emptiness, whereas those on other occasions are yogas with signs, in that they are mainly concerned with dualistic appearances, although they do involve meditation on emptiness.

Just as in Highest Yoga Tantra a divine body meditated on the stage of generation is called an impure divine body and one meditated on the stage of completion is called pure, here in the *Vairochanābhisambodhi*, a Performance Tantra, the divine bodies of the yogas with and without signs are respectively called impure and pure. Though the *Vairochanābhisambodhi* does not indeed indicate, either explicitly or implicitly, the bodies of the two stages in Highest Yoga Tantra, its thought is aimed at those, and thus it can be cited as a source for the two bodies in Highest Yoga Tantra, as was done by Chandrakīrti (see pp. 180).

In Performance Tantra the yoga with signs is in two types, external and internal, with each having four branches as in Action Tantra—self-base, other-base, sound, and mind. At the beginning of the process of deity meditation and mantra repetition one meditates on emptiness, delineating the absence of inherent existence of oneself and the deity through a reasoning such as that of dependent-arising—the fact that both oneself and the deity arise in dependence on their respective bases of imputation. One's own final nature and the final nature of the deity are the same, an emptiness of inherent existence.

To perform deity yoga one does not just withdraw ordinary appearances and then appear as a deity but causes the mind realizing emptiness itself to appear as a deity. Thus, it is essential initially to meditate on emptiness, cleansing all appearances in emptiness. One then uses that wisdom realizing emptiness as the basis of emanation of a divine body. This must be done at least in imitation of a consciousness actually doing this, for meditation on a truly existent divine body, instead of helping, will only increase adherence to inherent existence. Meditated properly, the appearance of a divine figure is the sport of the ultimate mind of enlightenment, first in imitation and later in fact.

In one mode of procedure the deity appears in full form instantaneously; in another, the wisdom first manifests as a moon and seed syllable that transform into the divine form. This latter type is like the procedure in Highest Yoga Tantra in which one contemplates, "The root of all phenomena included in the environment and the beings within it—mere wind and mind, appearing as a moon—am I." Although Performance Tantra does not have such an explanation of wind, the basic thought is the same in terms of the mind. One first generates the view realizing emptiness—at least in imitation—whereupon that mind ascertaining emptiness serves as the basis of emanation, appearing as a moon. This is said to be like the rising of a water bubble from water, for just as a water bubble is different from water but still has a nature of water, so the form of the moon disc is different from the pristine wisdom realizing emptiness and yet does not pass beyond being the sport, or nature, of that pristine wisdom.

The moon disc with seed syllable on top of it then changes into the body of the deity, here the great Vairochanābhisambodhi; this is the first branch, the self-base, or generation of oneself as a deity. The second branch, or other-base, is the imagination of a deity similar to oneself in front, a second Vairochanābhisambodhi facing oneself. Then, the third and fourth branches, mind and sound, consist of imagining a moon disc—the nature of which, again, is the wisdom realizing emptiness—in the heart of the deity in front with the form of the mantra syllables set upright around its edge facing inwards. One then engages in repetition. That is the external four-branched repetition.

The internal four-branched repetition involves generating oneself as Shākyamuni with Vairochanābhisambodhi at his heart inside an upright moon disc, which is like a two-sided mirror. The internal Vairochana has a moon at his heart with the mantra letters standing upright around its edge facing inwards. Meditation is done in this way until calm abiding is attained, at which point yoga without signs is begun.

The yoga without signs is cultivated within clear imagination of one's body as a deity's and is preceded by the four branches of repetition. The mode of meditation is first to reflect on the body as something not affected by good and bad since it is composed of matter; except for serving as a basis of consciousness, the body itself cannot feel anything. Then one analyzes whether or not the body inherently exists in the way it appears to exist so solidly. Through using a reasoning such as the body's not being an inherent existent one or many, one realizes its emptiness of inherent solidity.

The mind is similarly analyzed to discover its emptiness of inherently existent production, abiding, and disintegration. Then, the I that is designated in dependence on body and mind should be analyzed and settled as not inherent existent.

Buddhaguhya describes this process as beginning with identifying the subject, one's own divine body with the two factors of clear appearance and divine pride, and then settling its emptiness by any of three techniques:

1. the reasoning of its not being either an inherently existent one or many, or the reasoning of its not being produced from self, other, both, or neither;
2. a stabilizing meditation on the meaning of emptiness;
3. eliminating all conventional appearances [such as a divine body] and concentrating solely on the ultimate, the emptiness of inherent existence.

The first technique is based on an analytical reasoning as done in the Middle Way School. The second must refer to a stabilizing meditation on an emptiness, which one has ascertained earlier through analysis; however, repeated analysis would have to be done in order to enhance one's understanding, for stabilizing meditation alone—without the factor of great bliss as in Highest Yoga Tantra—is not sufficient because the mode of procedure for developing special insight in the three lower tantras—Action, Performance, and Yoga—is the same as that in sūtra, alternating stabilizing and analytical meditation.

The third is a case of viewing appearances themselves—wherever the mind alights—as empty of inherent existence, in contrast to the first technique, in which the emptiness of a particular subject is being ascertained through a reasoning such as the lack of its being an inherent existent one or many. The third is like the teaching on the Great Seal (*mahāmudrā*) in the Kagyupa (*bka' rgyud pa*) order that the more thoughts one has, so much more are the Truth Bodies, or emptinesses, realized.

In all three cases it is necessary to alternate stabilizing meditation and analytical meditation, for only in the stage of completion of Highest Yoga Tantra can mere stabilizing meditation on emptiness be done, the difference there coming from the feature of great bliss. Thus, by merely cultivating nonconceptuality and nonanalysis it is impossible to enter into the yoga of signlessness. Even after emptiness has been realized, powerful and repeated analysis is needed. Merely to set one's mind on the meaning of emptiness as realized earlier is the mode of cultivating calm abiding observing emptiness; in order to cultivate special insight it is necessary to analyze again and again. These two modes of meditation—stabilizing and analytical—are alternated until analysis itself induces even greater stabilization, at which point stabilization and wisdom are of equal strength, this being a union of calm abiding and special insight.

In Performance as well as in Action Tantra the meditative stabilization that is a union of calm abiding and special insight is used to gain feats for the sake of aiding sentient beings and accumulating merit quickly. These are gained in dependence on (1) external substances, as in the case of the feat of the sword, which is used for flying to lands of Knowledge Bearers where tantric practice is maintained; (2) internal imagination of discs representing earth, water, fire, or wind; or (3) achieving a meeting with a special deity such as Mañjushrī. Unlike Yoga Tantra, however, Action and Performance do not present means for actually transforming one's body [while still on the path] into a similitude of a divine body. In Yoga Tantra techniques are taught for the sake of actually transmuting this body into one of a Knowledge Bearer or of a tenth ground Bodhisattva.

II

The Great Exposition of Secret Mantra

The Stages of the Path to a Victor and Pervasive Master, a Great Vajradhara: Revealing All Secret Essentials

Parts Two and Three

Tsongkhapa

TRANSLATED AND EDITED BY

Jeffrey Hopkins

ASSOCIATE EDITORS:

Lati Rinpoche and Danma Lochö Rinpoche

CO-EDITED BY

Elizabeth Napper

INTRODUCTION

The presentation of the stages of the path in Action and Performance Tantras has two parts: (1) analysis of whether Action and Performance have self-generation and entry of a wisdom-being and (2) individual explanations of their stages of the path.

Controversy about Deity Yoga in Action and Performance

The analysis of whether Action and Performance Tantras have self-generation and entry of a wisdom-being [the deity's dissolving into the meditator] has two parts: stating masters' [varying] assertions and explaining the correct position among them.

Stating Masters' [varying] Assertions on Whether Action and Performance Tantras Have Self-Generation and Entry of a Wisdom-Being

Most earlier Tibetan lamas [mistakenly] said that although Action Tantras have meditation on a deity in front of oneself, they do not have generation of oneself as a deity and that in Performance Tantras, except for generating oneself as a pledge-being [symbolic of the actual deity] and generating a wisdom-being [the actual deity] in front of oneself, there is no entry of a wisdom-being into oneself:

1. because the *Wisdom Vajra Compendium*[1] [a Highest Yoga Tantra] says:

> One who is terrified [of single-pointed cultivation of deity yoga] and is very cleanly, who lacks the excellent bliss of a wisdom-being and pride in oneself as a deity, who is not an object of the unusual practice [of using desire in the path], and who practices with thoughts on the features of defects [such as birth, aging, and so forth] abides in Action Tantra.

> [and they wrongly assumed that] this passage explains that Action Tantras do not have self-generation and entry of a wisdom-being [whereas it indicates that *some* Action Tantras do not involve these in order to accommodate within their paths those unable to practice them]

> 2. and because [they wrongly concluded that the Performance Tantras] the *Vairochanābhisambodhi Tantra* and the *Vajrapāṇi Initiation Tantra* set forth generation of oneself as a deity but do not set forth entry of a wisdom-being into oneself.

[Moreover,] the following [Indian] commentators [wrongly] assert that both Action and Performance Tantra do not have self-generation. Shrīdhara's *Innate Illumination Commentary on the Difficult Points of the "Yamāri Tantra"* (*yamāritantrapañjikāsahajāloka*[2] [a Highest Yoga text]) says:

> Even in the Action and Performance systems [practitioners] do not engage in achievements and means of achievements over a long time; [rather] these arise from imagination because they complete feats through the power of deities that are found in paintings and so forth [that is, they imagine a deity in front of themselves from whom they, as ordinary beings, receive feats]. The Yoga Tantras have this feature: Through one's own deity yoga [of self-generation] one observes a deity as found in paintings and so forth and achieves concordant feats.

Jinadatta [wrongly] describes Action and Performance Tantra in a similar way in his *Commentary on the Difficult Points of the "Guhyasamāja Tantra"* (*guhyasamājatantrapañjikā*) [a Highest Yoga text]. Also, the *Explanation of the "Condensed Meaning of the Saṃvara Tantra"* (*cakrasaṃvaratantrarājaśambarasamuccaya-nāmavṛtti*) [a Highest Yoga text], which is said to have been written by Indrabhūti, [wrongly] says:

> From the approach of Action and Performance Tantras within the Secret Vajra Vehicle, [practitioners] depending on only a permission [rite] for practicing knowledge mantras seek to actualize a goal achieved through observation with signs—imagination having a view of oneself and a deity as different.

[The Assertion by Other Indian Commentators that Both Action and Performance Tantra Have Self-Generation]

Buddhaguhya's commentary[3] on the statement in the *Concentration Continuation Tantra*[4] [one of the four main general Action Tantras] that:

> The secret mantra concentrations
> Are said to be supremely secret.

says:

> "Secret" means unrevealed. The meaning is that though the secret mantra concentrations [such as deity yoga] are the essence of the branches for achieving all secret mantras [that is, feats], they are not taught in clear detail in the individual tantras. This is in order to accommodate migrators who are trainees but are unable to perform earnestly the branches of concentration, such as withdrawal [of the mind from external objects] and [stopping] vitality and exertion [breath and distraction]. These are mostly set forth in a nonmanifest manner in all [Action Tantras]; I will explain them later.

Thus, Buddhaguhya says that although the mantra concentrations, such as deity yoga, which he is yet to explain, are the essence of the causal branches for achieving feats, these are not taught clearly in other Action Tantras in order to accommodate within these tantras those who could not cultivate deity yoga one-pointedly through methods such as holding the winds inside, and so forth, which he is yet to describe. Buddhaguhya explains that these concentrations are, however, mentioned in an unclear way in other tantras.

Moreover, his *Commentary on the "Concentration Continuation Tantra"*[5] says:

> The activities to be done during the concentrations of secret mantra repetition are set forth in the *Susiddhi Tantra* (*susiddhi*), the *Questions of Subāhu Tantra* (*subāhuparipṛcchā*), the *Compendium of Imaginations* (*dpal rtog pa bsdus pa*),[6] and so forth, which are compendiums of the general rites of all Action Tantras. These [activities] are also described in tantras of specific [lineages and deities] such as the *Vairochanābhisambodhi: the Empowerment of Emanations*, the *Vajrapāṇi Initiation Tantra*, the *Essence of Enlightenment* (*byang chub kyi snying po*), the *Scriptural Division of the Knowledge Bearers* (*vidyādhārapiṭaka*), and so forth. In some they are explained nonmanifestly; in some, clearly, as when the *Susiddhi Tantra*[7] says:
>
> > When reciting with repetition,
> > Except for knowledge mantra and deity
> > Do not apprehend in thought at all [other]
> > Meditations though cherished as supreme.

and so forth. Also, Buddhaguhya[8] says:

> The *Vairochanābhisambodhi* [a Performance Tantra] clearly explains that, when doing repetition, mantra training is done through training in the four-branched repetition [which involves self-generation as one of its branches]. The *Vajrapāṇi Initiation* [a Performance Tantra] says, "Mañjushrī, when practitioners of mantra

> spontaneously achieve the pride of a deity, they dwell in proximity to all secret mantra [feats]." The *Scriptural Division of the Knowledge Bearers of Mantras* says, "One should concentrate on a deity [as found] in a painting and so forth:
>
> > Contemplate [the deity] with swaying ear-rings
> > And the movement of the small [jewel-] bag ichneumon.[9]
> > When striving at repetition in this way
> > Imagine in stages the feet and so forth."
>
> The *Compendium of Imaginations* teaches familiarization with the selflessness of phenomena and deity yoga in a great many passages; therefore, I will not cite them here. In such tantras the bodies of deities and the repetition that is performed prior to secret mantra concentration on sound [that is, before the concentrations of abiding in fire and in sound] are described.

Buddhaguhya says that meditation on a divine body, concentration performed while observing a mantra, meditation on the suchness of oneself, and so forth, are explained either clearly or unclearly, completely or incompletely in [Action] Tantras. He says that the four-membered repetition is taught very clearly in the *Concentration Continuation* [an Action Tantra] and in the *Vairochanābhisambodhi* [generally considered to be a Performance Tantra].

This master [Buddhaguhya] asserts that the deity yoga of the four-membered repetition and so forth is similar in both Action and Performance Tantras, and he says that the *Vairochanābhisambodhi*, for instance, can be an Action Tantra due to the trainee; therefore, except for dividing Action and Performance Tantras by way of their trainees, he does not divide them from the viewpoint of the tantras themselves.[10]

Varabodhi's *Clear Realization of Susiddhi* (*susiddhi-abhisamaya*)[11] says:

> Do not think that the stages of achieving a deity are not taught in Action Tantras. Though the Supramundane Victor did not teach these in most, they are taught as main subjects in the *Vajrapāṇi Initiation* and the *Ten Principles* (*daśatattva*).[12] In sum, all feats depend on a secret mantra deity and on suchness; if these are deficient, activities of pacification and so forth will not be achieved; hence, these can be understood through a guru's explanation and through a little analysis of the features of tantras.

Here Varabodhi's citation of the *Vajrapāṇi Initiation* [a Performance Tantra] as a source for the existence of deity generation in Action Tantra makes clear his assertion, like Buddhaguhya's above, that the deity yogas of Action and Performance Tantras are similar. His explanation that since the achievement of the manifold activities of pacification and so forth depend on deity and emptiness yogas, even Action Tantra must involve deity meditation is very good reasoning.

Correct Position Among the Assertions as to Whether Action and Performance Tantras Have Self-Generation and Entry of a Wisdom-Being

Question: Well, which among these different systems should be held here?

Answer: The assertion that there is no generation of oneself as a deity in Performance Tantra is not reasonable (1) because if the *Vairochanābhisambodhi* and the *Vajrapāṇi Initiation* are not considered to be Performance Tantras, it would be impossible to find a Performance Tantra, and if they are, self-generation is clearly set forth in them and (2) because the third chapter of Āryadeva's *Lamp Compendium of Practice* (*caryāmelakapradīpa*) also calls it a Performance Tantra saying, "The *Vairochanābhisambodhi,* a Performance Tantra, says . . ." Also, it is thought of the *Saṃpuṭa Tantra* (*saṃpuṭa*) and the *Hevajra Tantra* [both in the Highest Yoga class] that [Action Tantras] use in the path the desire of male and female deities' observing each other;[13] therefore, it must definitely be asserted that even Action Tantras have self-generation as a deity.

Question: Well, is this generation of oneself as a deity carried over from [the thought of] other tantras [such as the *Saṃpuṭa* and *Hevajra*] or does it come from the side of Action Tantras themselves?

Answer: With respect to this, some latter-day scholars [such as Butön (*bu-ston*)[14] wrongly] say:

> Just as it is said that Action Tantras do not have self-generation and entry of a wisdom-being, so it is clear that it is so in fact. Still, the two—Buddhaguhya and Varabodhi—say that Action Tantras have self-generation but do not set forth entry of a wisdom-being.
>
> [Possible "reasons" for this assertion]
>
> 1. The master Nāgārjuna speaks of self-generation and entry of a wisdom-being as well as initiation in his *Means of Achievement of the Retention of the Thousand-Armed and Thousand-Eyed Avalokiteshvara* (*sahasrabhujāvalokiteśvarasādhana*) [which is *based* on an Action Tantra]. Also, self-generation, entry of a wisdom-being, and so forth are described in *Means of Achievement* that are *based* on Action Tantras such as the *Means of Achievement of Mahākaruṇika* by the master Padmasambhava, the *Means of Achievement of the Eleven-Faced Avalok-*

iteshvara (*bhaṭṭārakaryaikādaśamukhāvalokiteśva-rasādhana*) by Lakṣhmi,[15] the *Means of Achievement of Sitātapatrāparājitā* (*sitātapatrāparājitāsādhana*), which is said to be by Chandragomin, the [two] *Means of Achievement of the Five Guards* (*pañcarakṣāviddhi*) by Ratnākarashānti and Jetāri [separate texts with the same title], the *Means of Achievement of Vimaloṣhṇīṣha* (*vimaloṣṇīṣasādhāraṇīvidhi*) by the Foremost Elder Atisha, and moreover the *Ocean of Means of Achievement* (*sādhanasāgara*), the *One Hundred and Fifty Means of Achievement,* the *Hundred Means of Achievement,* and so forth. [Thus it should be analyzed whether Buddhaguhya and Varabodhi mistook *Means of Achievement* based on Action Tantras for presentations of Action Tantra.]

2. Buddhaguhya and so forth assert that even the *Vairochanābhisambodhi* and so forth are Action Tantras; therefore, it should be analyzed whether [their position] is in consideration of mixing Action and Performance Tantras.

3. Or, perhaps [their position] is in consideration of explanations by other masters that it is suitable to apply the format of Yoga Tantra also to Action and Performance rites as is taught in the *Compendium of Principles* (*tattvasaṃgraha*) [a Yoga Tantra]:

> The essence, seal, mantra, and knowledge
> Explained in the [four] sections [of this tantra]
> Are all achieved through whatever mode one wishes,
> [The rites of Yoga Tantra] itself or [the others].

4. Or, just as deities similar to [Highest Yoga dei-

> ties] such as Pratisarā, Mārīchi, and Parṇashavarī, as well as their mantras, appear in Action Tantras, so Saṃpuṭa,[16] and so forth, [usually associated with Action Tantra] also appear in Highest Yoga Tantras. Hence, it should be analyzed whether the thought of Highest Yoga is being carried over to Action Tantra or whether the latter has obtained self-generation in its own right.

[To refute the second hypothesis:] It is not that Buddhaguhya did not find a clear description of self-generation in Action Tantra and thus took the *Vairochanābhisambodhi* and *Vajrapāṇi Initiation* [Performance Tantras], and so forth, as his sources because Buddhaguhya asserts that the four-branched repetition is clearly taught in the *Vajroṣhṇīṣha Tantra*, which is an Action Tantra. Thus Buddhaguhya's commentary on the statement in the *Concentration Continuation Tantra*[17] [which is a continuation of or supplement to the *Vajroṣhṇīṣha Tantra*],[18] "Flow to the bases, mind, and sound," says:

> This means that the characteristics of the branches of repetition and so forth, such as bases, mind, and sound, are not explained here [in the *Concentration Continuation Tantra*] because they were explained initially in this tantra [the *Vajroṣhṇīṣha*]. The characteristics that were explained there are these: "Sound" is [the forms of] mantra letters. "Mind" is the manifestation of a moon disc, which is the base of the mantra. A "base" is the entity of a body of a One-Gone-Thus. The second base is one's own [appearance in the] form of a deity. Furthermore, it should be known that since the characteristics of [stopping] vitality and exertion [breath and distraction], withdrawal [of the mind from external objects], and so forth were explained earlier in just this *Vajroṣhṇīṣha Tantra*, they are not described here in this

> section called the *Concentration Continuation Tantra,* which is related [with the *Vajroṣhṇīṣha* as its continuation or supplement].

Thus, since the assumption of the form of one's own deity and so forth were explained earlier in the *Vajroṣhṇīṣha Tantra,* they are not set forth here in the *Concentration Continuation Tantra,* which is part of it, and there is no one who does not assert that this [*Vajroṣhṇīṣha*] is an Action Tantra.

Buddhaguhya asserts that the four branches described here and in the *Vairochanābhisambodhi Tantra* are similar. His commentary on the *Concentration Continuation Tantra* says:

> For instance, the *Vairochanābhisambodhi Tantra*[19] says:
>
> > "The immutable" is the mind of enlightenment
> > [appearing as a moon].
> > The second ["immutable"] is called "sounds" [the
> > forms of the letters on the moon].
> > "Base" is to make the figure
> > Of one's deity as your own body.
> > That called the second base is a complete
> > Buddha,
> > The supreme of the two-legged [imagined in
> > front].
> > "Vitality" is explained as wind.
> > "Exertion" is mindfulness [that is, distraction].
>
> and so forth. Here [in the *Concentration Continuation Tantra*] also one should view in a similar way the characteristics of the bases and so forth that were explained earlier [in the *Vajroṣhṇīṣha Tantra*].

Therefore, if the meaning of the "bases" [in the passage from the *Concentration Continuation Tantra*], "Flow to the bases, mind, and sounds," could not refer to the base of generating oneself as a deity, one would have to assert that the two lines in the

Vairochanābhisambodhi Tantra, "'Base' is to imagine one's own body/ As that of one's deity," also would not indicate generation of oneself as a deity since there is no difference between them.

[To refute the fourth hypothesis:] In some *Imagination of Mārīchi* self-generation is indeed clearly described, and the conventions "stage of generation" and "stage of completion" [which are exclusively found in Highest Yoga Tantra] also indeed appear to be used. If these are taken as Action Tantra, it is clearly wrong, and if they are accepted as included within Highest Yoga [as is correct], they are not fit as sources for the existence of self-generation in Action Tantra.

Therefore, it is evident that the *Concentration Continuation Tantra,* as well as Buddhaguhya's commentary, are very clear with respect to Action Tantras' having self-generation in their own right, and this is also known through Buddhaguhya's quoting in his *Commentary on the "Vajravidāraṇā Tantra"* (*vajravidāranānā-maṭīkā*)[20] descriptions in the *Extensive Tantra of Vajravidāraṇā* of meditation on the six deities (see p. 104).

[To refute the third hypothesis:] Ānandagarbha's *Illumination of the Principles* (*tattvālokakārī*),[21] commenting on the first part [of the *Compendium of Principles Tantra*], says:

> Those who adhere to the rites of both [this Yoga Tantra] and Action and Performance Tantras, and so forth, should, through their [respective] rites, achieve the great seal and so forth, which are explained here [in the *Compendium of Principles*]. To indicate this meaning, [the *Compendium of Principles*] says:
>
> The essence, seal, mantra, and knowledge
> Explained in the [four] sections [of this tantra]
> Are all achieved through whatever mode one wishes,
> [The rites of Yoga Tantra] itself or [the others].

The four—essence, seal, mantra, and knowledge—which are

explained respectively in [the descriptions of] the great maṇḍala, retention maṇḍala, doctrine maṇḍala, and action maṇḍala in all four sections of the *Compendium of Principles* are said to be amenable to achievement even through both the rites of Yoga Tantras themselves and the rites of other Tantras, Action and Performance. Therefore, it is clear that also from the viewpoint of the *Compendium of Principles* self-generation, entry of a wisdom-being, and so forth are suitable [to occur in Action and Performance Tantra since it says that their rites may be used].

[To refute the first hypothesis:] Also, it is evident that in consideration of the similarity of the deities and mantras, such as Mārīchi, that are described in both Action and Highest Yoga Tantras, the *Ocean of Means of Achievement* and so forth—using them only as illustrations [for the sake of understanding]—frequently treat rites of generation and so on for deities explained in Action and Performance Tantras like Highest Yoga [and, therefore, it is clear that Buddhaguhya and Varabodhi were not relying on these illustrations from Highest Yoga as sources for Action and Performance].[22]

Question: Well then, what is the meaning of the passage from the *Wisdom Vajra Compendium* (p. 45)?

Answer: As Buddhaguhya says (p. 47), there are several types of trainees of Action Tantras who are frightened and terrified by the activity of single-pointed cultivation of deity yoga, who are not receptacles for using in the path deeds of desire—this being unusual in, or contrary to, the world—and who achieve the path through practices involving thoughts on features of faults such as birth, aging, and so forth, in conjunction with the conception of true existence. It is said [in the *Wisdom Vajra Compendium*] that such trainees do not have generation of oneself as a deity or entry of a wisdom-being, but this does not apply to each and every trainee of Action Tantra, as in the case of the *Vajroṣhṇīṣha Tantra* [which presents generation of oneself as a deity and entry of a wisdom-being]. Because such trainees are predominant in both Action and Performance, deity yoga is not obvious in the tantras, and even those tantras that have it are indeed not extensive. Nevertheless, the *chief* trainees of Action and Performance Tantras are not those who either do not like or are not able to cultivate one-pointedly a deity yoga by way of restraining vitality and exertion [breath and distraction], and so forth.

In accordance with the master Varabodhi's explanation (p. 50), even common beings practicing Action and Performance Mantra are said to achieve the great feats of the sword [for flying in the sky], the pill [for immediately becoming youthful], and so forth, as well as the manifold activities of pacification [such as of evil spirits or illness] and so on. The *Vajrapāṇi Initiation Tantra* clearly says that the achievement of these relies on deity and emptiness yogas:

> When practitioners of the Bodhisattva deeds engaging[23] in the Secret Mantra approach cause themselves to have the form of their own deity and with a mind free from doubt generate the pride [of being a deity] and whether going, standing, or staying still are always immovable [in this clear appearance and pride of a deity] though moving about, O Shāntamati, they are endowed with the ethics of a great Bodhisattva who is practicing the Bodhisattva deeds of the Secret Mantra approach.

Then it says that when they make effort at yoga and act in accordance with the ways shown by the deity, they are abiding in the conduct, and when they perform the activities of repetition, burnt offering, and so forth within that conduct, they are performing the deeds, and when making effort at the yoga of nondifference with a deity and holding the bases of the training, they practice the Great Vehicle, they attain feats of Secret Mantra, right after which it says, "Furthermore, a great Bodhisattva, a Bodhisattva practicing the Bodhisattva deeds who engages in the Secret Mantra approach, should always abide in signlessness [deity yoga conjoined with the view of emptiness]." At the end of that, it clearly says:

> Abiding in the conduct,
> Ethics, deeds, and bases
> Of the training laid down
> By the perfect Buddha,
> A māntrika achieves mantra [feats].
> The past Victors became Buddhas
> Through nonconceptual pristine wisdom,
> They taught that secret mantra [feats]
> Are achieved in the nonconceptual.
> The pure fruit of that is
> To become clear light by nature.
> For one who abides in conceptuality
> Feats do not arise.
> Therefore abandon conceptuality
> And contemplate a mantra form.

"Abandon conceptuality" is the eradication of conceptuality conceiving self [inherent existence] through the wisdom of selflessness; it does not mean to stop any and all types of conceptuality. "Contemplate a mantra form" is to meditate on a deity. The measure of firmness in deity yoga is indicated by "whether going, standing, or staying still are always immovable though moving about." When one has attained the capacity to hold the mind on the divine body in all types of behavior—whether in meditative equipoise or not—without the mind moving to something else, one has the capacity to remove the pride of ordinariness.

Although the two masters, Buddhaguhya and Varabodhi, do not describe entry of a wisdom-being into oneself [in their commentaries on Action and Performance Tantra], such entry is suitable, for it is described by many Indian scholars and adepts. Were it unsuitable, it would have to be because [trainees of these tantras] hold themselves and the deity—the wisdom-being—to be separate and do not believe in holding them to be one. However, this is not the case, because it is said that though the power of believing one's own body, speech, and mind to be undifferentiable from the deity's exalted body, speech, and mind all one's physical actions and movements are seals and all one's speech is mantra. For, in this way moreover the *Vajrapāṇi Initiation Tantra* says:

> A son or daughter of lineage[24] who has seen a maṇḍala, who generates the mind of enlightenment, who is compassionate, skilled in means and skilled in teaching the ways of letters—the door of Secret Mantra—should contemplate thus, "Separate from speech, there is no mind. Separate from mind, there is no speech. Separate from mind, there is no divine form. Mind itself is speech; speech itself is mind; divine form itself is also mind, and speech itself is also divine form." If mantra practitioners believe in this way that these are undifferentiable, they attain purity of mind. At those times when they have pure mind, they always view in all ways their own body to be the same as the deity's body, their own speech to be the same as the deity's speech, and their own mind to be the same as the deity's mind; then, they are in meditative equipoise.
>
> When at all times in all ways
> Māntrikas are in equipoise,
> Then they enter into a state of
> The sameness of body and so forth.
> Abiding in the state of sameness,
> Whatsoever movements of their limbs
> And whatsoever words spoken
> Are seals and secret mantras.

This is also the same in Action Tantra because, when there is generation of oneself as a deity, one must enact the pride that is the thought that one is the actual deity being generated, Vairochana, and so forth.

Therefore, to view one's body as a deity, one's speech as mantra, and one's mind as absorbed in suchness is not a distinguishing feature of Highest Yoga. It is definitely required also in the lower tantra sets.

Structure

The individual explanation of the stages of the path in Action and Performance Tantras has two parts: (1) the general structure and (2) the actual stages of the path.

General Structure of the Path in Action and Performance Tantras

The *Concentration Continuation Tantra*[25] [an Action Tantra] says:

> Through diligence to achieve secret mantra
> In three periods, this subtlety
> Is always known, O Pure One. The rites
> Of the ten branches are the activities.

It is said here that those who make effort at achieving mantra [deity yoga and all surrounding activities] know, that is, actualize, the conduct of knowledge mantra, which has the nature of deity yoga and is subtle [hard to realize] in that it is known through concentration in three sessions [every day]. Thereupon, feats [special yogic powers described in the chapter titled "Feats"] are achieved. The branches [of this process] are included in ten topics that Buddhaguhya's commentary[26] explains as:

1. place of practice,
2. self-principle,
3. knowledge mantra principle,
4. repetition principle,
5. concentration of abiding in fire,

6. concentration of abiding in sound,
7. concentration bestowing liberation at the end of sound,
8. rites of engaging in mantra practice,
9. rites of burnt offerings,
10. initiation rites.

Concerning those, the self, knowledge mantra, and repetition principles[27] are the concentrations of the four-branched repetition [described in the chapters "Self-Generation," "Generation in Front," and "Mantra Repetition"]. The concentrations of abiding in fire, abiding in sound, and bestowing liberation at the end of sound are the concentrations of the three principles, which will be explained later [in the chapter titled "Concentration Not Relying on Repetition"]. Those two [groups of concentrations] are the chief paths. The rites of engaging in mantra practice [described in the chapters "Prelimiaries" and "Mantra Repetition"] are rites prior and subsequent[28] to practicing those two groups of concentrations. Conferring initiation [briefly mentioned in the chapter titled "Structure"] makes [a trainee] into a receptacle suitable for meditatively cultivating these paths. [Rites of] burnt offerings [mentioned in the chapter "Concentration Not Relying on Repetition"] are performed when effecting the achievement [of feats after preliminary approximation] and when engaging in activities [of pacification of illness, demons, and so forth, increase of wealth, lifespan, wisdom, and so forth, control of resources, power, and so forth, and ferocity—expelling harmful beings, and so forth—after achieving such feats].

When through these approaches one gains ability, one achieves the manifold activities [of pacification, increase, and so forth that enhance progress on the path through amassing merit by helping others] whereby one completes the practices of enlightenment. In this way the meanings of both Action and Performance Tantras are included in the causal process of their trainees' enlightenment.

The Four General Action Tantras

Moreover, from among the four general Action Tantras, the *Questions of Subāhu Tantra* teaches the three [supramundane] lineages—One-Gone-Thus, vajra, and lotus—and furthermore the six lineages—[adding to those the three mundane lineages] pañchika, wealthy, and worldly, as well as their secret mantras, divisions of actions, and methods of pleasing—condensing what was extensively explained and not condensed in some tantras, explaining clearly what was taught only briefly in others, and teaching what was not mentioned in yet others. For the most part, it does not clearly describe the four-branched concentration and the concentrations of the three principles [abiding in fire, abiding in sound, and bestowing liberation at the end of sound] but clearly and extensively describes the remaining rites for achieving mantra as well as how to achieve the groups of activities [see the chapter titled "Feats"].

The *General Secret Tantra* (*guhyasāmānya*) mainly teaches the topics concerning making [trainees] into receptacles, for it shows how to draw the three thousand five hundred maṇḍalas of the three [supramundane] lineages and teaches the general rites for conferring initiation and so forth. The *Susiddhi Tantra* is not very clear on the six concentrations [the three principles of self, knowledge mantra, and repetition as well as the three concentrations of abiding in fire, abiding in sound, and bestowing liberation at the end of sound] but clearly teaches the rites for achieving mantras [feats], the ways of achieving the groups of activities, burnt offerings, pledges to be kept, and so forth, which are common to the three [supramundane] lineages. The *Concentration Continuation Tantra* teaches very clearly the six concentrations in general and in particular their branches, such as restraining vitality and exertion (*prāṇāyāma*), as well as the latter three concentrations [abiding in fire, abiding in sound, and bestowing liberation at the end of sound]. It is evident that these are also common to the three [supramundane] lineages.

The Main Headings

When one understands the presentations of these, one knows well how the meaning units of the individual Action Tantras and Performance Tantras are brought together. It is convenient to condense them under four headings:

1. the topic of conferring initiation, thereby making a receptacle suitable for cultivating the path;
2. the topic of keeping pledges and vows that are the basis for achieving feats;
3. then the topic of approximation for the sake of generating ability;
4. the topic of achieving feats for the sake of effecting one's own and others' welfare once one has gained ability.

Though there appear to be many [texts describing] means of achieving deities based on Action and Performance Tantras, it is evident that in terms of commentaries that accord with what occurs in these two tantras, the texts of Buddhaguhya and Varabodhi appear to be excellent; therefore, here I will explain Action and Performance Tantra according to them.

Action Tantra

Pledges and Vows

The stages of the path in Action Tantra has four parts: (1) how to become a receptacle suitable for meditatively cultivating the path, (2) having become a receptacle, how to maintain purity of pledges and vows, (3) how to perform prior approximation while abiding in the pledges, and (4) how to achieve feats once the approximation is serviceable.

How to Become a Receptacle Suitable for Meditatively Cultivating the Path

Since I fear that the maṇḍala rites together with the bestowal of initiations would make this text much too long, I will not write about them here. In my *Explanation of the Root Infractions*[29] I have already described, with respect to the two tantras [Action and Performance], mere entry into a maṇḍala and the initiations that are conferred on one who has entered. [Persons who have faith but are unable to keep the Bodhisattva vows and tantric pledges are allowed to enter a maṇḍala but are not conferred initiation. They are allowed to enter because viewing a maṇḍala with faith cleanses ill-deeds accumulated over many eons and plants predispositions for becoming a suitable receptacle in the future. Persons able to keep the Bodhisattva vows and tantric pledges are conferred the water and crown initiations in Action Tantra, with the addition of the vajra, bell, and name initiations in Performance Tantra.][30]

Having Become a Receptacle, How to Maintain Purity of Pledges and Vows

In my *Explanation of the Root Infractions* I have extensively indicated the vows taken at the time of conferring initiation [these being the Bodhisattva vows since tantric vows are limited to Yoga Tantra and Highest Yoga Tantra],[31] the root infractions of those vows, and so forth. Therefore, I will describe here the other pledges.

About them the "Chapter on Knowledge Mantra Discipline" in the *Susiddhi Tantra*[32] says:

> I will explain the discipline
> Of repeating secret mantra,
> Through abiding in which repeaters
> Will quickly attain the feats.
>
> Practitioners do not despise
> Any of the secret mantras
> Or any of the gods or any
> Great being of repetition.
>
> Wise persons do not fabricate
> Secret mantra rites or secret mantras
> And do not deride persons
> Who have a bad disposition.
>
> Even if the guru who reveals
> The maṇḍala becomes of bad deeds,
> They never deride that one
> With speech or with mind.
>
> Wise persons do not use
> Knowledge mantras in anger
> For suppression or for binding,
> Cutting, defeating, or fierceness.

They do not take up a secret mantra
Unless another grants permission.
Though knowing the rite they do not give secret mantras
To one without reverence and respect.

Those skilled in knowledge of tantra do not give
Secret mantras, seals, the details of rites,
Or explanations of tantras and maṇḍalas
To one who has not entered a maṇḍala.

Do not eat or step over any
Of the likenesses of weapons,
The likenesses of sentient beings,
And all the varieties of seals.

Intelligent practitioners
Do not deride the medicines,
They do not let filth touch them
Nor let their foot pass over them.

Those of the Great Vehicle and the intelligent
Should not debate [out of competitiveness].
Having heard about the strong Bodhisattvas
One should not disbelieve [their powers].

Never compete with practitioners
Through the use of mantras.
Do not engage in fierceness
Having angered at small faults.

Those dwelling in a repetition rite
Should not sing, dance, or play,
Nor wear garlands and colors
For the sake of making beauty.

Completely abandon
Stepping over [others], jumping,
Running, making clamor,
And physical bad forms.

Those dwelling in true practice
Should forsake false, cruel, altered,
Harsh, and divisive speech,
And not make much senseless talk.

Do not live with or
Argue with Forders,[33]
Nor repeat secret mantra with those
Of bad lineage such as butchers.

When the intelligent engage in repetition,
Except for just a mantra servant,
They do not talk at all
With others without purpose.

Do not rub the body with grain oils,
Also do not eat sesame.[34]
One wanting feats should completely
Forsake turnip, garlic, salts,

As well as the different
Varieties of sour condiments,
Sour yeast,[35]
Sesame candy, and red beans.

A repeater of secret mantra
Should forsake all foods of bringers of harm,[36]
All sacrificial food,
Kṛsara and milk-soup.

Do not mount chariots and so forth,
Nor step on lotuses and the like.
Do not let your foot touch
Food that has been thrown away.

A repeater of secret mantra
Should abandon all acts of charm,
Holding shoes and umbrellas [for show],
And all adornment[37] of the body.

Do not rub a foot with a foot,
Nor rub a hand with a hand.
Do not dispose of feces and urine in water,
Nor dispose of it near water.

Do not eat in just the hands,
Nor in a bronze bowl.
Also do not eat from the backs of leaves.[38]
The wise do not eat desirous food.[39]

A wise practitioner
Does not sleep with others
On beds or couches in uncleanliness
Nor supine, nor with face down.

Do not eat again and again,
Nor very little nor a whole lot.
Do not not eat at all,
Do not eat also what you have qualms.

Do not take pleasure in the strange,
Nor look at any entertainment,
Do not desire with a mind of attachment
Unbridled behavior[40] with regard to women.

Those dwelling in a repetition rite
Should not at all use food and activities
Without physical, verbal,
And mental restraint.

Skillful householder repeaters
Do not wear clothes of dyed color,
They also do not at all
Wear old or smelly clothing.

Do not deride yourself,
Do not dislike yourself,
Do not become depressed,
Nor let illness overpower you.

Except in response [to your guru]
You should not leave off secret mantra.
With obscured mind deride not [mantra repetition]
Nor let your firmness be loosened.

Repeaters should recite secret mantra
Without the mind straying to anything else,
Without many thoughts and without
A mind of desire for the unclean.

Do not perform rites for [expelling] demons
And do not perform protections or reversals.
Repeaters should not perform poisonous rites
With their own mantra or also through others.

Except when they are needed for practice
Do not use secret mantras in other ways.
Do not use secret mantras for
Competition or for testing prowess.[41]

The intelligent should repeat three times
And should bathe three times [every day].

and:[42]

Practitioners should especially
Do worship on the eighth,
Fourteenth, and fifteenth, and
For half the month of magical display.[43]

They should intensively make effort
In repetition, burnt offering, offering,
Likewise in keeping the vows,
And particularly in the meritorious.

and:[44]

Repeaters should always think of the sayings
In the discipline of knowledge mantra,
"Do this, do not do that,"
And the vows of the precepts.[45]

Night and day you should forsake
Desire for your own pleasure,
Be without carelessness toward
"Having done these, this should be done."

At night individually disclose
Deeds done heedlessly during the day.
Also those done at night disclose in the morning.
Thoroughly rejoice in what was done well.

Practitioners should earnestly dwell
In repetition, burnt offering, cleanliness,
Superior knowledge mantras, self-restraint,
And the discipline of knowledge mantra.

It is said that *kṛsara* (above, p. 70) is a stew of boiled black sesame, red bean, and rice mixed together.

With regard to the unsuitability of bestowing mantra on those who have not entered a maṇḍala, the *General Tantra* says:

> If those not having seen well
> A maṇḍala repeat mantra,
> They will not attain feats and
> After death will fall to a bad state.
>
> Whoever shows to them
> Rites of mantras and seals
> Also fall from their pledges and go
> To a hell of wailing sentient beings.

Therefore, it is in all ways unsuitable based only on a rite of permission for one who has not been allowed entry into a maṇḍala of any of the four tantras and received initiation to practice a deity and so forth and for a mantra to be granted to such a person. With regard to the way to purify the ill-deed if such is done, the same text says:

> If you fall from the pledges
> Just explained, you should repeat
> Your essence mantra
> A hundred thousand times.
>
> Or it is suitable to repeat a thousand times
> The retention mantra of mental nonobscuration,
> Or perform a burnt offering of pacification,
> Or it is suitable to enter a maṇḍala.[46]

You should strive in these ways and purify [the ill-deed].

Ratnākarashānti's *Precious Lamp, Commentary on the Difficult Points of the "Kṛṣhṇayamāri Tantra"* (*kṛṣṇayamāripañjikāratna-pradīpa*)[47] [a Highest Yoga Tantra] after setting forth those pledges, says:

> Though I have gathered these pledges from Action Tantras, yogis of the Great Yoga [Yoga Tantra] also should keep whatever are suitable in accordance with their area, time, and thought. Moreover, those who propound that they are yogis of the Great Yoga and wish to be unclean and unrestrained are intractable because in accordance with one's thoughts and so forth,[48] statements of looseness occur even in Action Tantras:
>
> > Being clean is suitable, being unclean is suitable,
> > Eating food is suitable, not eating is suitable,
> > Bathing is suitable, not bathing is suitable,
> > Through being mindful of one's deity,
> > achievement comes.
>
> but mostly yogis of even the Great Yoga do not transgress the above-mentioned pledges.

Thus, not only are these to be kept by those who have received Action and Performance initiations but also by those engaging in Highest Yoga. Therefore, identifying these and the root infractions, one should strive to be utterly unpolluted by root infractions, and even if one is polluted by other faults, they should be disclosed and purified in accordance with the statement that one should not be heedless of faults but at night amend those which occurred during the day and in daytime amend those which occurred at night.

Preliminaries

How to Perform Prior Approximation While Abiding in the Pledges

This has two parts: the reasons why prior approximation is needed and its stages.

The Reasons Why Prior Approximation Is Needed

The *Concentration Continuation Tantra*[49] says:

> "The concentrations of secret mantra"
> Are said to be supremely secret.
> Achievement will not occur without them
> For even the great ascetic sages.

Thus, it is said that if they do not have the two concentrations [with repetition and not relying on repetition], which will be explained [in this and the next four chapters], even sages striving at mantra and having ethics, disciplined conduct, and asceticism do not achieve [feats of pacification, increase, and so forth].

The Chapter on Feats in the *Vairochanābhisambodhi Tantra* also says:

> If one wishes to attain
> The great waves of wisdom
> Or the five clairvoyances[50]
> Or the feats of holding the knowledge mantras
> Or long life becoming a youth,

As long as this approximation
Is not done, so long are these not attained.

This fact is similar in both Action and Performance Tantras.

Therefore, in accordance with the statement in the Chapter on the Character of Mantras in the *Susiddhi Tantra*:

After analyzing one's lineage,
Nature, powers, and activities
Approximation to secret mantra[51]
Agreeable to one's own mind is begun.

you should:

- attain well an initiation in a maṇḍala of the three lineages [One-Gone-Thus, lotus, or vajra], come to possess the Bodhisattva vows and mantra pledges, and become skilled in the stages of what to do,
- whereupon you should assemble in complete form the place, companions for practice, and so forth with their characteristics as taught in the *Susiddhi Tantra* and the *Questions of Subāhu Tantra,*
- and then you should perform the preliminary approximation cultivating the two concentrations [with repetition and not relying on repetition] together with their branches.

With respect to initiation, the *General Tantra* says:

One who has been conferred initiation well
In a maṇḍala of the One-Gone-Thus lineage
Becomes a master of the maṇḍalas
And so forth of all three lineages.

It is said that if initiation is obtained in a maṇḍala of the One-

Gone-Thus lineage, you become a master of all three lineages; with initiation of the lotus lineage, you become a master of the lotus and vajra lineages, and with that of the vajra lineage, you become a master of just that lineage. Nevertheless, you still must receive the oral transmission of the meditation and repetition of the mantra being practiced.

Stages of Approximation

This has two parts: concentration with repetition and concentration not relying on repetition.

Concentration with Repetition

This has three parts: how to perform the preliminaries to the four-branched repetition, the actual concentrations of the four-branched repetition, and how to conclude[52] the concentration of the four-branched repetition.

How to Perform the Preliminaries to the Four-Branched Repetition

This has four parts: (1) what to do initially in the place of dwelling, (2) how to bathe outside and enter the place of practice, (3) having enrobed and sat on the cushion, blessing the offerings into magnificence, and (4) protecting oneself and the place.

What to Do Initially in the Place of Dwelling

Making the seal and reciting the mantra of the general lineage.[53] Daily, when you have risen from bed in the early morning for the first session and at the beginning of other sessions, you should construct the pledge seal of whichever of the three lineages you are practicing and then utter the [respective] secret mantra.

One-Gone-Thus Lineage

Having turned up the palms, bend the two forefingers a little (seal 1); having placed this on the head, say:
Oṃ tathāgata-udbhavaye svāhā.

Lotus Lineage

Join the palms; then form them in the manner of a blossoming lotus (seal 2); having placed this at the heart, say:
Oṃ padma-udbhavaye svāhā.

Vajra Lineage

Reverse and join the palms; join the two thumbs and two little fingers (seal 3); having placed this at the navel, say:
Oṃ vajra-udbhavaye svāhā.

Respectively, these are the seals and mantras of the One-Gone-Thus lineage such as Uṣhṇishavijaya, the lotus lineage such as Avalokiteshvara, and the vajra lineage such as Vajravidāraṇa.

Homage to the Buddhas and Bodhisattvas. Then, observing all the Buddhas in the ten directions, bow down at their feet with this mantra:
Oṃ sarva-tathāgata kāya-vāk-citta-vajra-praṇamena sarva-tathāgata-vajra-pāda-vandanaṃ karomi.

Offering yourself. Then, offer your body, saying:

> If until I am in the essence of enlightenments, I totally and thoroughly offer myself at all times to all Buddhas and Bodhisattvas abiding in the ten directions, may the great Buddhas and Bodhisattvas please take me. Please bestow upon me the unsurpassed feat [Buddhahood].

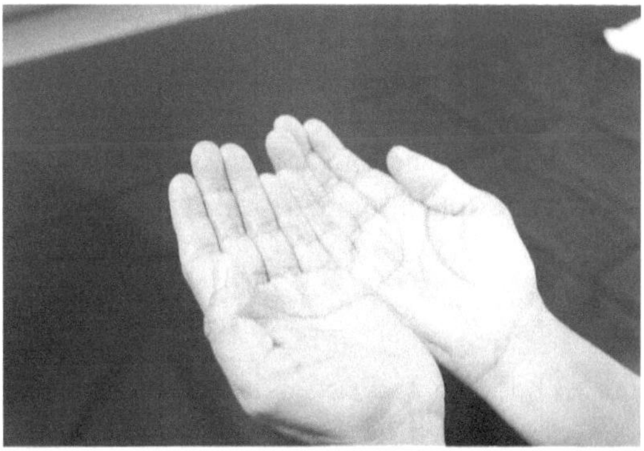

Seal 1. Pledge seal of the One-Gone-Thus lineage

Seal 2. Pledge seal of the lotus lineage

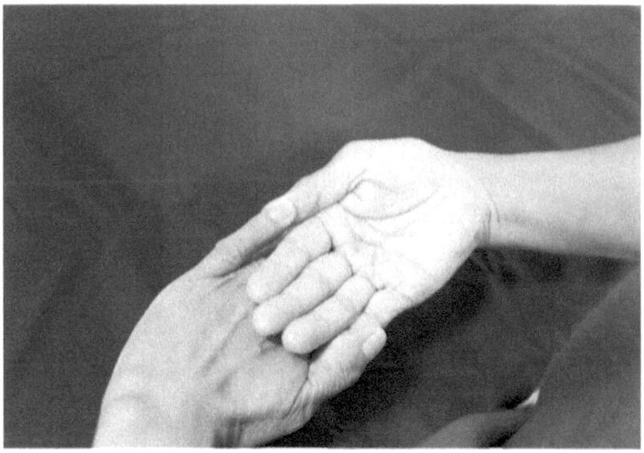

Seal 3. Pledge seal of the vajra lineage

Refuge and altruistic mind generation. Then, go for refuge and generate the altruistic mind of enlightenment with:

> To Buddha, Doctrine, and Supreme Community
> I go for refuge until enlightenment.
> To achieve the welfare of myself and others
> I will generate the mind of enlightenment.
>
> Listen, O Buddhas and Bodhisattvas
> Abiding in the ten directions,
> I now for the sake of perfect enlightenment
> Will generate the mind of enlightenment.

Protection through secret mantra and seal. Then create protection with the seal and mantra of the Fierce Unobscured One.[54] The seal is to interlace the fingers of the two hands, making a fist; align and straighten the two little fingers; set the two thumbs beside the forefingers, the tips of which are joined (seal 4). The mantra is: *Oṃ vajra-krodha mahābālā hana daha paca vidhvaṃsaya ucchuṣma krodha hūṃ phaṭ.*

Create protection with this mantra also when eating, drinking, urinating, and defecating.

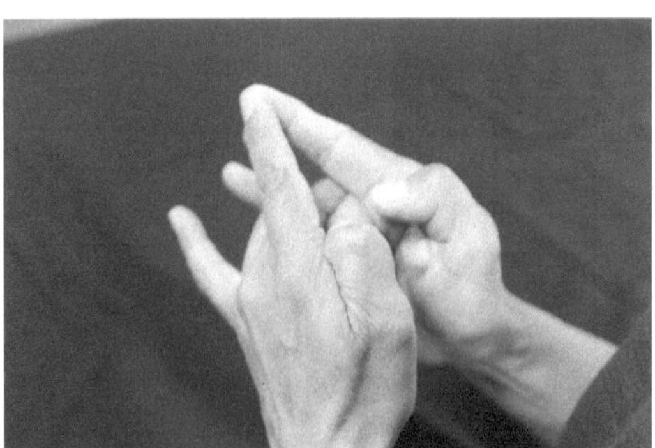

SEAL 4. SEAL OF THE FIERCE UNOBSCURED ONE

Reflection on purity. Then, think that these letters with interconnected flames—*ma,* which is the entity of Vairochana on a moon at one's heart, and *ha,* which is the entity of Achala at one's head—are stirred. Say:[55]
Oṃ svabhāva-śuddhāḥ sarva-dharmāḥ svabhāva-śuddho 'haṃ
(*Oṃ naturally pure are all phenomena, naturally pure am I*).
Believe that [all phenomena are][56] naturally pure.

Going outside. Then, come out of the dwelling place; use the toothstick [for cleaning the teeth] and so forth. Collect and remove [the dirt and dust] in the temple and so forth.[57]

How to Bathe Outside and Enter the Place of Practice[58]

Then, in order to bathe go to a shore where beings do not gather and where there is no fright.

Picking up earth. Interlace the fingers of the two hands on the outside and bend them. Align and straighten the two forefingers, placing the two thumbs at their base (seal 5); touch this seal to clean earth, and say:[59]
Oṃ nikhanavasude svāhā.

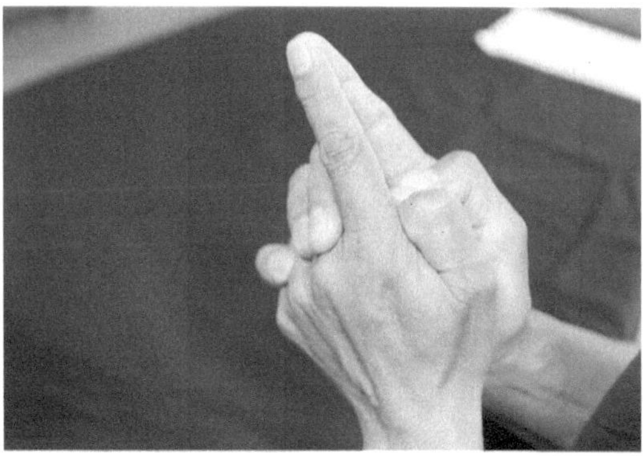

Seal 5. Seal of picking up earth

Pick up the earth, and dividing it into three portions, put these in a clean place. With respect to that, first construct whichever of the three pledge seals indicated earlier (pp. 79–80) is appropriate and then pick up the earth.

Self-protection. Then, create self-protection through Amṛtakuṇḍali. Pressing the nails of the little fingers with the thumbs, form the remaining fingers into a symbol of a vajra; then, crossing [the arms], place these on the shoulders (seal 6). Press the lower lip with the upper teeth and look with a fierce gaze; say:
Namo ratnatrayāya, namaṣcaṇḍa-vajrapāṇaye, mahāyakṣasena-pataye, namo vajra-krodhāya, tadyathā oṃ hulu hulu tiṣṭha tiṣṭha bandha bandha hana hana amṛte hūṃ phaṭ.

Expelling obstructors in the body. Say:
Oṃ hana hana amṛte hūṃ phaṭ.

Bind the two fists inside; having let out and straightened the forefingers, cast this from the head to the feet (seal 7). Thereby, expel obstructors from the body.

Creating vajra armor. Then say:
Oṃ vajra-agni-pratipataye svāhā.

Having turned up the palms, set the two ring-fingers between the two interlaced little fingers. Align and straighten the two middle fingers, and bend the forefingers to the third joint of the middle fingers. Joining the two thumbs, place them in the center (seal 8). Making this seal, put on the vajra armor [to prevent obstructors from entering].

From that seal make the seal of vajra armor. Having spread out the two forefingers, form them in the manner of a vajra (seal 9). Say:[60]
Namo ratnatrayāya oṃ khakili hūṃ phaṭ.

Make the armor [imagining vajra armor], touching the head, the tops of both shoulders, heart, and neck.

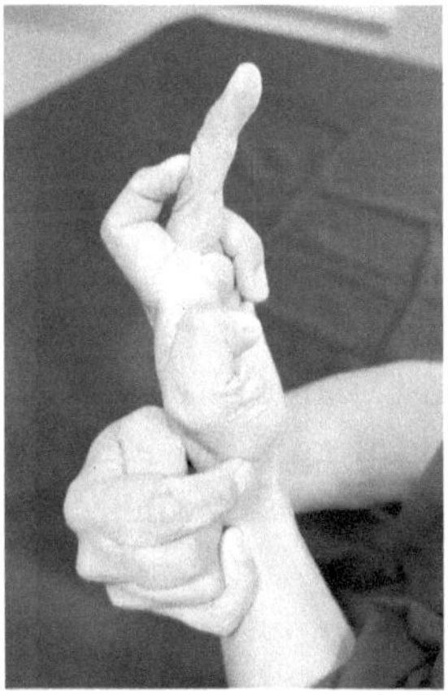

SEAL 6.
SEAL OF AMṚTAKUṆḌALI

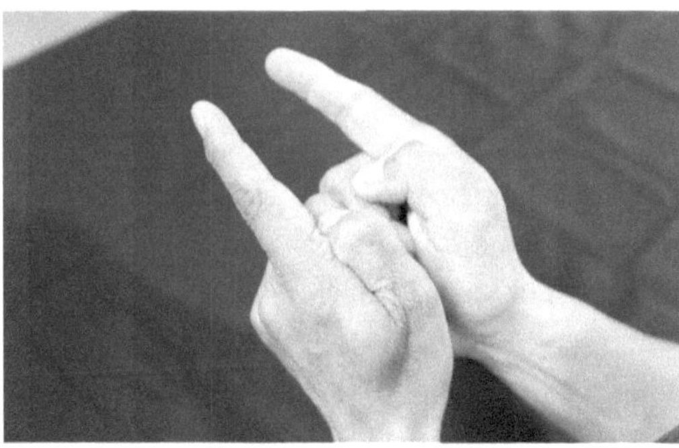

SEAL 7. [SEAL OF EXPELLING OBSTRUCTORS FROM THE BODY]

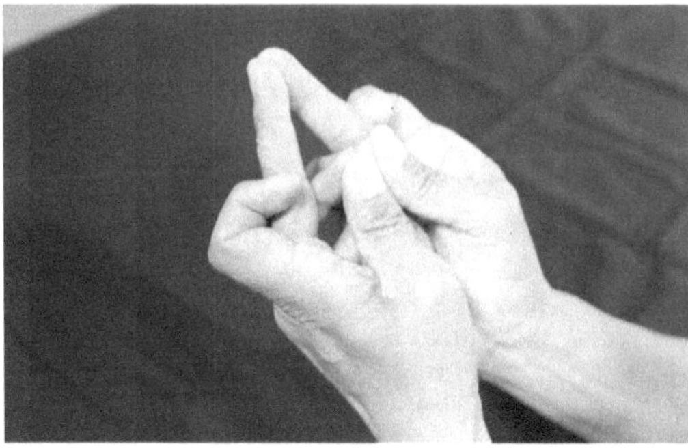

SEAL 8. [SEAL OF PUTTING ON VAJRA ARMOR]

Dispelling obstructors. Then say:[61]
Namo vajrāya hūṃ hana dhuna matha vidhvaṃsaya udsarāya phaṭ.

Press the two middle fingers of the left hand with the thumb, and forming the forefinger and little finger in the manner of a circlet, stick them in the middle joints of the middle fingers. Form the three middle fingers of the right hand in the manner of a vajra and place this in the area of the waist (seal 10). Touch earth or water with this seal of dispelling obstructors. Since [Varabodhi] explains that this dispels obstructors, first touch earth and water.

Casting mantra into the water. Then, cast this mantra into the water:
Namo ratnatrayāya, namaṣcaṇḍa-vajrapāṇaye, oṃ hana hana vajra vajraṇaha.

Sprinkling the earth. Say:
Oṃ kīlikīla vajra hūṃ phaṭ.

With the thumb of the left hand press the nail of the little finger, and form the remaining fingers into a symbol of a vajra (seal 11); touch this seal of Kīlikīla to the water, and sprinkle the earth with the water.

Mantrafying the earth. Then, pick up one portion of the earth, having mantrafied it seven times with:
Oṃ vajra hara hūṃ.

Wearing the bathing cloth, enter into the water just to the disappearance of the navel, and bathe [washing below the navel with the first portion of earth].[62]

Ablution. Then, wash the hands with the second portion of earth. Say:
Oṃ śruti smṛti dharini hūṃ ha.

Having turned upward the palm of the right hand, place the forefinger at the base of the thumb and put the thumb at the center joint of the forefinger (seal 12); perform ablution [of the tops of the

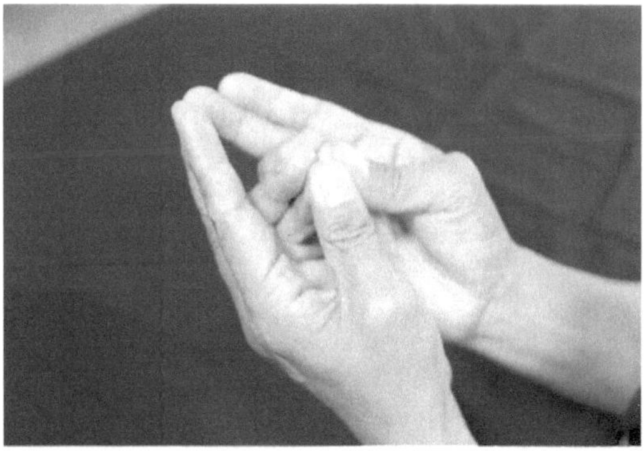

SEAL 9. SEAL OF VAJRA ARMOR

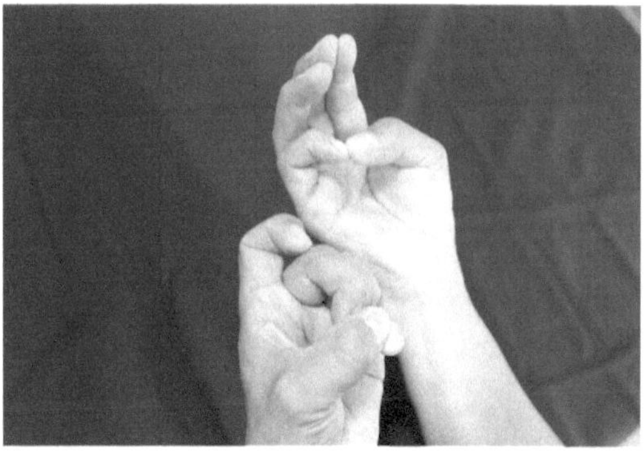

SEAL 10. SEAL OF DISPELLING OBSTRUCTORS

SEAL 11. SEAL OF KĪLIKĪLA

shoulders, mouth, nose, eyes, and ears] with this seal of Sarasvati. The *Questions of Subāhu Tantra* says to perform ablution[63] at this point; it seems that the master Varabodhi holds that just the seal and mantra serve as ablution.

Protecting and tying up the hair. Then, say:
Oṃ susiddhikari svāhā.
Tying up the hair on the head, create protection.

Mantrafying, circling, and rubbing earth on the body. Pick up the third portion of earth, and mantrafy it:
Oṃ bhūr jala hūṃ phaṭ.
Turning it to the right, face it to the sun, and then rub it on the [entire] body.[64]

Stirring the water. Then, recite:
Namo ratnatrayāya, namaṣcaṇḍa-vajrapāṇaye, mahāyakṣa-sena-pataye, namo vajra-krodhāya daṃṣṭotkaṭa bhairavāya tadyathā, oṃ amṛtakuṇḍali khakha khāhi khāhi tiṣṭha bandha bandha hana hana, garja garja, visphoṭāya visphoṭāya sarva-vighnāṃ vinayakāna, mahā-gaṇa-pati jivita antakarāya svāhā.
Having turned upward the palm of the right hand, bend the middle and ring fingers, and press them with the tip of the thumb. Bend slightly the forefinger and the little finger (seal 13). Stir the water with this seal of water-stirring.

Offering to the Three Jewels. Say:
Oṃ rate rate buddhāya svāhā.
Offer three handfuls of water to the Three Jewels.

Pouring water on the head. Then, say:
Oṃ amṛte hūṃ phaṭ.
Pour three double handfuls on your head and wash your hands. With that mantra confer initiation on yourself with three double handfuls of water.

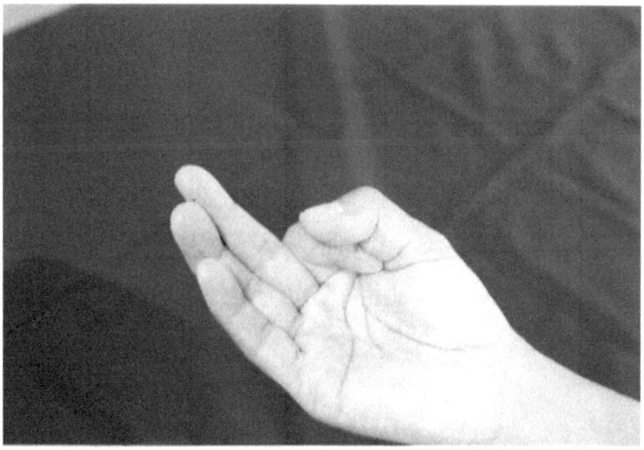

SEAL 12. SEAL OF SARASVATI

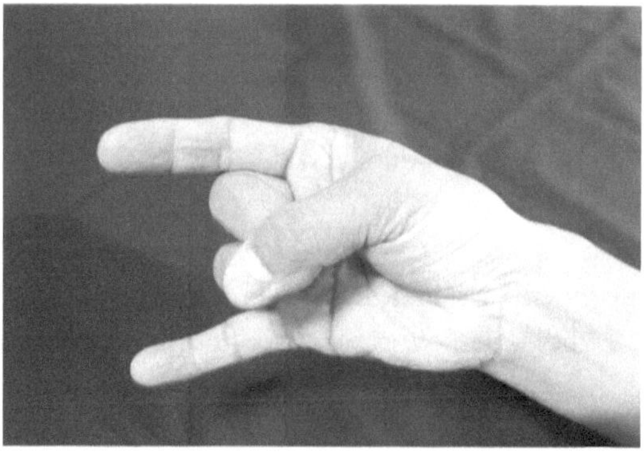

SEAL 13. SEAL OF WATER-STIRRING

Inviting the deity and bathing his/her body. Mentally invite your own deity and ask him/her to reside on a lotus [imagined in front of yourself].[65] Bathe his/her body, saying:
Oṃ sarva-tathāgata-amṛta svāhā.

Then, if repetition is to be done in the temple, repeat the mantra[66] twenty-one times while in the water.

Importance of bathing. The Chapter on Repetition in the *Susiddhi Tantra* says:

> The wise should not apply those
> Repetitions done without
> Restraint or cleanliness to the number
> Of repetitions that are prescribed.

Thus it is said that repetitions done without the cleanliness of bathing and so forth cannot fulfill the count of repetitions; therefore, you should abide in cleanliness.

If extensive bathing cannot be accommodated, it is clear that it is sufficient to bathe with earth and water until the grime is removed; the *Questions of Subāhu Tantra* says:

> Five masses of earth at the anus, three to the [sexual] sign,
> Three for the left, and seven for the two hands,
> Or use earth and water until
> You become free of defilement.

Entering the temple and engaging in the pledges. Then, go up to the temple; having washed the feet, face east or north and do the ablution,[67] whereupon enter the place and, visualizing the deities vividly, do homage [as on p. 80].[68] Then, repeat this engagement in the pledges:
Oṃ viraja viraja mahāvajri, sata sata sarate sarate, trayi trayi virdhamani saṃbhañjani taramati siddha-agretaṃ svāhā.

Having Enrobed and Sat on the Cushion, Blessing the Offerings into Magnificence[69]

Removing contamination. Then, pour scented water in the palm of the hand; repeat the essence mantra of the appropriate lineage [three times][70] [*jinajik, ārolik,* or *vajradhṛk*]; and sprinkling the water on top of the head, clear away defects of contamination and so forth.

Sprinkling the cushion and sitting. Having sprinkled the cushion

[made] of *kuśa*[71] grass or other material together with [reciting the mantra of] Kuṇḍali (p. 84), sit on the cushion in either the lucky, lotus, or vajra cross-legged manner.[72]

Putting on the circlet and so forth. Then, affix a circlet to the wrist of the right hand and a sprinkler [made] of *kuśa* grass to the ring finger of the right hand. Tie on the *ze'u kha* [a piece of red silk or cotton bound on the head] and [tie up the hair as an][73] image of the crown protrusion, as explained earlier (p. 88) [with the mantra *oṃ susiddhikari svāhā*].

With respect to the circlet, an uneven number of threads spun by a girl should be wound and tied in an uneven number of knots. Having affixed one rosary bead of the appropriate lineage [such as a seed of *putranjiva roxburghii* for the One-Gone-Thus lineage][74] in the center, repeat the mantra of your own [respective lineage]. These are the knowledge mantras of the circlets, [the mantras of] the lineage mothers:

One-Gone-Thus Lineage

Oṃ ruru spuru jvala-tiṣṭha-siddha-locane sarva-artha-sādhani svāhā.

Lotus Lineage

Homage to the Three Jewels. Homage to the Bodhisattva, the great being, the Superior Avalokiteshvara.

> May I cure all illness
> Of all sentient beings
> Through seeing, hearing,
> Touching, or remembering me.

Tadyathā kaṭe vikaṭe kaṃkaṭe kaṭa vikaṭe, kaṃkaṭe bhagavati vijaye svāhā.

Vajra Lineage[75]

Oṃ kulandhari bandha bandha hūṃ phaṭ.
It is explained that when the circlet has been anointed with incense, the mantra should be repeated a hundred times.[76] Concerning the benefit of these, the Chapter on the Knowledge Mantra Discipline in the *Susiddhi Tantra* says:

> Through these you will not be
> Overpowered by obstructors.
> Through saying these you will quickly
> Attain feats and become pure.

Concerning the sprinkler [made] of *kuśa* grass, the *Susiddhi Tantra* says:

> Those who have individually repeated
> The three syllables of the lineage essence,
> Jinajik, ārolik,[77] vajradhṛk,
> Should put on the ring finger
> A sprinkler [made] of *kuśa* grass.
> When practitioners strive,
> Their hands become pure through this.

The mantra to be cast in the *ze'u kha*—the skull binder made from red silk or cotton—is the mantra to be cast in clothing that will be set forth below [p. 146]: *Oṃ rakṣa rakṣa mānā sarva-buddha-adhiṣṭhana ātma civara svāhā*]. Clothing should [also] be implanted with that mantra and then worn.

Holding the vajra.[78] Make a three-pointed vajra from wood pierced by lightning, *nimba* (*azadirachta indica*), a charred piece of funeral wood, sandalwood, or other [wood]. Wash it well; rub on red sandalwood [in a water solution] and generate [that is, imagine] it as a fierce Susiddhi [after reflecting on its emptiness]. Having invited a likeness of him, perform offering and so forth. At the initial cer-

emony [after making the vajra], repeat a thousand times and on other occasions seven times:
Oṃ dhuna vajra hā.
Make this petition:

> Supramundane Victor, abide in me out of empathy. Please perform all my actions [such as protecting from obstructors].

When making offerings and so on to the action vajra, hold it with the left hand. Every day make offerings to it and mantrafy it seven times with his mantra [given just above]. The *Susiddhi Tantra* says that through holding it obstructors, false leaders, and harmers will take fright and leave.

Dispelling obstructors.[79] Then, preceded by refuge and generation of an altruistic mind of enlightenment [as done earlier, p. 82], repeat into the scented water with the mantra either of all the activities of [the appropriate among] the three lineages (p. 95) or of Kuṇḍali, explained earlier, *namo ratnatrayāya* and so on (p. 84). Clear away obstructors in the flowers and so forth through sprinkling [them with scented water]. Dispel [the obstructors] with scented water put in the left hand [into which] the appropriate[80] secret mantra of the lineage lord or lineage essence such as *jinajik* [for the One-Gone-Thus lineage, *ārolik* for the lotus lineage, and *vajradhṛk* for the vajra lineage has been repeated].

Generating magnificence. Then, from the seal of dispelling obstructors explained earlier (p. 86–87, seal 10), take hold of the [left] middle finger with the three middle fingers of the right formed in the manner of a vajra (seal 14). With this seal of generating magnificence distribute [the magnificence] on top of the perfume, flowers, and so forth and repeat the mantra of generating magnificence. Think that through these the offerings have become marvelous divine articles. The mantras of the three lineages are:

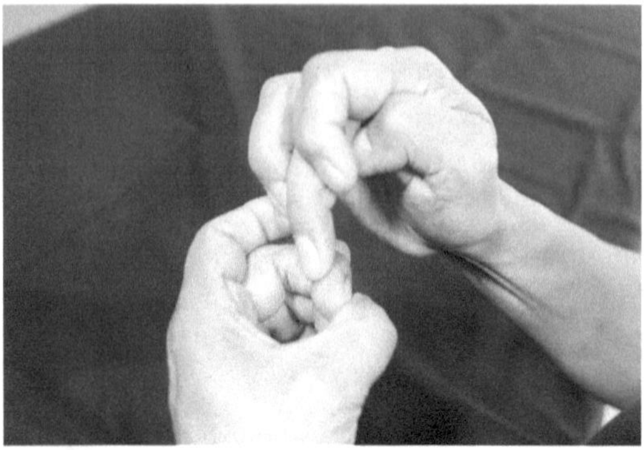

SEAL 14. SEAL OF GENERATING MAGNIFICENCE

One-Gone-Thus Lineage

Oṃ tejaḥ tejaḥ sani siddhi sādhaya hūṃ phaṭ.

Lotus Lineage

Oṃ divya divya dhipaya, aveśa mahāśrīyaye svāhā.

Vajra Lineage

Oṃ jvala jvalaya bandhṛ hūṃ phaṭ.

Then, bless them into magnificence with the mantra of Kuṇḍali explained earlier (p. 84), and repeat the essence mantra of the appropriate lineage (p. 93).

SELF-PROTECTION[81]

Either make the seal and mantra expelling obstructors in the body explained earlier (p. 84) or protect yourself with another that you know. Then repeat the mantra for all activities of [the appropriate among] the three lineages or the mantra of Kuṇḍali into the scented water and sprinkle it on yourself, dispelling obstructors. The mantra of Kuṇḍali is *namo ratnatrayāya . . . amṛṭe hūṃ phaṭ.* (p. 84). The mantras for all activities of the three lineages are:

One-Gone-Thus Lineage

Oṃ traṃ bandha svāhā.

Lotus Lineage

Oṃ namo mahā-śrīyāyai, sau me siddhi siddhi sādhaya, śivi śivaṃkari, abhaha, sarva-artha-sādhani svāhā.

Vajra Lineage

Oṃ kīlikīla vajra hūṃ phaṭ.

Place-Protection[82]

Circle of Protection. Meditate on the circle of protection. Repeat into the scented water seven times:
Oṃ kīlikīla vajri vajri bhur bandha bandha hūṃ phaṭ.
Perform sprinkling in all directions.

Creating the ritual dagger. Make the ritual dagger seal. Form the middle and ring fingers of both hands mutually like circlets, and join the tips [of the ring and middle fingers] at the base of each.

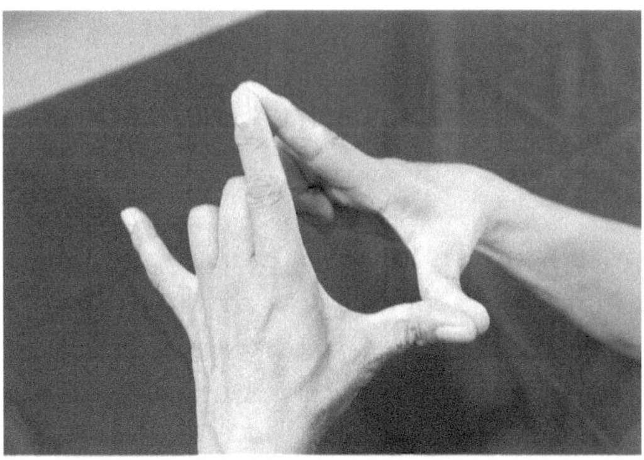

Seal 15. Seal of the ritual dagger

Align and straighten the two little fingers and forefingers; form the thumbs in the manner of a ritual dagger and set this on the earth (seal 15). Recite the mantra just explained [for the circle of protection] and implant the obstructors with the fierce Vajra Daggers [generated as fierce deities]. Think that thereby they have become immovable.[83]

Fumigation. Infuse them with the fumes [of powdered incense] in which you have repeated:
Oṃ susiddhikara jvalita, ananta-murtaye jvala jvala bandha bandha hana hana hūṃ phaṭ.

Think that the upper gods[84] are bound [the lower having been bound in the last step]. That mantra is a general one for the three lineages. [Otherwise] for the One-Gone-Thus lineage say:
Oṃ jvala hūṃ.

For the lotus lineage say:
Oṃ padmini bhagavati mohaya mohaya, jagad mohani svāhā.

In both the [*Susiddhi*] *Tantra* and Varabodhi's *Clear Realization* a separate one does not appear for the vajra lineage.

Binding obstructors. Then sprinkle the area and surroundings with the scented water into which the lineage essence mantra (p. 93) has been repeated. Think that all obstructors of the directions are bound by this mantra: *Bhrūṃ oṃ amṛtodbhava udbhava hūṃ phaṭ, namo ratnatrayāya, namaṣcaṇḍa-vajrapāṇaye, mahā-yakṣa-senapataye, oṃ sumbhani sumbha hūṃ, gṛhṇa gṛhṇa hūṃ, gṛhṇapaya gṛhṇapaya hūṃ, ānayaho bhagavān vidyā-rāja hūṃ phaṭ svāhā.*

That[85] is the secret mantra of the knowledge kings of the three lineages.

Creating a fence. Then, from the dagger seal (seal 15), make the fence seal, extending the two thumbs upward (seal 16). Say:
Namo ratnatrayāya, namaṣcaṇḍa-vajrapāṇaye, mahāyakṣa-senapataye, tadyathā oṃ sara sara vajra-prakara hūṃ phaṭ.

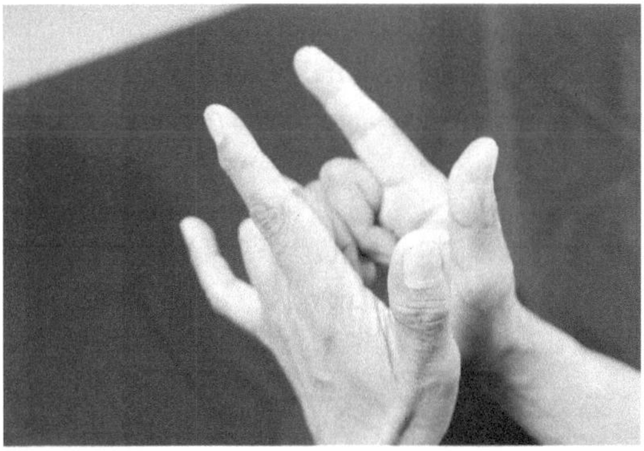

SEAL 16. FENCE SEAL

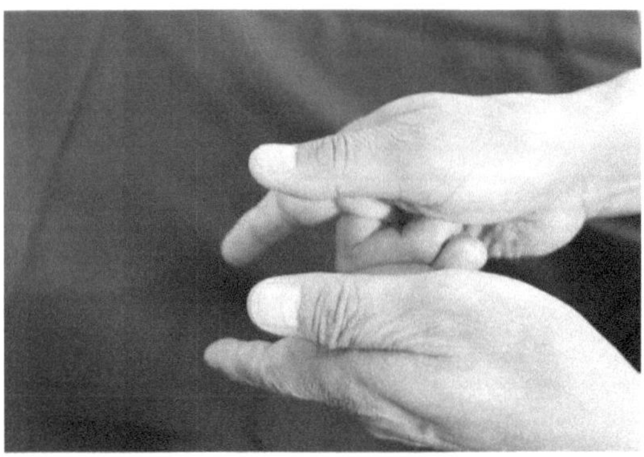

SEAL 17. LATTICEWORK SEAL

Think that thereby a vajra fence[86] encircles [the area] without break.

Creating a latticework. Displaying the fence seal itself (seal 16) upside down, move it in a circle (seal 17). Think that a vajra latticework or tent emerges on top of the vajra fence [like a roof, saying]:

Namo ratnatrayāya, namaṣcaṇḍa-vajrapāṇaye, mahāyakṣa-senapataye, oṃ visphu-rakṣa-vajrapāṇi hūṃ phaṭ.

Then, empower these [that is, the fence and roof] with the mantras and seals of Kuṇḍali and Kīlikīla explained earlier (pp. 84 and

86), seals 6 and 11; for the Kīlikīla mantra see p. 95).[87] The *Susiddhi Tantra* explains that the two fierce ones [Kuṇḍali and Kīlikīla] are always associated with the fence, latticework, and daggers surrounding the house [in the sense of abiding there as protection].

Closing off the area. Then, make fists; press the nails with the thumbs. Let out the forefinger and encircle from the middle (seal 18). Thinking that a blazing mass of fire covers all the directions of the fence, close off the area [saying]:[88]
Namaḥ samanta-vajranāṃ, oṃ tara tara, turu turu, maṭa maṭa, bandha bandha, sarvatra apratihate, sasime samabandha, kuru kuru tara tara samanta-vajre, samanta-vajre, kuru amale kuruṇa, maye tutaye tutaye, bara bara, kara kara sumima samanta, vidhvaṃsaye jvalāya svāhā.

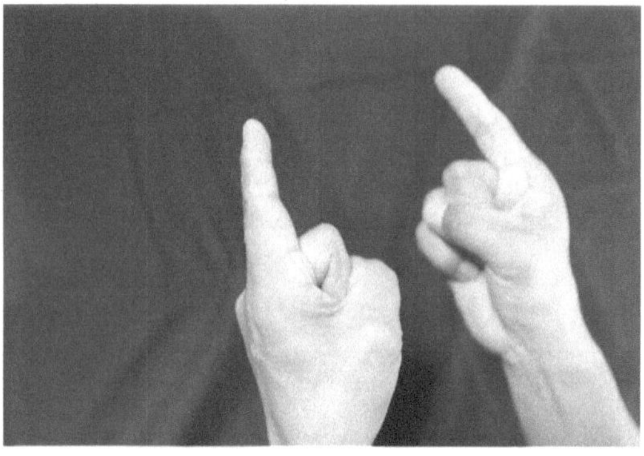

SEAL 18. [SEAL OF CLOSING OFF THE AREA]

Self-Generation

The presentation of the actual concentrations of the four-branched repetition has two parts: the concentrations of the branches of repetition and how to perform repetition in dependence on the branches.

The Concentrations of the Branches of Repetition

The *Concentration Continuation Tantra*[89] explains that initially offerings are made to a deity [generated, that is, imagined, in front of the meditator], after which one generates oneself as a deity:

> Only having first made offerings
> To the image of the deity's body
> Within contemplating the presence of a One-Gone-to-Bliss
> in front,
> Then those endowed with wisdom dwell in yoga.

Buddhaguhya's commentary says:

> Offering is just an illustration; hence, observing cleanliness, protecting oneself and the place, inviting the deity, and so forth should be performed because without having done these there is no way to make offering to the deity. [The rites of] cleanliness and so forth [through to offering] can be known in[90] all [texts on knowledge mantra, and so forth].

Hence, Buddhaguhya asserts the stages [of practice] this way [with generation of a deity in front first and self-generation afterwards], but Varabodhi's *Clear Realization of Susiddhi* explains that first one generates oneself as a deity and then invites the deity and makes offering and so forth; although the former appears to be more convenient for stages of meditation (see p. 109), I will explain [the order] in accordance with Varabodhi since at this point I am mostly depending on his text.[91]

The explanation has two parts: (1) generating oneself as a deity and (2) offering and so forth to the wisdom-being invited in front.

Generating Oneself as a Deity

Straighten your body and leave it that way.[92] Reverse the senses from the varieties of objects to the inside. Having made your neck like a peacock's, gently breathe in and out. Open your eyes just a little and aim them at the point of your nose. [Gently] press teeth with teeth, and touch your tongue to the palate.

Observing all the [various] groups of sentient beings, generate the great compassion that assumes the burden of freeing them from suffering. Then, with striving generate the [altruistic] mind of enlightenment thinking, "For their sake I will attain highest enlightenment," and [within that aspiration] amass the collections of merit [through cultivating deity yoga, and so forth] because all achievements of virtue while abiding in that mind induce omniscient wisdom, and virtues blessed into magnificence with this mind induce limitless happiness even in cyclic existence.

Ultimate deity. Then the *Concentration Continuation Tantra*[93] indicates cultivation of an ultimate mind of enlightenment [a wisdom directly realizing emptiness in the continuum of a Bodhisattva] with:

> Afterwards, freed from the limbs
> [Your own suchness is] not discriminated [by others]—
> Thoroughly devoid of discrimination, and subtle.

> Unmoving and clear, mental analysis dwells in its presence.

[After offering and so forth to a deity invited in front,[94] you should reflect on the ultimate deity, your own suchness that is freed from the branches, or senses, in that the senses do not ultimately exist. It is not discriminated by others in that it is not apprehended by others and thus is formless. It is thoroughly devoid of discrimination in that it does not apprehend forms and so forth; it is subtle, for it is without inherent existence. Your mental analysis should remain in the presence of the suchness of self in the sense of revealing it; that analysis should be unmoving—stable and free of excitement—and clear, that is, free of laxity.]

The self imputed by the [non-Buddhist] Forders (*tīrthika*) does not exist even conventionally; therefore, a "self" is only imputed to just these five aggregates [forms, feelings, discriminations, compositional factors, and consciousnesses. The stanza above] should be taken [as indicating] how [the step of realizing] the suchness of such a self should be done.

The time [for contemplating this] is after making offering and so forth to the invited deity [in Buddhaguhya's order of first generating the deity in front]. With respect to how it is done, when an analytical consciousness concerned with the ultimate [that is, emptiness] makes investigation, [the self] is not discriminated, that is, apprehended, by the eye consciousness and so forth of others' continuums; also, that the self discriminates, that is, apprehends, other objects is abandoned because the branches such as eyes and so forth are released, that is, are not [ultimately] established. Thereby, truly existent apprehended-object and apprehending-subject are refuted; hence, [suchness is] the emptiness of duality; this is how oneself should be considered.

Nevertheless, thinking, "Who could stop this appearance of [external] objects due to internal mistake like a dream consciousness!" one might conceptualize that a nondualistic consciousness truly exists. To this, it is said [that suchness is] "subtle" because the absence of inherent existence [of all external and internal phenomena] is very subtle. Through this, it is shown that the ultimate suchness of self is devoid of all signs of the proliferations [of inherent existence].

The mode of meditation is indicated by the line, "Unmoving and clear, mental analysis remains in its presence," which will be explained below (pp. 162–64). Varabodhi's explanation[95] also appears to be similar in meaning to Buddhaguhya's.

Just as the suchness of oneself is ultimately free from all [conceptual and dualistic] proliferations, so is the suchness of the deity. Therefore, create the pride of the sameness of oneself and the deity in terms of nonconceptual perception of the undifferentiability of those two, like a mixture of water and milk. Concentrate without appearance [of the two as different] until your knowledge is very definite. This is the ultimate deity.

Meditating thus on the emptiness of all [coarse and subtle] selves of persons and other phenomena is the same essential as when, in other tantras, prior to meditating on a deity, one says the mantra *svabhāva* and so on [*Oṃ svabhāva-śuddhāḥ sarva-dharmāḥ svabhāva-śuddho 'haṃ* (Oṃ naturally pure are all phenomena, naturally pure am I.)] and meditates on its meaning.

Sound deity. Rising from that,[96] imagine the resounding of the tones of the mantra of the appropriate deity; this is the sound deity. It does not appear in Varabodhi's *Clear Realization of Susiddhi,* which at this point describes meditation on that mind [of the ultimate deity] in the aspect of a moon disc. Both masters [Buddhaguhya and Varabodhi] are similar in this respect [in that Buddhaguhya also describes in the next step a moon disc, which is an appearance in form of the ultimate deity above which the sounds of the mantra resound].

Letter deity. Then, think that [the mind realizing the ultimate deity] appears in the sky in the aspect of the written letters of the mantra of the appropriate deity. Think that the mind having the aspect of [realizing] the suchness of oneself and the deity as undifferentiable has become a moon disc and that on it [the letters] are set in order [the sounds of the letters mixing with the form] like very pure mercury adhering [that is, mixing completely with] grains of gold.[97] This is the letter deity.

Except for only a description in Varabodhi's *Clear Realization of Susiddhi*[98] of [the mantra here as] "the mantra to be repeated," neither of the two masters clarifies the point; however, it is apparent that [not just a long mantra but also] a short one such as *oṃ bhrūṃ svāhā,* which is explained in the *Ocean of Means of Achievement* as the mantra of Vijaya of the One-Gone-Thus lineage or *oṃ māricyai maṃ svāhā* for Mārīchi of the One-Gone-Thus lineage is also sufficient. The same should also be understood for Avalokiteshvara [*oṃ maṇi padme hūṃ*] and so forth of the lotus lineage and for Vidāraṇa and so forth of the vajra lineage.

Form deity. Then, Buddhaguhya says no more than that light emits from the moon; however, according to Varabodhi's explanation,[99] forms of the deity being meditated emerge at the points of variegated lights that have arisen from the moon and mantra. They fill all the sphere of the sky and through emanating great clouds of offerings make splendid offerings to all the Victors. Also, they emanate great clouds from which a rain stream of ambrosia descends, extinguishing the fires of the hells and satisfying those [beings with whatever they want]. Then, the light as well as the divine bodies return and enter the moon disc that is one's mind. Meditate on this as the appropriate deity [that is, the moon as well as the letters are transformed into the deity's physical form] and create the pride of nondifference from yourself. This is the form deity.

It is also suitable to consider extinguishing the sufferings of the hells as just an illustration [of relieving others' misery] and to apply this to other sentient beings [hungry ghosts, animals, humans, demi-gods, and gods—relieving them of their particular miseries and satisfying their wants through a rain of ambrosia].

Seal deity. Then, about the seal deity, Buddhaguhya's *Commentary on the "Concentration Continuation Tantra"* says, "Having risen also from that, make the seals at the gathering [which is a point four finger-widths above the hair line], crown of the head, and so forth as well as their branches [that is, mantras]." Thus, in accordance with the individual tantra's explanation to construct the seals of the crown protrusion, hair-treasury [one coiled hair in the middle of the brow], eyes, and so forth, and to recite mantra, bless into magnificence the crown and so forth of the appropriate deity from among the three lineages, touching those places with the seals and mantras. This is the equivalent of blessing into magnificence the eyes and so forth in other tantra sets [through the imagination of letters or deities in those places].

If you do not do it that way [using the specific seals and mantras for those places, you may use the general mantra and seal of the lineage].[100] Varabodhi[101] says, "Then, having constructed the pledge seal of one's own deity, bless into magnificence the heart, the point between the brows, neck, and tops of shoulders." Hence, it can be done with the [general] pledge seals and mantras of the three lineages explained earlier (pp. 79–81). You should understand that for Vijaya, Sitatāpatraparajita, and Mañjughoṣha, for instance [who are of the One-Gone-Thus lineage], it should be done with the seal and mantra of the One-Gone-Thus lineage [and similarly with those of the lotus and vajra lineages for their deities.

Sign deity. For the sixth deity, Buddhaguhya's *Commentary on the "Concentration Continuation Tantra"* speaks of "aspected conventional meditative stabilization" and "conceptual deity."[102] In other places the term "sign deity" is used. This should be understood as meditating on just the deity [as which you have been] generated.

Sources

Buddhaguhya[103] describes meditation in this manner by way of the six deities in commentary on the meaning of the *Concentration Continuation Tantra*[104] where it says:

> Having set oneself thus,
> Meditate with the mantra minds.

"Mantra minds" are the six deities, called the six aspects of secret mantra. "Meditating them" is explained as suffusing the mental continuum with these. [The six deities are not described in the *Concentration Continuation Tantra* itself but] are clearly set forth in the *Extensive Vidāraṇa Tantra,* which Buddhaguhya's *Commentary on the "Vidāraṇa Tantra"*[105] cites:

> Having first bathed, a yogi
> Sits on the vajra cushion
> And having offered and made petition
> Cultivates the six deities.
> Emptiness, sound,[106] letter, form,
> Seal, and sign are the six.

Buddhaguhya says, "Making oneself into Vajrapāṇi by way of the six manifest enlightenments—the emptiness of the Buddha or Bodhisattva who has entered [oneself], and so forth." This is the equivalent of deity generation by way of the five manifest enlightenments[107] in other tantras [Yoga and Highest Yoga].

With respect to this mode [of self-generation by way of cultivating the six deities] Buddhaguhya's *Commentary on the "Concentration Continuation Tantra"*[108] also says, "These are the general stages for cultivating the minds of secret mantra; they likewise should also be applied to descriptions in other aspects." Buddhaguhya thus asserts that [the six deities] should be used in all the various generation rites of deity yoga in Action Tantra.

Modes of Meditation

There are two types of meditation on the six deities (see also p. 158):[109]

1. With concentration (*dhyāna*): engaging in many observations by way of many aspects, contemplating the six deities in series or contemplating the color, hand symbol [and so forth] of the deity in series;

2. with meditative stabilization (*samādhi*): dwelling on the body of the deity as contemplated [formerly] with concentration but [now] by way of one aspect, not many, because meditative stabilization is described as one-pointedness of mind.

The *Concentration Continuation Tantra*[110] says:

> Meditate with the mantra minds.
> Restrained, dwell in meditative stabilization.
> Thoroughly restrain vitality and exertion.

The first line "Meditate with the mantra minds," and the second line "Dwell in meditative stabilization," indicate the two modes of meditation. The rest speaks of restraining vitality (*prāṇa*) [breath] and exertion (*āyāma*) [distraction] when meditating with meditative stabilization.

The stages of this [restraining of breath and distraction when meditating with meditative stabilization] are these: Prior [to meditative stabilization], position the body so that it has the essential points as explained earlier (p. 100), and having meditated through to the form deity[111] without the distraction of thought elsewhere, assume the pride of clear appearance as the deity. Then the wind [or energy] that leaves and enters through the eyes, ears, nose, mouth, navel, male or female organ, anus, and hair-pores is [called] vitality (*prāṇa, srog*). Exertion (*āyāma, rtsol ba*) is "mindfulness" (*dran pa*) [not in the usual sense of keeping a virtuous object in mind but] in the sense of becoming distracted to another object of observation that you have taken to mind. Therefore, bind these two in this way: stop the exhalation and inhalation of breath; withdraw inside movements of the breath throughout the body like a turtle's retracting its limbs and drinking water with the tongue by means of the upwards-drawing wind. Also, withdraw inside the usual intense movement of the unequipoised mind out from the community of the senses. Nevertheless, leave your eyes a little open, raise your face a little, and set yourself in one-pointed meditative equipoise, observing your own body clarified as a deity. The observation should be done like that of a person dwelling in a cave and looking outside [in the sense that one is as if inside the divine body, observing it from within].

The passage from the *Vairochanābhisambodhi* quoted earlier (p. 54) establishes that the meaning of vitality and exertion (*prāṇāyāma, srog rtsol*) is as given above. In another way, vitality (*prāṇa*) is as described above, but here *āyāma* means to *stop* exhalation and inhalation and sever the continuum of their movement.

Hold [your breath] in that way with whatever capacity you have [all the while observing one aspect of the divine body]. Then, when unable, let the breath out gently; relax, viewing yourself clarified as a deity, and then act again as before [stopping breath and distraction and observing the same one aspect of the divine body]. The method for resting when tired from meditating will be explained later [in the chapter titled "Mantra Repetition"].

Here, in order for the divine body to appear clearly, meditative stabilization in which the mind remains for a long period [on one object] must be generated. Since the horse of the mind is wind [that is to say, since the mind rides on wind, or currents of energy], Buddhaguhya's *Commentary on the "Concentration Continuation Tantra"* speaks of holding the wind, in consideration that it is easier to hold the mind to one object of observation when the wind is held:

> The mind—the monarch—surrounded by a retinue of mindfulness, meditative stabilization, mental engagement, and so forth is asserted as being mounted on the horse of vitality (*prāṇa*); when the horse of vitality [wind] is held, the mind—the monarch—as well as the retinue will definitely be held. For another [text] says, "Vitality [wind] is to be stopped; when it is stopped, one's mind as well as mindfulness, intellect, mental engagement, and so forth will definitely be held."

Although concentration also requires restraining [vitality and exertion], it operates on many objects of observation and, therefore, does not require restraining like that necessary for meditative stabilization to operate on one object. Hence, the *Concentration Continuation Tantra* says, "Restrained, dwell in meditative stabilization" (p. 106) with regard to meditative stabilization and not concentration.

To what point should this be performed? According to the *Vajrapāṇi Initiation Tantra* quoted earlier (pp. 57–59), it should be performed until attaining the capacity to stop the pride of ordinariness by means of the clear appearance of a deity as well as by means of the pride of being a deity in all modes of behavior. Therefore, it is not sufficient just to hold the mind to the appearance of a divine body; once the pride [of being a deity] is made firm, the mind must also be held to that; both [clear appearance and pride] are necessary. These points will be explained at length on the occasion of the stage of generation in Highest Yoga Tantra.

In Highest Yoga the wind yoga of holding the winds is prescribed after deity yoga has become firm; however, here it is said that it should be done simultaneously with holding the mind on the divine body. [In Highest Yoga Tantra the holding of the winds, or the stopping of vitality and exertion, specifically refers to stopping the movement of the winds in the right and left channels and thus is performed during the stage of completion and after attaining steady clear appearance of the deity in the stage of generation. Hence, even in Highest Yoga Tantra the stopping of vitality and exertion *as explained in the lower tantras* for the sake of withdrawing the mind inside and setting it on the appropriate object as long as one likes is also performed in connection with the early stages of holding the mind on the divine body.][112]

Although the master Varabodhi did not explain these [two types of meditation], I have described them in accordance with the master Buddhaguhya's clear exposition of the meaning of the [*Concentration Continuation*] *Tantra*. It is evident that they are very important.

It is convenient to do this combination of wind yoga and holding the mind on the divine body as found in the six deities *after* inviting the wisdom-being [the deity in front], offering, praising, and so forth [since one is thereafter free to remain withdrawn]. It is not convenient to invite the wisdom-being after [self-generation since one would have to be disturbed from single-pointed equipoise]. Therefore, on the occasion of initial practice, the order should follow Buddhaguhya [performing generation in front first and self-generation afterwards].

On occasions when one has performed prior approximation and then bestows initiation [on another], or performs a rite of cleansing [others' obstructions, and so forth] related with a vase, or achieves feats for oneself or others [such as increasing wealth] and so forth, whichever of the two orders is done appears to be the same. If self-generation is done after [generation in front], perform the offering and praising to [yourself generated as a deity] in accordance with what is prescribed by other masters who composed *Means of Achievement* for Action and Performance Tantras. [Offering and praising would be done twice, once for the deity generated in front, as explained in the next chapter, and again for oneself after generating oneself as a deity.] When self-generation is performed beforehand, it is permissible to perform the offering and praising [of the two deities—the one generated in front and oneself] at the same time if these are not done separately.

During self-generation other masters say to meditate on one's own appropriate deity completely [with retinue and so forth]. However, according to these masters [Buddhaguhya and Varabodhi] the main deity of the individual lineage is sufficient on the occasion of self-generation during initial approximation. When achieving one's own and others' aims, once prior approximation is finished, it is better—during self-generation—to meditate on the deity in complete form as explained [in the rite with surrounding figures, and so forth].

[In connection with self-generation] it is suitable to perform the entry of the wisdom-being [that is, the dissolving of the actual deity into oneself imagined as that deity], conferring of initiation [on oneself by an invited initiation deity], seal implanting [the affixing of the seal, or sign, of the lineage through imagining the lineage lord at the crown of the head after initiation], and so forth as explained by other masters. However, there also is no contradiction in acting in accordance with these two masters' not describing these.

Generation in Front

The presentation of how to make offering and so forth to the wisdom-being invited in front has six parts: (1) generation of the residence, (2) inviting the resident deity and asking the deity to sit, (3) displaying seals, (4) offering and praising, (5) disclosure and so forth, and (6) cultivating the four immeasurables.

Generation of the Residence[113]

In front of yourself in the direction where a painting [of the deity] or the like has been arranged, imagine a ground of many precious substances covered with golden sand. Bless it into magnificence with:

Oṃ calavī hūṃ svāhā.

On top of it, imagine a great ocean of milk [that is, of white color] free from such faults as scum and adorned with flowers such as lotus, *utpala,* and so forth with many flocks of jewel birds flying overhead. Bless these into magnificence with:

Oṃ vimāla-dhaha hūṃ.

In the center, imagine the square Mount Meru, adorned from its four sides with sets of stairs made from gold, silver, sapphire, and topaz. All over it are wish-granting trees well grown and adorned with a thousand flapping victory banners. On the top of the mountain imagine a lotus stalk adorned with many precious substances, having petals of various jewels, golden corolla, and anthers of topaz with silver lines surrounding the top of its center. Many *yojanas* in breadth, the lotus stalk rises out of the center of Mount Meru, and from it hundreds, thousands, ten thousands, and ten millions of lotus latticeworks emerge.

From the [position] of palms in homage interlace [the fingers] and press the left thumb with the right (seal 19). Bless [the imagined residence] into magnificence, repeating a hundred times:[114]

Namaḥ sarva-tathāgatānāṃ sarvathā udgate spharaṇa-himaṃ gaganakhaṃ svāhā.

Also, mentally imagine a canopy [appearing] above the residence in an instant. Although Varabodhi's *Clear Realization of Susiddhi* does not mention meditation on an inestimable palace [as a residence for the deity] at this point, it does later,[115] saying, "Ask him to come again, together with an inestimable palace."

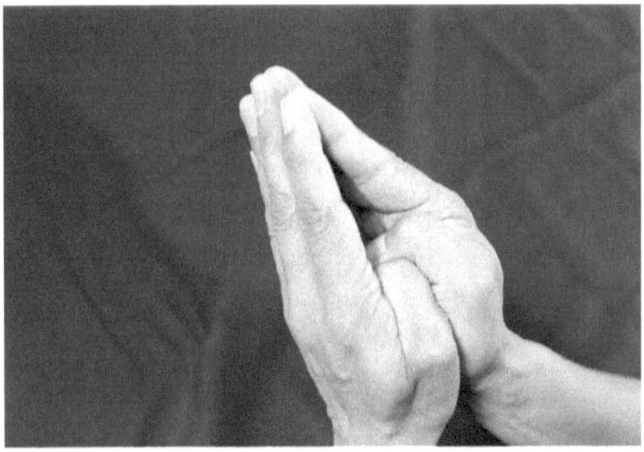

SEAL 19(A). [SEAL OF BLESSING]

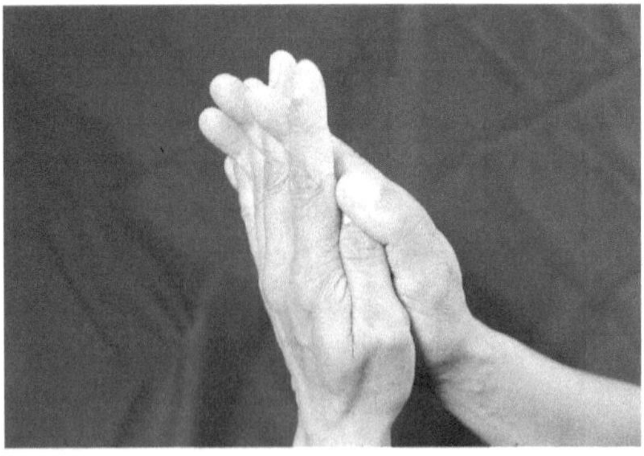

SEAL 19(B)

Therefore, an inestimable palace should also be generated. [One first imagines an empty inestimable palace into which the deity comes with deity's own palace, which fuses with the former, much like a wisdom-being fusing with a pledge-being.] Furthermore, it can be generated all at once in the center of the former lotus just as were the others [the land, ocean, trees, and so forth] without being generated from syllables. Or it can be generated from *bhrūṃ* [imagining the syllable, which turns into the palace]. It is similarly permissible to generate a second lotus [inside the palace] as the deity's seat.

These two masters [Varabodhi and Buddhaguhya] do not speak of generating an inestimable palace or of other seats in self-generation, but other masters' *Means of Achievement* mention thrones supported by lions, and so forth, seats of living beings [such as a deer], generation inside a reliquary for Vijaya, and so forth.

Inviting the Resident Deity and Asking the Deity to Sit[116]

Preparing an oblation

Invitation must be done with oblation [like drink offered to a visitor]. It must, therefore, first be achieved [that is, it must be prepared, cleansed of obstructors, and made magnificent]. The oblation vessel can be gold, silver, stone, wood, or other than those; a copper vessel is auspicious in common for all [activities, whether of pacification, increase, or ferocity]. In such a vessel offer oblation of [ground] barley and milk for pacification [of illness, demons, and so forth] and high feats (see p. 169); offer oblation of [ground] sesame and yogurt for increase and middling feats; offer oblation of cow urine and rice with *kodrava* [a common grain] or blood for ferocity and low feats. Offering oblation of a mixture of [ground] parched rice, fragrant incense, white flowers, *kuśa* grass, and sesame in pure water is auspicious in common for all activities [pacification, increase, and ferocity].

Set out [whatever has been chosen] and suffuse it with incense. Bless the oblation into magnificence, repeating seven times either the mantra of the knowledge king (p. 96), the essence mantra of the general lineage (p. 93), the mantra of all activities of the individual lineage explained earlier (p. 95), or the mantra of inviting a deity [to be explained two paragraphs below].

Inviting the deity

Then, face in the direction where the painted figure or the like is; bow down (as on p. 80), and kneel on the ground; construct the seal of invitation by intertwining the fingers, turning the palms upward, aligning and straightening the two forefingers, and beckoning with the two thumbs (seal 20). Say:

> Due to [my] faith and [your compassionate] pledges
> Come here, come here, O Supramundane Victor.
> Accepting this oblation of mine
> Be pleased with me through this offering.

At the end of the mantra [described in the next paragraph], add *ehyehi*.[117] Holding the vessel, offer it in a line with your head for the One-Gone-Thus lineage, and in a line with the chest and navel for the other two lineages [lotus and vajra respectively]. Think that because of this wisdom-beings similar to those [imagined deities] come [that is, the actual deities come to receive the offerings].

With respect to the mantra, invite a male deity with the mantra of the knowledge mantra king (p. 96); invite a female deity with the mantra of the knowledge mantra queen. Or do it with [the deity's] individual mantra. Or the *Susiddhi Tantra* says that invitation with the general essence mantra of the lineage, such as *jinajik ehyehi* for Vijaya [of the One-Gone-Thus lineage and similarly *ārolik ehyehi* for the lotus lineage and *vajradhṛk ehyehi* for the vajra lineage] is supreme.

Furthermore, the Chapter on Invitation, in the *Susiddhi Tantra*[118] says that when the deity to be invited is standing, sitting, or

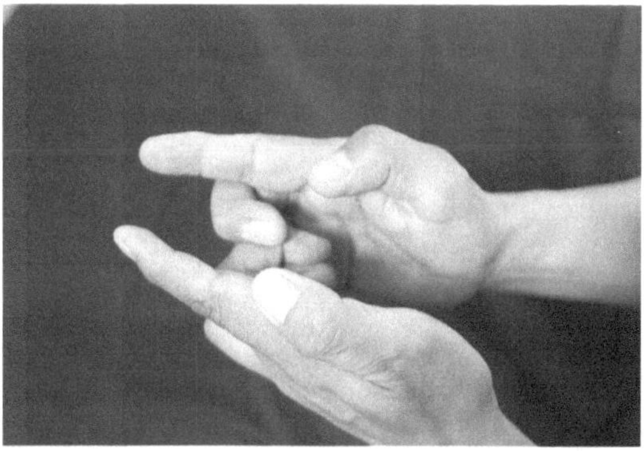

SEAL 20. SEAL OF INVITATION

bent to one side, one should assume that form and then make the invitation with oblation. Also, it says that, if the oblation has not been obtained as prescribed [in the rite], one should ask for the deity's patience and make the invitation with whatever has been obtained.

With regard to how many deities to invite, the *Concentration Continuation Tantra*[119] says [to do it with full retinue]:

> Dwell always to fulfill concentration
> Approaching the body of a Victor
> With all the many Knowledge Mantra Ones and Fierce Ones
> As well as Secret Mantra Ones and so forth.

It is as Buddhaguhya's commentary[120] on this explains:

> Imagine the body of a One-Gone-Thus in front of yourself. Imagine that in an instant the sphere of space is pervaded and the perimeter surrounded by Knowledge Mantra Ones, Secret Mantra Ones, Fierce Ones, male and female Emissaries, and so forth. You also dwell in their center with divine pride. Also, those Knowledge Mantra Ones and so forth always dwell in the presence of the Victor. Thereby, through performing deity yoga the māntrika also approaches a Victor.

Offering a Seat

Then, [offer a seat to the deity with the appropriate seal and mantra]. The seal of the lotus posture (seal 21) is to display the pledge seal of the lotus lineage, which was explained earlier (seal 2, p. 80). The seal of the vajra posture (seal 22) is from the seal of the lotus posture to form the three fingers like a vajra. The seal of the heroic posture (seal 23) is from the seal of the lotus posture to join the middle fingers as one. The mantras respectively are:
Oṃ kāmalāya svāhā,
Oṃ vajra-asani hūṃ phaṭ,
Oṃ vajraka hūṃ phaṭ.

In accordance with the explanation to offer an appropriate seat, offer it with those, and ask the deity to sit. Or, offer a seat while reciting the stanza:[121]

> It is good that the compassionate Supramundane Victor has come,
> I am meritorious and fortunate.
> Taking my oblation, please pay
> Heed [to me] and grant [my request].

and the stanza:

> From compassion for myself and migrators,
> As long as I make offering
> May the Supramundane Victor please remain [here]
> Through your powers of magical creation.

Displaying Seals[122]

Then, say:
Śaṃkare samaye svāhā.

Display the pledge vajra seal: press the nail of the little finger with the thumb of the right hand, and form the remaining fingers like a vajra (seal 24).

Seal 21. Seal of the lotus posture

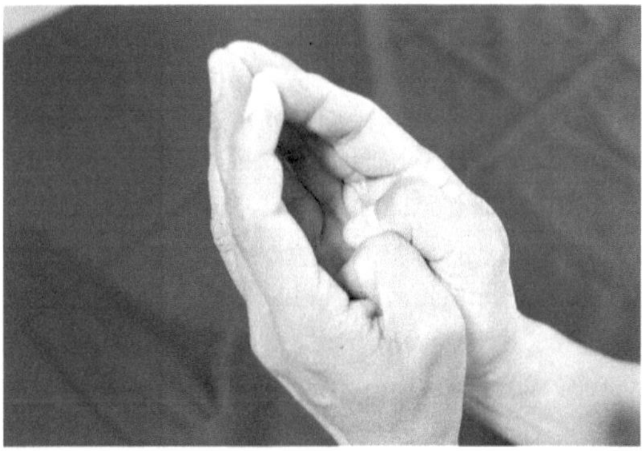

Seal 22. Seal of the vajra posture

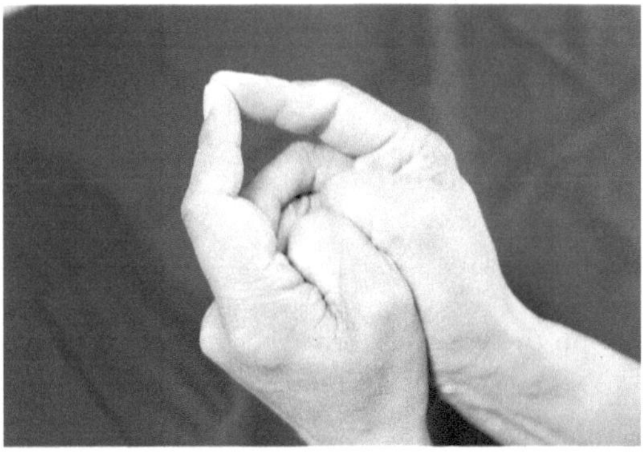

Seal 23. Seal of the heroic posture

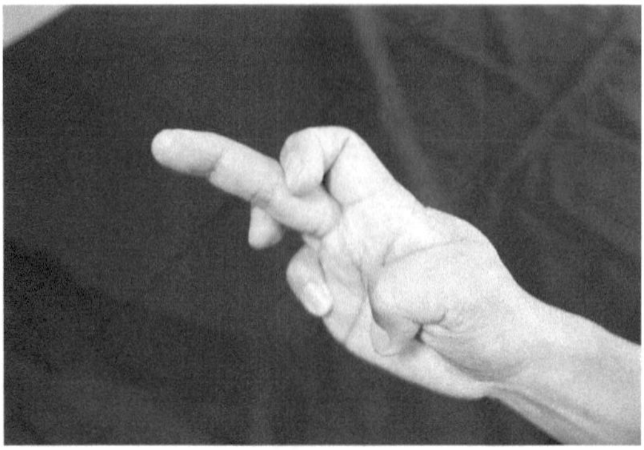

SEAL 24. PLEDGE VAJRA SEAL

Then, displaying the seal of the [appropriate among the] three lineages, say [the appropriate among] the three essence mantras, *jinajik, ārolik,* or *vajradhṛk*. With respect to the seals, for the One-Gone-Thus lineage make the two hands into fists together, and display the two thumbs (seal 25). For the lotus lineage insert the left thumb inside and display the right thumb (seal 26). For the vajra lineage display the left thumb (seal 27).

Then construct the great pledge seal of the lineage (seals 1–3, p. 81) and revolve it. Do it thus, for this is said to afford great protection from all evil deeds by obstructors who arrive after [the achievement of deities due to one's own karma and conceptions], and so forth. If this is not done, drive away these obstructors by repeating the mantra of the appropriate Fierce One into white mustard seed [which is then scattered].

PRESENTING OFFERINGS AND MAKING PRAISES

Presenting Offerings[123]

As before (pp. 93–94), perform the dispelling of obstructors, cleansing, and generation of magnificence with respect to the articles of offering. Since the *Susiddhi Tantra* says also to cleanse them while repeating the [eight] mantras of presenting offerings [as

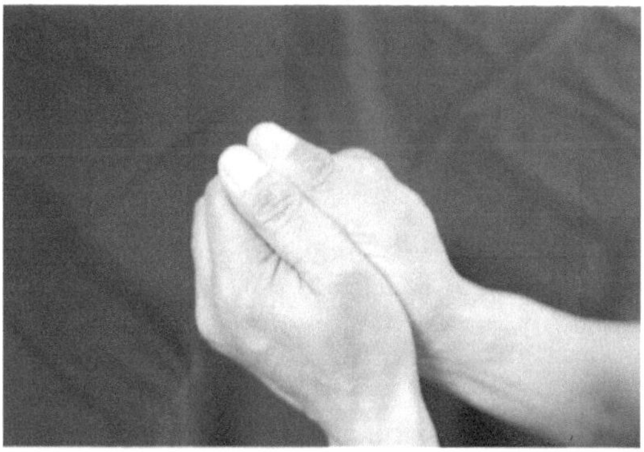

SEAL 25. SEAL OF THE ONE-GONE-THUS LINEAGE

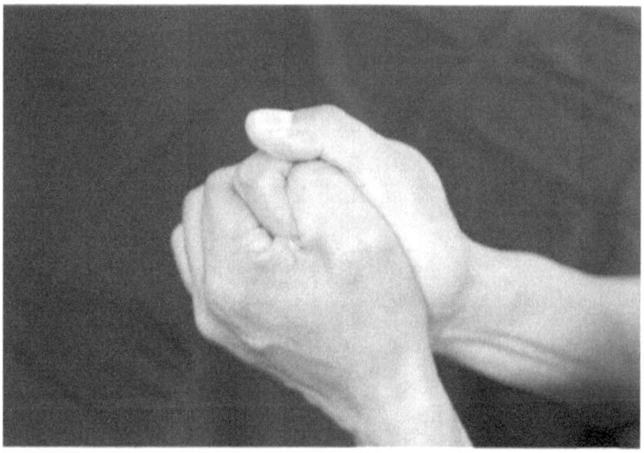

SEAL 26. SEAL OF THE LOTUS LINEAGE

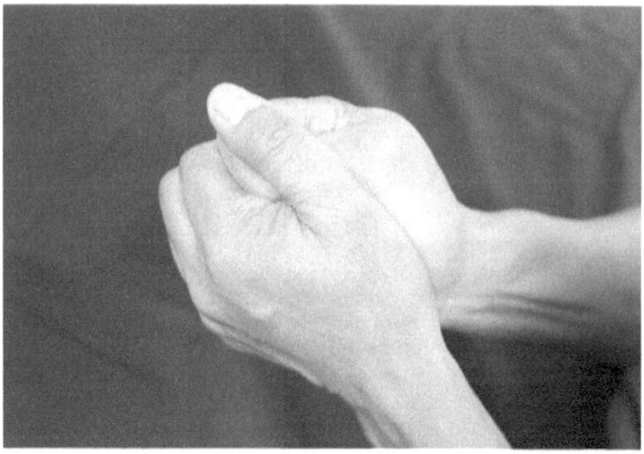

SEAL 27. SEAL OF THE VAJRA LINEAGE

given below] or the mantra of the appropriate particular lineage, these are also necessary.

Offering oblation. Then, construct the seal of oblation; interlace the little fingers and the ring fingers inside; bend the forefingers to the third joint of the two middle fingers that have been aligned and straightened. Join the two thumbs to the sides [of the hands] (seal 28). Say:[124]

> You have come blissfully, Supramundane Victor.
> Come here and please be seated.
> Receiving my oblation also,
> Please take pleasure in mind from this.
> I have respect for you.

At the end of the deity's mantra, offer oblation, saying:[125]
Arghaṃ pratīccha svāhā.

Offering a footbath. Construct this seal: make the forefinger and thumb of the fisted right hand like a pincers, take a flower from the vessel for bathing the feet, and gradually release the fingers (seal 29). Putting "footbath" in place of "oblation" in the above stanza, offer the footbath with:
Oṃ pravarasatkaraṃ pratīccha svāhā.

Offering a bath. Then actually offer a bath to the reflection of the image in a mirror if one is obtainable. If not, make the seal of washing the body: having turned up the palms, join the tips of the forefingers and tips of the thumbs (seal 30). Say:
Oṃ sarva-devatā-acinta-amṛta svāhā.

Imagine washing the deities' bodies with great clouds of perfumed water [which have risen from][126] many precious gold vases and so forth filled with fragrant perfumes.

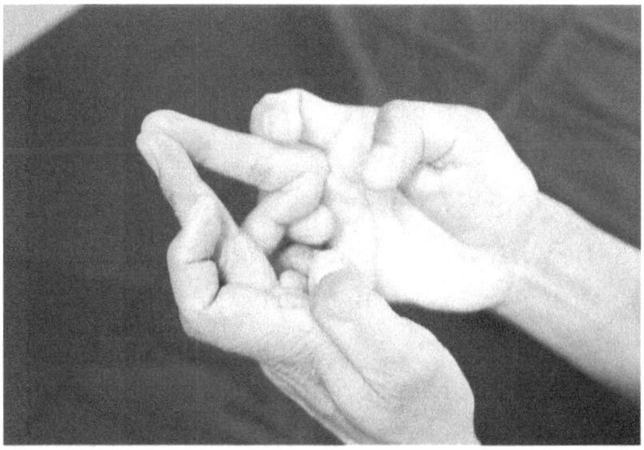

Seal 28. Seal of oblation

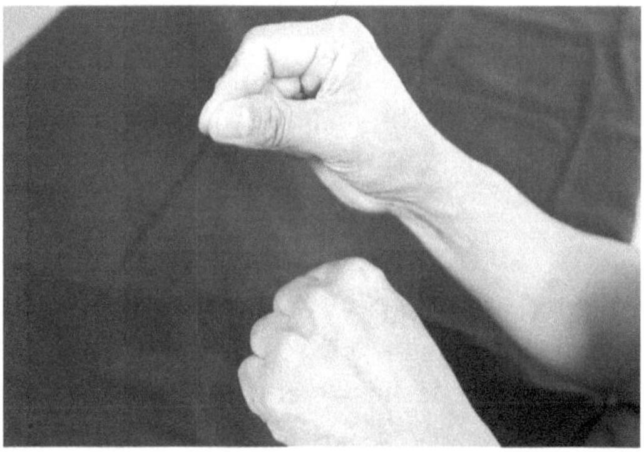

Seal 29(a). [Seal of a footbath]

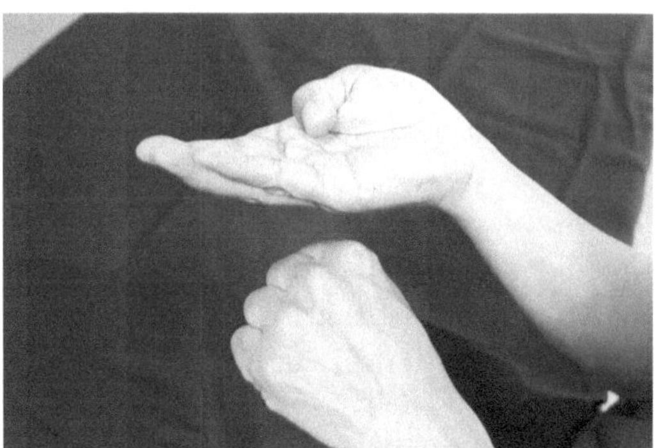

Seal 29(b)

Offering clothing, adornments, and music. Then, mentally offer clothing and adornments. Offer music, and mentally raise up melodies of praise.[127]

Offering perfume. Then, make the seal of perfume: with the left hand hold the wrist of the right hand that is making [the seal of] bestowing refuge (seal 31). Offer the perfume:

> I offer with faith these perfumes
> Of wholesome divine substances
> Arisen from the clean, most clean.
> Receiving them, be pleased with me.
> *Āhara āhara sarva-vidyādhari pūjite svāhā.*

Except for the lamps, use this mantra of offering for the other three [flowers, incense, and food] also.

Offering flowers. Make the flower seal: interlace the fingers of both hands; make the forefingers into one inside the hand and form them in the manner of a bracelet; put the thumbs, formed in the manner of a lotus, beside them (seal 32). Offer flowers with:

> I offer with faith these flowers
> Of auspicious divine substances
> Grown from the clean, most clean.
> Receiving them, be pleased with me.
> *Āhara āhara sarva-vidyādhari pūjite svāhā.*

Offering incense. Make the seal of incense: join together the little, ring, and middle fingers of both hands. Bend the ones in front at the base of the nails of the others; stretch the two forefingers at an angle, and put the two thumbs at their side (seal 33). Offer incense with:

> With faith I offer divine
> Substances made with perfume,

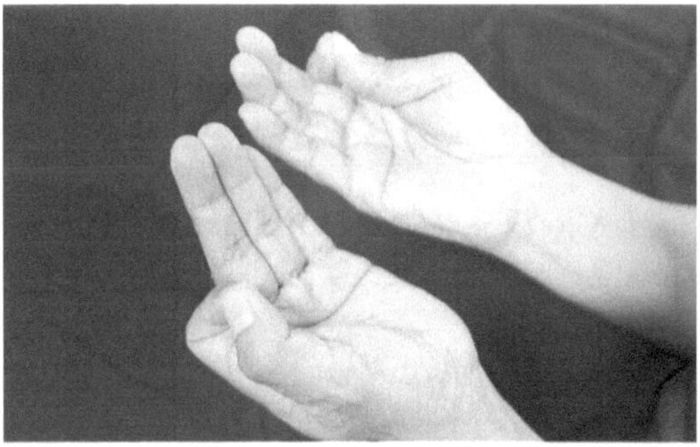

SEAL 30. SEAL OF WASHING THE BODY

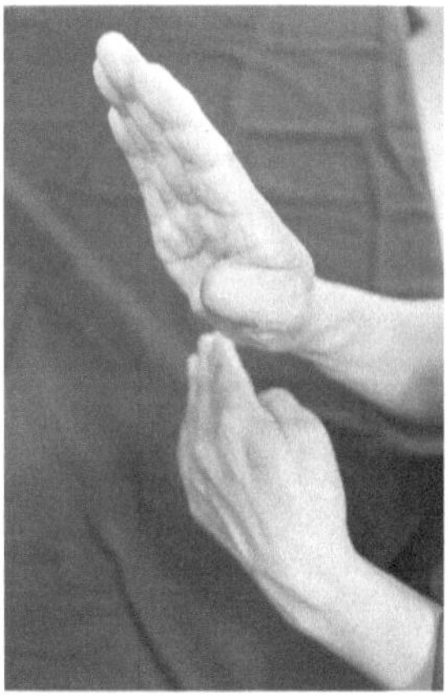

SEAL 31. SEAL OF PERFUME

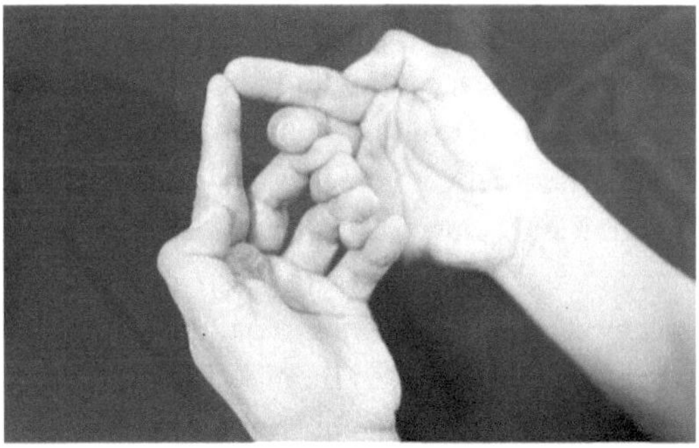

SEAL 32. FLOWER SEAL

Pleasant essences of the forest.
Receiving them, be pleased with me.
Āhara āhara sarva-vidyādhari pūjite svāhā.

Offering food. Make the seal of divine food: from cupped palms, bend the forefingers slightly (seal 34). Offer food with:

I offer with faith these foods
Of mantra, pleasant
Essence of medicines.
Receiving them, be pleased with me.
Āhara āhara sarva-vidyādhari pūjite svāhā.

Offering lamps. Make the lamp seal: join and straighten the thumbs and middle fingers; make the hands into a fist (seal 35). Offer lamps with:

I offer with faith these dispellers
Of darkness, conquering harmers,
Auspicious and virtuous.
I beg you to receive these lamps.
Ālokāya ālokāya vidhādhare pūjite svāhā.[128]

[Comments]

If the articles of offering mentioned for the particular deities of the individual lineages are not obtainable, mantrafy the offering articles of another lineage with the mantras of the lineage [being practiced] and offer them.

If the oblation and below are not actually obtainable, [the *Susiddhi Tantra* and Varabodhi's *Clear Realization*] say that one should make the [respective] seals and mantras and, having visualized the articles of offering mentally, offer them. With respect to the flowers and so forth, paintings of them are also suitable for offering. Even

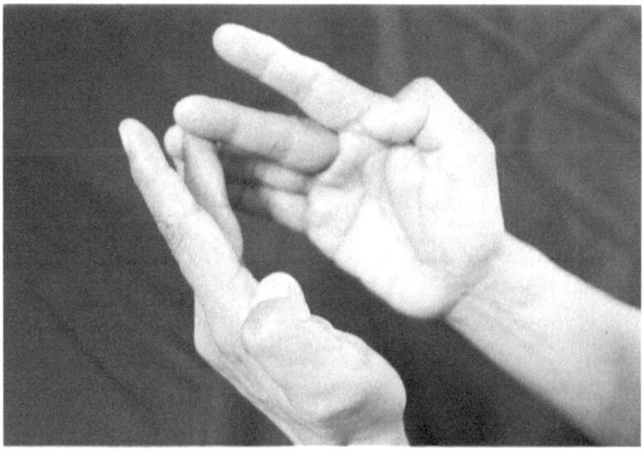

SEAL 33. SEAL OF INCENSE

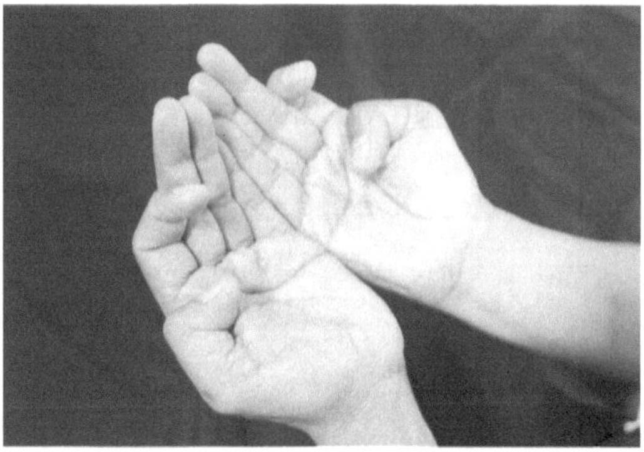

SEAL 34. SEAL OF DIVINE FOOD

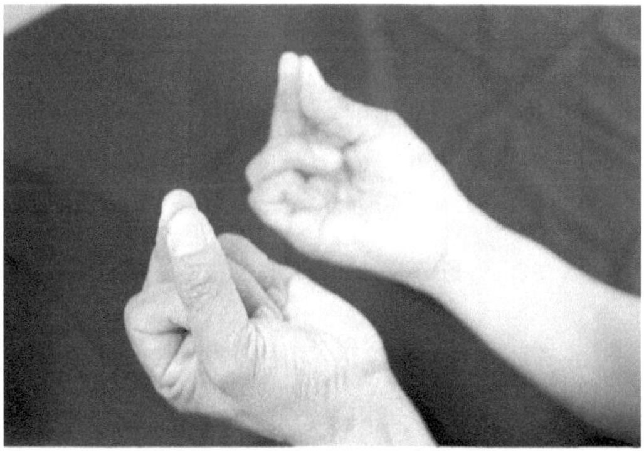

SEAL 35. LAMP SEAL

with respect to actually obtained offerings, it is said that since the mind precedes everything, mental offerings have a great difference [and thus should be given along with external ones].

Having in this way made whatever offering is possible, here also repeat one hundred times the mantra of blessing into magnificence the place explained earlier as repeated a hundred times (p. 112).

Making Praise[129]

Then, make praises to the Three Jewels and the lords of the three lineages in accordance with what is said in the *Susiddhi Tantra*.

Obeisance to the Three Jewels

Homage to the One-Gone-Thus,
Protector with great compassion,
Omniscient teacher, oceanic
Field[130] of merit and attainments.

Homage to the pacifying doctrine,
Through purity separating from desire,
Through virtue liberating from bad migrations,
In all ways the supreme ultimate.

Respectful homage also to the spiritual community,
Released, teaching the path of release,
Thoroughly dwelling in the learnings, excellent of fields
[For accumulating merit], possessing good qualities.

Obeisance to the Lords of the Three Lineages

Homage also to Mañjushrī,
Bearer of the appearance of a youth,
Vividly adorned with the lamp of wisdom,
Dispeller of the three worlds' darkness.

Homage to the always empathetic,
Whose name is Avalokiteshvara,
Composite of all excellent qualities,
Strongly praised by all the Buddhas.

Homage to Vajrapāṇi,
Powerful and fierce,
Virtuous king of knowledge mantra,
Tamer of the hard to tame.

Also, make specific praise of the particular relevant deity, and repeat a hundred times the mantra of bringing forth praise: *Namaḥ sarva-buddha-bodhisattvānāṃ, sarvatra saṃkurumita avijñā-rāshini namo stute svāhā.*

Disclosure and So Forth[131]

Disclosure

With strong contrition for ill-deeds done formerly and firm resolve to refrain from doing them henceforth, disclose ill-deeds:

Ones-Gone-Thus residing in all
Directions of the worlds,
Foe Destroyers, and Bodhisattvas,
I ask you to heed me.
Whatever ill-deeds I have
Committed in any lifetime,
Or disturbed by the power of desire,
Stupidity, or anger in cyclic existence
In former lives or this life,
Whatever ill-deeds I did,
Asked others to do, or admired
Even a little, even slight ones
Unconscientiously done with

Body, speech, or mind to Buddha, Doctrine,
Or Spiritual Community
Or to gurus, father or mother,
Foe Destroyers, Bodhisattvas,
Or to any object of giving,
Or other sentient beings,
Educated or uneducated—
Having mentally collected all these
I bow down in great respect
To the perfect Buddhas and children
Manifest before me now
And disclose individually
And repeatedly my mistakes
With pressed palms and saddened mind.
Just as the perfect Buddhas know
The ill-deeds that I have committed,[132]
I make individual disclosure.
Henceforth I will not do such.

Refuge

Go for refuge with strong intent:

So that the sufferings of living beings might be pacified
I respectfully go for true refuge
To Buddha, Doctrine, and Spiritual Community
As long as I remain alive.

Admiration

Set in equipoise, I take admiration
In the varieties of doctrinal usage.

Entreaty and Supplication

To generate nonconceptual knowledge
I entreat you to turn the wheel of doctrine
And not to pass away from sorrow
Until [all] trainees are satisfied.[133]

Prayer-Wishes

Just as the earlier Buddha Children
Made prayer-wishes,
I also with a virtuous mind
Plant prayer-wishes in that way.
May all beings have happiness,
Peace, and freedom from disease.
May I be capable in all activities
And also possess [all good] qualities.
May I be wealthy, generous,
Intelligent, and patient,
Having faith in virtue, memory of
Former births in all lives, and empathy.

Say those with one-pointed attention to the meaning.

Cultivating the Four Immeasurables[134]

Then, observing all creatures stricken with suffering, dwell in compassion thinking, "May they separate from all suffering"; dwell in love thinking, "May they possess all happiness"; dwell in joy thinking, "May they become happy with the bliss of Buddhahood"; and dwell in equanimity thinking "May they pass from sorrow with the unsurpassed nirvāṇa of a Buddha" [which is an equanimity devoid of the conceptions of apprehended-object and apprehending-subject as inherently existent].

Then, say:

In order to pacify the suffering
Of limitless realms of sentient beings,
To release them from bad migrations,
Release them from afflictions,
And protect them completely from
The varieties of sufferings when
The discomforts of cyclic existence crowd in,
I will generate the altruistic mind of enlightenment.
May I always be a refuge
For all destitute sentient beings.
May I arrive as a protector of the protectorless,
A support of those without support.
May I become a refuge for those without refuge,
Maker of the miserable happy,
And may I cause the pacification
Of all sentient beings' afflictions.
May whatever virtuous actions I have
Accumulated in this and other lives
Assume the aspects of the collections
Called merit and pristine wisdom.
May whatever effort I make
By way of the six perfections
Be of benefit to all beings
Without there being any exception.
Making effort until enlightenment,
I will strive at actions temporarily
And limitlessly over lives so that
In short all the afflictions
Of all sentient beings may be
Pacified and they be freed.

Generate a mind of enlightenment that will definitely suffuse the mental continuum, thinking, "I will attain Buddhahood in order to liberate stricken migrators."

Meditation in this manner on a deity in front is explained by both masters [Buddhaguhya and Varabodhi] as on an invited wisdom-being [who comes from the deity's natural abode to the place of meditation] rather than as new generation [as was done in self-generation]. Other masters assert that having taken the invited deity as the basis of accumulation [of merit through offering and so forth] and after amassing accumulations [of merit], one causes the wisdom-being [the invited deity] to enter oneself generated as a deity, whereupon one performs meditation and repetition. No more than a few describe performing [meditation and repetition] while observing the deity in front, and they assert that when one becomes fatigued from deity meditation, repetition is performed from that point.

Since deity yoga is the main means for achieving feats, here also the mind, as explained before, should be held on the clarification of oneself as a deity. From time to time also visualize the body of the deity like yourself in front and keep the mind on it as long as possible [within maintaining a less emphasized observation of yourself as a deity during that period]. These two [self-generation and generation in front] are the branch of the "base" among the four branches of repetition;[135] it is treated as two in those [four].

Mantra Repetition

The presentation of how to perform mantra repetition in dependence on the branches has three parts: (1) how to assemble the rosary and count, (2) how to perform repetition observing what objects, and (3) how to reinstate the repetition if unfavorable conditions arise.

How to Assemble the Rosary and Count[136]

You should meditatively cultivate deity yoga as explained as long as you do not tire; if you tire, then with respect to the material for the rosary for doing repetition [of mantra] at the end of having [intensively] meditated, [seeds of] *putranjiva roxburghii* (*putrajīva*) are best for the One-Gone-Thus lineage, lotus hearts for the lotus lineage, and *rudrākṣa* (berries of the *elaeocarpus ganitrus*) for the vajra lineage. The *Susiddhi Tantra*[137] says that if these are unobtainable, *lung tang* [?], conch, crystal, pearl, coral, jewel, ivory, clay, various seeds, and so forth are suitable. The *Questions of Subāhu Tantra* explains that lead, copper, and bronze are also suitable.

With respect to the number [of beads], you should use 1008, 108, 54, or 21. Pierce the beads and wash them with the five cow-products [a mixture of milk, yogurt, butter, dung, and urine gathered from orange-colored cows that eat clean grass and drink clean water].

With respect to the string, you should thread the beads with three strands wound together, spun by a girl. Having tied the knot, you should make offerings to the gods. Then, placing the rosary in your cupped palms, bow down to the lamas and gods. Then, to initially achieve [that is, empower] the rosary repeat the appropriate mantra of the three lineages one hundred and eight times:

One-Gone-Thus Lineage

Namo ratna-trayāya, oṃ adbhute vijaya siddhi siddharthe svāhā.

Lotus Lineage

Namo ratna-trayāya, namo aryāvalokiteśivarāya, bodhisatvāya, mahā-satvāya, oṃ amṛtaṃ gale śrīya śrīmalina svāhā.

Vajra Lineage

Oṃ kīri kīri rautriṇi svāhā.

When performing repetition [after the initial consecration], you should join the palms and pay homage to the lamas and gods.[138] Put the mantra rosary in your cupped palms, and repeat the [appropriate] mantra seven times:

One-Gone-Thus Lineage

Oṃ bhagavati siddhi-siddhaya, siddhārthe svāhā.

Lotus Lineage

Oṃ vasu-mati-śrīye svāhā.

Vajra Lineage[139]

Oṃ vajraya jatanajeye svāhā.

Then, raise the rosary to the heart; extend the middle and little fingers of either the right or left hand. Putting the forefinger behind, count with the ring-finger and thumb for all activities or with the forefinger for the fierce. The *Questions of Subāhu Tantra* explains that when repeating one should hold the action vajra explained earlier (p. 92–93) [in the other hand], but if it is unobtainable, one should clench a vajra fist.

How to Perform Repetition Observing What Objects

This has two parts: repetition observing the form of letters and repetition observing the sound of letters.

Repetition Observing the Form of Letters

This has two parts: repetition observing the form of letters at the heart of a deity visualized in front [of you] and repetition observing the form of letters at your own heart.[140]

Repetition Observing the Form of Letters at the Heart of a Deity Visualized in Front

The *Concentration Continuation Tantra*[141] indicates this with:

> Flow to the bases, mind, and sound.
> Dwell on the immutable secret mantra base [the deity].
> Repeat secret mantra without losing the branches.
> If becoming tired, rest yourself.

This is drawn out as meaning that secret mantra should be repeated. With respect to how to do this, repetition should be performed within the context of not losing the four branches [the two bases—self-generation and generation in front—as well as mind and sound] or letting them degenerate.

With respect to "bases," there are two; the first is creation of the pride of your being a deity, and the second is meditation of a deity in front similar to yourself. "Mind" is a moon [disc] set in the heart of the deity in front, the third branch. "Sound" is the series [of letters] of the mantra to be repeated set [around the edge of] the moon, the fourth branch. "Flow to them" is the repeater's adhering to them by way of uninterrupted observation.

The base, in observation of which repetition is performed, must not deteriorate from the appearance of a deity through becoming very familiar with the meditation, due to which the text says, "Dwell on the *immutable* secret mantra base." This is the base where the secret mantra of mind [appearing as a flat moon disc] and sound [the letters set around the edge of the disc facing inward] are placed [that is, the deity in front].

In brief, having restrained vitality and exertion as explained earlier (pp. 106–8), observe simultaneously all three branches in front [the *deity* in front with a *moon* at the heart on which the *letters* of the mantra stand][142] within the complete form of the four branches of repetition [that is, within also maintaining pride in oneself as a deity] and perform repetition. When exhaling, view your own body meditated as a deity [without repeating the mantra], and then do as before [holding the breath, observing the deity, moon, and letters in front, and repeating the mantra].

Resting at the End of a Session

Resting is for the sake of abandoning distraction; the base being rested is yourself—your fruition body [which is explained in the next paragraph. In brief,] leave off contemplating your body as a divine body [in intense one-pointed meditation,] and rise contemplating the fruition body. [This means to leave the contemplation in stages and appear again as a divine figure like an illusion, as is now explained.]

With respect to the stages of leaving the contemplation [when tired]:[143]

- leave off [observation of] the sounds of the mantra letters being repeated through observing the form of the letters [set on the moon at the heart of the deity in front],

- leave the letters through observing the moon without them,
- leave the moon through observing only the body of the One-Gone-Thus [in front],
- leave the body in front through contemplating only your own divine body,
- leave it through contemplating the form of the letters [of the mantra standing on the moon disc],
- leave them through observing their sounds,
- leave them through observing the divine Wisdom Body,
- leave off contemplating the Wisdom Body through contemplating the Truth Body—this being the suchness of self unapprehendable [as inherently existent],
- then, contemplate as your fruition body [the re-emergence of yourself as a deity] appearing like a magician's illusion, a mirage, and so forth.

This is the meaning of resting yourself.

The other [steps in the above description] are easy to understand; the meaning of "Leave it [your own divine body] through contemplating the form of the letters" and so forth refers to viewing the letter deity, sound deity, moon disc, creation of pride in the sameness of the suchness of yourself and the deity, and the suchness of self free of [dualistic] proliferations [in a manner similar to that] when they occurred in the initial [self-]generation [but in reverse order].

[Buddhaguhya] says that resting here is done in order to avoid distraction; therefore, [as described above] when distracted by conceptual proliferations, withdraw the observation in [reverse] order and finally set in meditative equipoise on emptiness. Then, since you are to rise like an illusion, it is not that you should not maintain the pride of being a deity when leaving the session. Other masters who composed *Means of Achievement* for deities based on Action Tantra frequently describe divine pride for all modes of behavior.

Repetition Observing the Form of Letters at Your Own Heart

The *Concentration Continuation Tantra*[144] indicates this with:

> Likewise, contemplate a mental purity [a moon disc],
> Possessing immutability and letters,
> Which is imagined for your mantra. It moves
> From the base [in front] to the base [yourself].

In this, "Likewise" indicates that this is a mode of observation other than the former; "a mental purity" is to be contemplated. Since it arises from the mind [in the sense that it is a manifestation of the mind realizing emptiness], it is "mental," the moon at the mind-heart area (*thugs ka,* center of the chest). Since it is unpolluted by the defilements of desire and so forth, is complete in all aspects, and appears without defilements, it is a "purity." It possesses the series of mantra "letters" (*yi ge, akṣara*),[145] which are "immutable" (*mi 'gyur ba, akṣara*) since they do not deviate from vivid appearance due to thorough meditation; also, since the mind appearing as a moon and possessing the "letters" (*yi ge, akṣara*) does not change (*mi 'gyur ba, akṣara*) nor become separate from them, it possesses "immutability." Such a moon is also "imagined for" the sake of a place to set "your mantra."

In short, restrain vitality and exertion as explained before (pp. 106–8). A moon, on which the mantra series is set, dwells in the heart of the "base," which is the One-Gone-Thus's body being meditated in front of yourself, not too distant and a little higher than yourself. The moon as well as the letters standing on it "moves to the base," which is yourself meditated as a deity—that is, together with the inhalation of air, it moves to your own mind-heart area. Observing it, perform [mental] repetition until exhaling breath. When the wind [breath] is let out, emit [the moon disc and letters] with it, and contemplate them as dwelling in the deity's mind-heart area. Again, as before, move it to your own mind-heart area and perform repetition.

Repetition Observing the Sound of Letters

The *Concentration Continuation Tantra*[146] says:

> Having again bound the mind through withdrawal
> And restrained vitality and exertion,
> Join the mind of secret mantra to the mantra
> And begin mental repetition.
>
> Otherwise, by means of just this rite[147]
> Whispering [the mantra] is also suitable.
> One wishing feats of mantra knowledge
> Should not perform other repetition.

Repetition should be performed while the mind observing the sounds of a secret mantra is joined to the mantra. Furthermore, the nonequipoised mind operating as usual should again be withdrawn and retracted; with vitality and exertion [breath and distraction] restrained as before (pp. 106–8), repetition should be performed. This is a case of initially visualizing the four branches of repetition, after which you should not [mainly] observe the form of the mantra to be repeated or the moon and so forth, but should perform repetition within [mainly] observing the tones; do this not as if listening to another recite the mantra but within observing the proclamation of the mantra sounds while you yourself repeat it [mentally or in whisper].

Buddhaguhya's commentary says that mental or whispered[148] repetition should be performed with the rite of just this observation of mantra tones but that when vitality and exertion are restrained, whispered repetition is impossible [since the breath is stopped]. His commentary also relates the restraining of vitality and exertion as well as mental and whispered repetition to the two earlier [repetitions, performed while observing the form of the letters on a moon disc at the heart of the deity in front and at one's own heart, which therefore can also be understood to have mental and whispered repetitions].

Question: If each of the three observations [(1) observing the form of the letters on a moon disc at the heart of the deity in front, (2) observing the form of the letters on a moon disc at one's own heart, and (3) observing the sound of letters] involves both types of repetition [mental and whispered], what is to be done first?

Answer: Initially perform whispered repetition; then, when the mind is not distracted to other [objects], restrain vitality and exertion and perform mental repetition. [This process] is described as being done in stages beginning with the coarse. Buddhaguhya's commentary[149] explains:

> Since the first [of the three] involves observation of a deity [in front], moon, and mantra series, it has three [main] objects of observation. The second has two [main] objects of observation, just the moon and the mantra [at one's own heart]. The last observes just the sound and, therefore, has only one [main] object of observation.

One person is to perform these three in order.

Varabodhi[150] describes repetition with the mantra set in one's own heart and in the heart of the deity in front. Although no more than this appears [in his description, the meditation should proceed] in accordance with Buddhaguhya's detailed explanation of the meaning of the *[Concentration Continuation] Tantra*. Other Indians who composed *Means of Achievement* based on Action Tantra also describe an imagination in which one makes offerings to Buddhas and achieves the welfare of sentient beings with beams of light emanating from the mantra series; [at the points of the beams deities emerge, emanating clouds of offerings to the Buddhas, Bodhisattvas, and so forth, and clouds of rain relieving the sufferings of all sentient beings.]

How to Repeat

About what to do when repeating, the fifth chapter of the *Questions of Subāhu Tantra* also says:

> When performing repetition be not fast
> Nor slow, be not loud nor very soft,
> Do not [repeat] while speaking nor while distracted.
> Lose not the vowels, anusvāra, or visarga.

and:

> Reversing quickly from the objects to which
> A lazy, desirous, and nonvirtuous mind
> Is distracted and runs, apply the mind well
> To the supreme letters of secret mantra.

and the *Susiddhi Tantra* as quoted earlier (p. 48) says that when repeating, one should not take to mind even high objects other than the objects of observation of that occasion, the deity and so forth.

For pacification and increase repeat softly, and for ferocity repeat such that others would hear.[151] When you arrive at the initial and final bead [of the rosary while counting repetitions] of the mantra, pay [mental] homage to the deities. When [the full count of] the beads is finished, look with your eyes at an image such as in a painting, or at a basis of worship,[152] or the seats [on which they sit].

The periods of recitation involve a session at the morning watch [see p. 143], half-sessions at the dawn and post-dusk watches, and either a half, a third, or a quarter of a session or a little repetition at noon. The burnt offerings involved in repetitions prescribed for the day may be made at night, and those prescribed for the night during the day, but making them right after repetition is superior.

With regard to the number of repetitions, the *Susiddhi Tantra*[153] says:

> In general perform a hundred thousand repetitions
> For as many syllables as there are
> When the count is fifteen or below.
> Three hundred thousand repetitions are prescribed
> For the count of syllables until thirty-two.
> When the syllables are more than that, do ten
> Thousand for prior approximation.

It is not necessary [to perform mantra repetitions] for both the central and surrounding deities, as is the case with other tantras. [In Yoga and Highest Yoga Tantra separate repetitions are necessary for each of the deities surrounding a central figure.]

How to Reinstate the Repetition if Unfavorable Conditions Arise[154]

If while reciting you become sleepy, yawn, sneeze, cough up phlegm, expel gas, or must urinate, defecate, and so forth, it is said that you should immediately set down the rosary and, having walked about [to relieve sleepiness] and so forth, do the ablution (see p. 86) and then start from the beginning of the count. Do not add [the new repetition] onto the earlier count [of that particular cycle of the rosary when the interruption occurred]. Also, the *Susiddhi Tantra* says that if through nonconscientiousness another deity's repetition is done, you should mentally plant a petition [to your deity] and begin the repetition again and that repetitions do not count when one is affected by obstructors, afflicted by illness, has become loose, nonconscientious, physically or mentally depressed, misses the time prescribed for the ritual, is unrestrained or unclean, and it explains that if bad dreams [such as going in darkness, wearing tattered clothes, becoming dirty, being bitten by a poisonous animal, sliding down a mountain of sand] arise at night, repetition during the [next] day does not count unless one repeats the mantra of the lord of the lineage (p. 96) a hundred times [to overcome the bad signs]. It is also said there that though one might complete the entire count through repeating half in one place and half in another, all such repetition is to no avail.

With regard to missing the time of a rite or repetition or doing it at a wrong time, the morning period is from the dawning of half of the sun until a full-length shadow [is cast, that is, when the shadow of a stick is the same length as the stick]. At noon there is a period of eight or nine water-clock hours [192–216 minutes]. The afternoon period is from when a full-length shadow remains until half of the sun has set. Those are the periods of the day. The period of the beginning of night is from the setting of half of the sun through half the post-dusk time. The second period is from half dawn time until half of the sun appears.

It is important to know the explanations in Varabodhi's *Clear Realization*[155] that activities of fierceness, invisibility, and so forth as well as cemetery activities are performed from midnight on and that pacifications and so forth are performed at opposite times [in the morning before noon] because it says that repetitions performed at the wrong time do not count.

[After completing a repetition rite] do as is presented in Varabodhi's *Clear Realization*:[156]

> When a repeater has finished repetition,
> By repeating twenty-one times
> [The mantras of] the mother and lord
> Of the lineage [the count] is always protected.

Mañjughoṣha is the lord of the One-Gone-Thus lineage; Avalokiteshvara of the lotus lineage, and Vajrapāṇi of the vajra lineage. Lochanā is the mother of the One-Gone-Thus lineage; Pāndaravāsinī of the lotus lineage, and Māmakī of the vajra lineage.

How to Conclude the Concentration of the Four-Branched Repetition[157]

Offering the Virtue

After the number of repetitions for the session is completed or exceeded, make the vase seal: put the middle-finger of the right hand behind the ring-finger, and put the middle-finger of the left hand behind the ring-finger; then join them [respectively]. Wrap the middle and ring-fingers of the left hand with the right forefinger, and wrap the middle and ring-fingers of the right hand with the forefinger of the left. Place side by side and straighten the two little fingers, and place the two thumbs at the center joint of the forefingers (seal 36).

Offer the virtue:

> I offer this virtuous root of mine to the Supramundane Victor as a cause of such-and-such feat. O Protector, please bestow such-and-such feat.

It is unrefined talk to assert that with this seal the rosary is offered [to the deity] when not performing repetition and is taken back when repeating.

Asking Forbearance and so Forth

Then, ask for forbearance for the fault of not having the circumstances to do the rite exactly according to the tantra, and make offering, praise, and so forth as before (pp. 118–27).

Requesting Departure

From the seal of invitation (seal 20) extend outside the two thumbs, making the seal of requesting departure (seal 37). At the end of your [particular] essence mantra or the general essence mantra add *gac-*

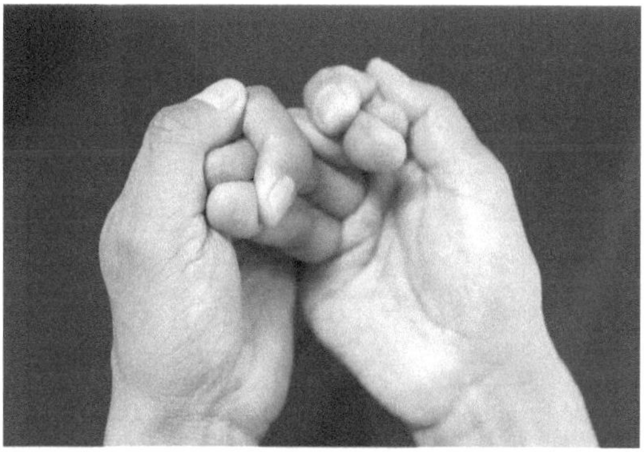

SEAL 36. VASE SEAL

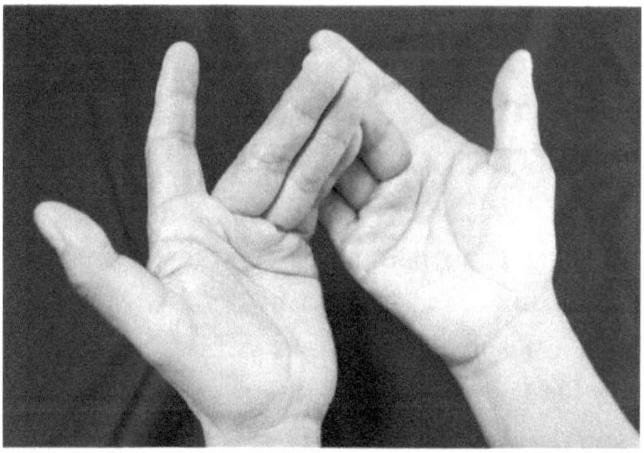

SEAL 37. SEAL OF REQUESTING DEPARTURE

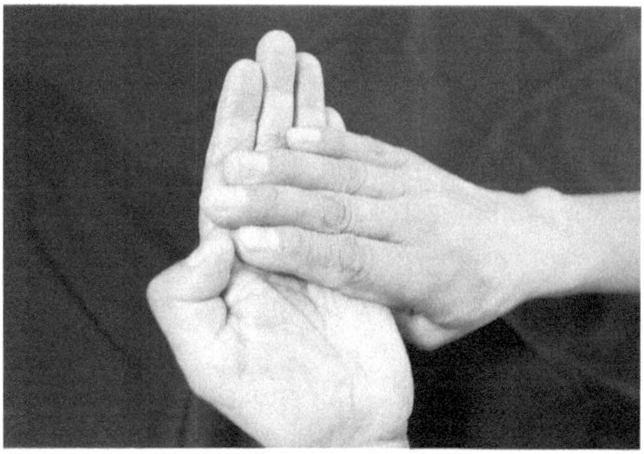

SEAL 38. SEAL OF UNEQUAL LIMBS

cha and ask the deity to depart along with the inestimable mansion. Then place the right palm on the left hand that has been turned up; join the tips of the crossed fingers to the base (seal 38); put this directly [in front]. Circle this seal of unequal limbs from the left, and free the directions and intermediate directions bound before, as well as [the upper and lower gods], with:
Oṃ hulu hulu caṇḍali-mataṃ givi svāhā.

Between Sessions, and so forth[158]

Then [within the firm pride of being a deity] do such [activities] as reading a book of the perfection of wisdom, cultivating the six recollections [of Buddha, doctrine, spiritual community, giving, ethics, and deities], establishing maṇḍala or bases of worship (*stūpa*), and so forth.

The offering vessels should be washed daily; the flower offerings should be refreshed three times [daily]. Robes such as the upper one should be mantrafied and washed, scented, or sprinkled three times daily. The upper robe should always be worn when repeating, making burnt offering, offering, and so forth, except when sleeping or reclining. Do not remove the lower robe except when sleeping or bathing, and do not let it become sullied with sweat. The mantra [to be cast in the robes] is:
Oṃ rakṣa rakṣa mānā sarva-buddha-adhiṣṭhana ātma civara svāhā.

Also, make food offerings (*gtor ma, bali*) in accordance with the statement to make them for spirits on the occasion of approximation.

Tie seven knots in a red string wound by a girl and dyed with poppy juice or camphor. Repeat a thousand times:
Oṃ āhara āhara bandhāni śukra-dharaṇi siddhārthe svāhā.
By tying it on the waist at night, it protects against emission.

You should perform the repetition rite as explained above, having bathed at the three times—morning, noon, and afternoon with the method [described on pp. 83–89).

Having fasted for one day each half-month, mantrafy a hundred times [a mixture of] the five cow-products—milk, yogurt, butter, dung, and urine of an orange-colored cow—as well as *kuśa* grass and water. Facing the east, squat, and drink it in any oblation vessel of about three "ounces" (*srang*). The *Susiddhi Tantra*[159] says that if this is done one will be purified for a half-month and that whatever is eaten—unsuitable food and so forth—will be cleansed. The mantras of the three lineages for this are:

One-Gone-Thus Lineage

Namo bhagavate uṣṇīśāyaṃ viśuddhe viraja śivi śantikare svāhā.

Lotus Lineage

Oṃ yaśoje svāhā.

Vajra Lineage

Namo ratnatrayāya, namaṣcaṇḍa-vajrapāṇaye, mahāyakṣa-senapataye, oṃ śikhi śikhi, nirmale, prabhesvare, tejo tejo vati svāhā.

Concentration Not Relying on Repetition

This has two parts: (1) explaining the concentrations of abiding in fire and in sound and (2) explaining the concentration on the end of sound.

Explaining the Concentrations of Abiding in Fire and in Sound

The *Concentration Continuation Tantra*[160] sets forth the three—the principle of abiding in fire, the principle of abiding in sound, and the principle of the end of sound:

> The secret mantra abiding in fire bestows feats.
> The abiding in sound bestows yoga.
> The end of sound bestows liberation.
> These are the three principles.

Buddhaguhya's commentary says that meditation on the six deities and [all steps] prior are preliminaries for both concentrations [with repetition and not relying on repetition] and that at this point the forms of Secret and Knowledge Mantra [deities] and so forth are to be manifested. Therefore, in order to generate these concentrations there must first be vivid appearance by way of the six deities as well as an ability to abide continuously in that vivid appearance, and furthermore, they must be done *within* visualization of deity yoga.

Abiding in Fire

The *Concentration Continuation Tantra*[161] says:

> Māntrikas having awareness bind to the self [that is, the mind]
> The phenomena arisen from the nondistinguished [mental consciousness].
> Dwelling on what transcends the branches [that is, the eyes and so forth],
> They should perform concentration without adherence.
>
> When contemplating adhering in mind
> To the immutable letters [that is, the sounds] strung together,
> Uninterrupted like the sounds of a bell
> And set in series called "sound,"
>
> They should intensively contemplate them as dwelling in fire—
> Quiescent, free from words, having the branches [the mantra letters],
> With a nature of having stopped vitality
> And exertion and having forsaken sleepiness.

The stages of this are as follows. *The first four lines* indicate initial contemplation of the suchness of self; these are drawn out as meaning that concentration should be performed. By whom? By "māntrikas." How? They should cease "adherence"; here this means to cease the conception of true existence and not to cease mere adherence to [or conception of] a conventional deity [for māntrikas still appear in the form of a deity and conceive that they are the deity]. They "dwell on"—do not rise from—[realization of emptiness,] freedom from the proliferations [of inherent existence][162] that "transcends the branches"—[conventional phenomena such as] the eyes and so forth—in that these have been delineated as not ultimately established.

With respect to the mode of dwelling [on emptiness], that which is "nondistinguished," or cannot be apprehended, by the eye sense consciousness and so forth is the mental consciousness; the main mind and mental factors concomitant with it are to be "bound to the self"—the mind—in the manner of the nonarising of entanglements, whereupon one dwells on that [freedom from the proliferations of the conception of inherent existence]. Moreover, if one "has awareness," that is, wisdom, one can investigate suchness [the emptiness of inherent existence].

The second and third stanzas. Then, upon rising from that [in the sense of ceasing to concentrate solely on emptiness], when the two:

1. the principle of the sound deity, which is the appearance [of that wisdom] in the aspect of the mantra of one's deity being heard, or in the aspect of its resounding, and
2. the suchness of self

become clear through the yoga of contemplating them as one, like milk mixed in water, māntrikas dwell in the deity yoga the nature of which is sound.

[The lines] are put together to mean that "they contemplate within adhering in mind" to the letters [that is, sounds] of the mantra joined, or set, in series. One might wonder whether the forms of the letters are to be arranged in series; therefore, it says, "series called 'sound,'" [that is, the sounds] of the mantra letters, "like the sounds of a bell." In order to define this, it says "letters strung together." "Immutable" means that the sounds of the letters appear uninterruptedly and without fluctuation, whereby they are like the continual arising of the external sounds of a bell being rung [repeatedly. Māntrikas] should concentrate on those sounds without adhering to their true existence.

Then, contemplate a fire, burning like the tongue of flame of a butter lamp, at the mind-heart of your [body] clarified as a deity, and think that the series of sounds described above dwells there.

Because it lacks the harm of heat and so forth, it is "quiescent." Since it is "free from words" whispered or mentally repeated, [the series of sounds] lacks those two types of repetition. It uninterruptedly possesses "the branches," the individual letters of the appropriate mantra.

In order to prevent excitement while contemplating in this way, it says to stop vitality and exertion [breath and distraction] because when these are not stopped, the mind lacks equipoise, like cattle. Prevention of slackness or laxity is indicated by "having forsaken sleepiness," since sleepiness is included in the class of slackness. This [concentration] does not have the aspect of one's own reciting mantra mentally but is like listening to another's reciting mantra; one's own mind appears in the aspect of the tones of the mantra dwelling in the midst of the fire.

Buddhaguhya's commentary[163] says:

> Perform this concentration until the external and internal signs of no hunger or thirst and so forth occur, whereupon one can achieve what one wants.

The "external signs" are not to be affected by hunger or thirst. The internal sign is to have generated meditative stabilization in dependence on bliss and warmth through the force of observing fire and performing wind yoga.

Buddhaguhya's commentary[164] says that this [concentration of abiding in fire] may be performed after repetition or on other occasions by those practicing the four-branched repetition for the sake of generating the power of mantra and of setting the mind in equipoise. Hence, since abiding in fire causes repetitions to become powerful and causes the mind to stabilize [the *Concentration Continuation Tantra* (p. 149)] says that it bestows feats [in the sense of bringing one closer to the achievement of feats].

Abiding in Sound

The *Concentration Continuation Tantra*[165] sets forth the concentration of abiding in sound with:

> Having placed [a divine body, which is] the base
> Of the immutable [mantra letters,] in a very peaceful
> Tongue of flame with brilliant pure light
> On a subtle stainless moon disc dwelling at the heart,
>
> Then contemplate the sounds while abiding in bliss.
> Or, having set the [written] letters
> On the immutable base [the moon disc],
> Contemplate solely the sounds themselves.

A "*subtle* stainless moon disc" is contemplated "at the heart" because if it were large it would be difficult to eliminate conceptuality [since the larger the object is, the greater is the tendency of the mind to stray]. "Having placed" a divine body, which is "the base of the immutable" mantra letters, in the earlier "tongue of flame" dwelling in [the center of] the moon disc [at the heart], then leave that and [mainly] concentrate on solely the mantra sounds. When exhaling, observe your own divine body [that is, the larger divine body, not just the one in the tongue of flame on the moon disc at the heart].

Here, when you observe the sounds, you should not [mainly] observe the deity and moon, or fire; hence, this is different from the two modes of the four-branched repetition [observing the form of the letters and the sound of the letters] and the abiding in fire. Doing it this way is because [as Buddhaguhya reports] other texts say that if you observe form when performing concentration on sound or being touched by wind, your mind will be distracted.

[With regard to the variant mode of this concentration indicated by the last three lines of the second stanza in the citation from the *Concentration Continuation Tantra*] the mind of enlightenment realizing suchness dwells singly in an aspect devoid of [dualistic] appearance; therefore, it is called "immutable"; hence, the moon that symbolizes it is also called "immutable." One observes the written syllables of the mantra on the moon disc and then, leaving them, concentrates on solely the tones of the sounds.

Hence, this is different from the observation of sound in the four-branched repetition because there, having rested the mind [through observing] the divine body, one later [mainly] observed only the sounds [in the repetition observing the sounds of the letters], whereas here, having rested [through observing] the written syllables, one observes the sounds. Buddhaguhya's differentiation of them thus in his commentary is from the viewpoint of the objects of observation; however, the main difference is that formerly one observed the tones of the sounds within mental repetition, whereas here one observes the tones of the mantra free from the aspect of one's own repetition [and, instead of that, observes the tones of the mantra as if hearing another is reciting it or it is merely resounding], because these [concentrations of abiding in fire and in sound] are again and again described as not relying on repetition.

On this occasion also, Buddhaguhya's commentary sets forth wind yoga for stopping vitality and exertion [breath and distraction].

Explaining the Concentration on the End of Sound

This has two parts: the stages of leaving the state of sound and the actual concentration on the end of sound.

Stages of Leaving the State of Sound

The end of sound is the suchness free from the two extremes [of inherent existence and no conventional existence] in which one has left completely even an abiding in the mere mantra sounds. When it has been cultivated, one is released from the two obstructions [to liberation from cyclic existence and to omniscience] and attains the liberation that has as its nature the Truth Body. About this also, the *Concentration Continuation Tantra*[166] says:

> A Victor knows the abandonment of the branches [or states]
> Of the lords of knowledge mantra—the dependent
> appearance
> With the limbs [of a deity], that called "sound" [whispered
> repetition],
> Mental [repetition], and purity from words [the
> concentrations of abiding in fire and sound].

This indicates the stages of the path through familiarization with which the concentration on the end of sound bestowing the liberation of the Truth Body is granted, whereby it clearly indicates the general stages of the path and the point where emptiness is meditated. [Realization of emptiness was cultivated earlier at the time of the suchness of self, and a sense of it was maintained throughout all the subsequent yogas; however, here the yoga is not merely conjoined with the *force* of emptiness yoga; rather, the mind of deity yoga actually realizes emptiness. Also, here instead of a divine form, mantra letter, or sound, emptiness is the *main* object.] Buddhaguhya's commentary[167] says:

> Yogis engaging in the practice of secret mantra actualize the Truth Body through the stages of completely leaving the states of appearing with the limbs of secret mantra [a divine body], of sound [whispered repetition], of mental [repetition], and of purity from words [the concentrations of abiding in fire and in sound, which are free from whispered and mental repetition]. Therefore, it is said that if one has meditated on the end of sound—the nature of which is the element of [a Superior's] attributes (*dharmadhātu*)—liberation is bestowed.

[In the stanza above from the *Concentration Continuation Tantra*] "knowledge mantra" is just an illustration; hence, it also encompasses secret mantra. The lords of knowledge and secret mantras are those having the aspects of the goddess and god whom you are practicing. Their "branches" are the factors, or states, related with those deities. The "abandonment" of them means to leave those states gradually. Moreover, from among the four states:

- The first is to appear with the limbs of the māntrika's own deity in dependence on having stopped vitality and exertion [breath and distraction] as well as on asceticism, concentration, and so forth; this is one's own appearing in a divine body.
- The second is the branch called "sound," the mantra state of performing whispered repetition.
- The third is the branch of mind, the state of performing mental repetition of mantra.
- The fourth is a purity from whispered and mentally repeated words—the concentrations of abiding in fire and in sound, in which the mind appears in the aspect of mantra sounds [as if recited by someone else or the reverberation of the mantra].

The way to abandon these is to make the former firm and then move to the latter. Buddhaguhya's commentary[168] says:

> The stages of gradual abandonment in stages from the coarse by one wishing for liberation are as follows:
>
> 1. Having performed withdrawal, asceticism, concentration, [stopping] vitality and exertion, and so forth, one makes firm a very gross meditative stabilization through observing the image of one's deity.
> 2. Having thoroughly abandoned apprehension of that very coarse meditative stabilization through[169] observing secret mantra sounds in whispered repetition, one makes firm a coarse meditative stabilization.
> 3. This apprehension of the coarse is also thoroughly

abandoned through the subtle meditative stabilization of mental sound.

4. Then, having also completely abandoned that, one abides in the very subtle meditative stabilization of secret mantra imagination [free from repetition].
5. Having also abandoned that, one who wishes release earnestly performs the meditative stabilization of observing the Truth Body.

[The stanza from the *Concentration Continuation Tantra* on p. 155 is taken in two ways:] "A Victor knows the stage bestowing liberation when emptiness is meditated after gradually leaving the four branches [that is, the four states described above]." Or: "O Lord of Knowledge Mantra, when you leave those branches, you will become a Victor knowing the divisions of mantra meaning." If the stanza is taken in accordance with the latter explanation, it agrees with Buddhaguhya's summary exposition of the "bestowal of liberation at the end of sound."[170]

Question: If it is necessary also to leave off observing the divine body, why is the "end of sound" described as merely leaving sound?

Answer: To leave the first branch [appearance as a deity] is to leave the place [or basis] of mantra *sound* because the māntrika who appears as a deity is the repeater of mantra. To leave the two middle branches [the stages of whispered and mental repetition] is to leave the compositional activity [involved in making] mantra *sound,* and to leave the last branch [abiding in fire and abiding in sound] is to leave the very nature of mantra *sound;* therefore, it is suitable to call the leaving of these a leaving of sound. Since not any of these appear in the face [of the ascertainment factor] of concentration observing suchness, it is said that they are left at this time [though they may still appear to the appearance factor of that concentration].

Here [with respect to the concentrations of Action Tantra] three meditative stabilizations are to be generated: observing a divine body, observing a divine speech mantra, and observing suchness, the divine mind. The first is a "very gross," or very coarse, meditative stabilization. The second is subtler than that, and the third is very subtle; hence, the order is definite, since they must be generated in the mental continuum in stages, from the coarse.

Concerning this, initially it is necessary to generate a composite of the two, *clarity* of the divine body and *dwelling* for a long time on it. Therefore, clear appearance must be achieved by means of concentration having many aspects because it arises from again and again taking to mind the aspects with which one is familiarizing, as is the case with conditioning to desire or fright [whereupon their objects appear vividly to the mind. Also] if [the mind] is not set one-pointedly [on the divine body], then even though clear appearance arises, one will not remain on a single object of observation as much as one wishes; hence, it is [also] necessary to fixate by means of one-pointed meditative stabilization as explained earlier (pp. 105–8).

About the way to attain a serviceable mind through such means the fifth chapter of the *Questions of Subāhu Tantra* says:

> Look at the point of the nose and abandon conceptuality.
> When, though moving about, one is immovable
> And a purity from states of unclarity is attained,
> The mind is certain to become serviceable.

As it says, the factor of stability, which is an immovability despite moving about,[171] must be free from laxity because stability that lacks an intensity of clarity does not preclude laxity.

Prior to repetition it is very important to achieve firm meditative stabilization observing a deity; the *Questions of Subāhu Tantra* says:

> In people having one-pointed mind
> Mentally arisen joy is strongly produced.
> Through joy physical pliancy is attained.
> Through physical pliancy they have the fortune of bliss.

> Through physical bliss, one-pointed mind, and meditative
> stabilization
> At that time repetition becomes unobstructed.

In my *Stages of the Path Common to the Vehicles* I have explained the way of flawlessly achieving the meditative stabilization of one-pointed mind, the initial generation of mental pliancy from having achieved [meditative stabilization], the generation of physical pliancy in dependence on that, the achievement of fully qualified calm abiding after that, and the generation of only a similitude of calm abiding prior to that;[172] therefore, I will not elaborate on these points here.

In all four tantra sets the time of initially achieving a fully qualified calm abiding is mostly when being instructed in deity yoga. Therefore, if you do not distinguish between fully qualified calm abiding and a similitude of it and do not differentiate finely the time of achieving calm abiding in accordance with how it occurs in the great texts, you will not know the extent to which you must be led when initially being instructed in deity yoga.

When in that way meditative stabilization observing a [divine] body becomes firm, you leave that and train in meditative stabilization observing a speech mantra. "Leaving" should be understood as setting aside the training of continuously holding the mind on the [divine] body and mentally apprehending another object of observation, but it does not preclude the later [continued] clear appearance of the deity because there are many descriptions of observing a deity during the three repetitions [observing the form of letters at the heart of the deity in front and at one's own heart and observing the sounds of the letters] as well as during abiding in fire and abiding in sound.

Among the three types of observation of mantra, observation of the coarse means to observe the form or the sound of letters and perform whispered repetition; this is a training in repetition such that only you can hear the sound while continuously holding the mind on the aspect of [written] syllables set on the moon or on the aspect of the tones, without scattering to anything else. When this repetition yoga—during which a mantra is repeated in speech and the mind does not scatter to anything other than the appropriate object of observation—becomes firm, you leave that training and train in the subtle; this is done until the two factors—(1) mere mental repetition without reciting the mantra in speech and (2) the mind's holding to either the aspect of the written form or the tone of the syllables without scattering to anything else—become firm. With the attainment of firmness, these are also left, and you train in the two very subtle concentrations [abiding in fire and abiding in sound] whose nature is sound. Just your own mind realizing the suchness of self appears in objectification in the aspect of mantra sounds and blazing fire; hold your mind on that. Through sustaining such until the signs as explained before (p. 152) are eventually gained, [the concentration of abiding in fire] becomes firm, and then it also is left, whereupon you train in the yoga of undifferentiable union of two—your own mind (1) in its objectified factor vividly appearing as having the aspect of the mantra tones and (2) in its subjective factor abiding on just the series of mantra sounds without scattering to anything else. The firming of this is the meaning of "The abiding in sound bestows yoga," (in the *Concentration Continuation Tantra;* see above, p. 149).

[During deity yoga] for example, your own mind in its objectified factor manifests simultaneously in the aspects of the face, arms, and so forth of a deity while it abides one-pointedly on its object of observation, and similarly here in these two [concentrations of abiding in fire and abiding in sound], there is a steadiness of mind in which the appearance of the former letters [that is, sounds] in the series vividly manifest even when the aspects of the latter [sounds] dawn.

Actual Concentration on the End of Sound

In that way, through the force of wind yoga stopping vitality and exertion [breath and distraction] in order to hold the mind [on its object] starting from [observing] the divine body and going through abiding in sound and through the force of holding the mind on many coarse and subtle objects of observation such as observing fire, a divine body, and so forth, (1) a very firm factor of stability, as explained in the *Questions of Subāhu Tantra* (p. 158–59), (2) a special joy and bliss in body and mind, and (3) pliancy—physical and mental serviceability—are generated, and in particular through the force of long cultivation of wind yoga and observation of fire, bliss and warmth and, based on them, powerful meditative stabilization—blissful, clear, and nonconceptual—are indeed generated; however, even these are not called the stage of completion [which only occurs in Highest Yoga Tantra]. Because you have not yet gained a path eliminating the conception of self [inherent existence]—the root of cyclic existence—you leave abiding in sound and, cultivating the concentration bestowing liberation at the end of sound, meditate on emptiness [for the sake of achieving a union of calm abiding and special insight realizing emptiness].

That [the *Concentration Continuation Tantra* and Buddhaguhya's commentary] only briefly describe at this point how to meditatively cultivate this is in consideration of its having been explained earlier on the occasion of meditation on the suchness of self [when explaining the ultimate deity, see p. 101. Therefore, the earlier description must be utilized here in explaining [the concentration on the end of sound].

Moreover, as explained earlier (pp. 100–2), the [coarse and subtle] selves of persons and [other] phenomena are refuted by scripture and reasoning, and you should first seek the view of the middle way, realizing that all phenomena are not ultimately established because a mere nonconceptuality in which this view has not been found does not have even the slightest meaning of meditation on emptiness.

With respect to how to meditatively cultivate the view when it is found,[173] you must meditate within possession of the two features mentioned in the *Concentration Continuation Tantra,* immovability and clarity (see quote, p. 101).[174] If you analyze too much with the view of selflessness, excitement is generated and [the mind] wavers; therefore, you should single-pointedly sustain just that ascertainment—inducing firm understanding of the meaning of selflessness—and not analyze a great deal. [However,] if having performed such stabilizing meditation, you fixate too much, [the mind] will not spread into individual analysis of phenomena and will become wholly nonconceptual, unable to diffuse when it should. Since calm abiding is then predominant, the factors of calm abiding and special insight will not be equal. Also, if you fixate too much in that [state], slackness or laxity and lethargy are induced, whereby [the mind] becomes lax and lethargic, like, for example, when due to too much analysis special insight predominates, excitement is finally generated. Therefore, you should perform both *analysis* training in the dexterity of analytical wisdom and *stabilization* in one-pointedness; Buddhaguhya's commentary[175] says:

> Now, to indicate that the nature of the pristine wisdom of the suchness of self is without slackness and excitement, [the *Concentration Continuation Tantra*] says "unmoving and clear." In that, "unmoving" is synonymous with "nonwavering." This also expresses that a yogi with excited wisdom should stop excitement, which is characterized by a nonpacification of movement in a mind that is accustoming to conceptuality thoroughly analyzing phenomena. Therefore, it speaks of an immovable mind, pacified in the path.

Thus, having cited a scriptural source [from the *Concentration Continuation Tantra*], Buddhaguhya says that since too much analysis is a fault, one should perform stabilizing meditation [at that time]. His statement that the wisdom differentiating phenomena has the character of excitement means that if one analyzes too much, excitement is finally generated. How could it mean that wisdom itself is a case of excitement!

Buddhaguhya's commentary[176] also says:

> Similarly, "clear" means pure; it is synonymous with being devoid of the faults of lethargy and so forth. This also indicates that a yogi gone solely into calm abiding should stop the factor of lethargy, which is discordant with analyzing phenomena and is characterized as slackness of mind over-fixating in equipoise even when analyzing phenomena.

This also means that when one stabilizes too much, lethargy and laxity are finally generated and that these are factors discordant with thorough analysis of phenomena; it does not indicate that calm abiding itself is slackness and lethargy.

In the same fashion, the last of Kamalashīla's [three works on the] *Stages of Meditation* (*bhāvanākrama*) also says:

> When, due to having meditatively cultivated special insight, wisdom becomes too dominant, calm abiding is lessened whereby, like a butter-lamp set in a breeze, the mind wavers, due to which suchness is not seen very clearly; therefore, at that time you should meditatively cultivate calm abiding. Also, when calm abiding is predominant, you will, like a person asleep, not see suchness very clearly; hence, at that time you should meditatively cultivate wisdom. When, like two oxen yoked as a pair, both are engaged equally, you should abide without application [of the antidotes to a predominance of either] as long as body and mind do not become adversely affected.

Act in accordance with his statement: when one from between calm abiding and special insight is predominant, meditatively cultivate the other a great deal, making them become equal, and meditate.

Do not hold that you have attained mastery over nonconceptual meditation upon the factor of calm abiding having become predominant in an imbalanced calm abiding and special insight.

Also, do not hold the system of the Chinese abbot [*Mahāyāna Hvashang*] in which it is held that all analytical meditations of individual investigation are hindrances to full enlightenment upon not identifying the measure of the object of negation by reasoning [in the view of selflessness] and thinking that all conceptuality whatsoever, "It is such-and-such," are conceptions of true existence and hence that all these are refuted in the Middle Way texts. The root text and commentary to the *Concentration Continuation Tantra* clearly speak to this; Buddhaguhya's commentary[177] says:

> Thus, although the suchness of self has the character of being experienced as without the branches [the five senses], without observation, without form, without aspect, unmoving and clear, it is asserted as just not having forsaken the path of analysis. Therefore, [the *Concentration Continuation Tantra*] says that "mental analysis remains in its presence." "Mental" is wisdom; its operating on its object is "analysis" and thus "mental analysis." This mental analysis, having the character of the illumination of wisdom, dwells in the presence of the suchness of self; [thus, the *Concentration Continuation Tantra* says that] "mental analysis dwells in its presence." The passage explains that although the nature of self-knowledge is nonconceptual, the illumination of wisdom engages in analysis in the presence [of the suchness of self].

This establishes that the wisdom of individual analysis is not fit to be forsaken even on the occasion of meditating on suchness.

In brief, during the concentrations of abiding in sound and below, calm abiding is achieved, and with the end of sound special insight is cultivated; also, because if during this process the wisdom of individual analysis is excessive, the former factor of stability disintegrates, performing analytical and stabilizing meditation alternately, you should attain a union of calm abiding and special insight.

In order to achieve the limitless varieties of activities of special feats just as they are described in Action and Performance Tantras, they must be preceded by the four-branched repetition and the concentrations of the three principles [abiding in fire, abiding in sound, and bestowing liberation at the end of sound]; however, there is no certainty that such is needed in order to achieve many minor feats. [Great feats such as living for a great eon require the completion of all the above concentrations to the point where a meditative stabilization that is a union of calm abiding and special insight observing emptiness is attained, whereas lesser feats such as pacifying illness or increasing intelligence do not.][178]

Feats

How to Achieve [Common][179] Feats Once the Approximation is Serviceable

The *Susiddhi Tantra*[180] says:

> Very supreme activities are achieved
> Through special repetition.
> Even during prior approximation
> Ordinary activities will be achieved.

and the *Questions of Subāhu Tantra* says:

> Having first repeated a hundred thousand like the rite,
> Then engage in achieving secret mantra.
> Then feats will quickly be attained.
> One is not long afflicted with secret mantra rites.

and the *Concentration Continuation Tantra*[181] also says:

> If all the principles of knowledge mantras,
> The rite of the suchness of self, and
> The supreme principles of repetition are known,
> People will attain feats.

Thus, since these say that when preceded by the yoga of the four-branched repetition, feats are achieved, prior to achieving pacifying, increasing, or fierce activities—such as increasing wisdom and the lifespan, and so forth—you must perform approximation and then apply yourself to the activities. [Upon finishing the first stage, the approximation, either the same rite is used in modified form in a second stage called "achieving," or rites of burnt offering are performed, and so forth; the third stage is the activity or feat itself, using it for the benefit of others.] This is the system of all four tantras.

Lineage.[182] Pacifying, increasing, and fierce activities are respectively achieved by way of [the mantras of] the One-Gone-Thus, lotus, and vajra lineages. Supreme, middling, and low feats [within the common] are achieved similarly. Pacifying activities are to pacify untimely death, illnesses, epidemics, harmers, and contagion. Increasing activities are to increase the lifespan, youth, magnificence, power, qualities [of realization, and so forth], and desired objects [such as resources]. Fierce activities are to kill, expel, [confuse], and so forth [harmful beings].

Season.[183] During the waxing [from the first to the fifteenth] of the last month of winter, the second month of autumn, the first and second months of spring, and the first month of summer, supreme feats and pacifying activities should be achieved; there are no obstructors with respect to the first [that is, supreme feats within common feats]. It is auspicious to perform pacifying activities mostly in the autumn; increasing, in the winter; fierce, in the late spring. Middling and lesser feats should be practiced during the wane [from the sixteenth to the thirtieth] of those five months [last month of winter, second month of autumn, first and second months of spring, and first month of summer].

Time.[184] The time for high, middling, and low feats and for pacifying, increasing, and fierce activities are respectively morning, post-dusk, and midnight or noon. Also, pacifying activities [should be achieved] from the first day of the month until the fifteenth; increasing, from the fifteenth to the fifteenth; fierce, during the wane.

Times auspicious for all activities are the first half of the first month, lunar or solar eclipse, and the first, third, fifth, seventh, and thirteenth days of the month as well as times of the appearance of the constellation pushya[185] (*skar ma rgyal*).

Place.[186] High, middling, and low feats should be practiced respectively on mountains and so forth, lake shores and so on, and other places concordant with mantra; they should not be done in dilapidated houses, and so forth.

Posture.[187] Use the lotus cross-legged posture for pacifying activities; the lucky posture for increasing activities; press one foot with the other for fierce activities. Face the north, east, and south [respectively].

Agent.[188] Since each lineage also has the three feats and the three activities—pacifying, increasing, and fierce—the activities of pacification and so forth are achieved by way of the lineage lord, mother, and fierce one.

Divisions.[189] With respect to how feats are divided into three [high, middling, and low], there are many approaches. From the approach of entity, the high are knowledge-bearing [such as being able to proceed to a pure land with one's usual body], clairvoyance, knowing all treatises [immediately upon reading], and so forth. The middling are invisibility, essence-extraction [empowering a pill so that all nourishment can be gained from it or so that one immediately turns into a youth], speedy feet, and so forth. The low are control of others, killing and expelling [of harmful beings], and so forth.

The three from the approach of lineage have already been explained (p. 168). From the approach of signs [which are external indications of having attained capacity], there are three by way of substances blazing [with fire], giving off smoke, and giving off heat.

By way of base, there are feats of (1) [enhancing] the body [so that it becomes free from disease, youthful, and so forth], (2) [using] substances [such as leaves, swords, and so forth for gaining feats], and (3) [changing ordinary] resources [into marvelous ones]. By way of speakers, there are [feats achieved through] mantras [set forth] by Superiors, deities, and those above the earth [*yakṣa*, Smell-Eaters, and so forth].

Though the [deity] bestowing a feat [on a particular practitioner] might be supreme, there are cases of a low feat being granted due to the practitioner's not striving at approximation. However, if the approximation is done well, there are instances of a low [deity's] granting a supreme feat through [the deity's] requesting such from another [higher deity].

Analyzing dreams.[190] Prior to [the stage of effecting] the achievement of a feat, the technique for examining omens of whether the feat will be achieved or not is to fast on the full moon day or any auspicious day of the moon's waxing and then analyze dreams for one or three nights. You should bathe with the bath-oil of *dhātri* (*emblica officinalis*) and fragrant perfume, perform the ablution, put on new clean clothes, offer oblations during the post-dusk period as explained before (pp. 113–14, 120), and invite your deity. Suffusing the offerings with white sandalwood and so forth as well as [mixed] incense, make the offering. Offer many good food offerings containing yogurt. Offer one hundred and eight burnt offerings of butter and burnt pourings [in a fire] of *sarjarasa* sticks (*Vatica Robusta*) according to the activity.

Make seven knots in a string wound by a girl and, having mantrafied it seven times with the mantra of your deity, tie it around the left upper arm. Make a petition to the deity to reveal in a dream whether that which is intended to be effected will be achieved or not. Then, contemplating yourself as like your deity, lie down while reciting the deity's mantra on a mattress of *kuśa* grass strewn with many flowers. Then if you dream joyful dreams of the Three Jewels, your deity, Bodhisattvas, the four types of retinue [monks, nuns, male and female lay devotees], mountains, elephants, waterfalls, obtaining jewels and clothing, and so forth, you should begin the [stage of] achievement.

Effecting the achievement. Then, to effect the achievement, perform the many things that are prescribed [in the particular text] such as for achievement by means of burnt offerings or by mere repetition-meditation of mantra, and so forth; three times [each day] make offerings, disclose ill-deeds, admire [your own and others'] virtue, plant aspirational wishes, read books of the perfection of wisdom, make maṇḍalas, maintain vows, and do those things that are to be maintained three times, while changing clothes thrice daily. If, having become unconscientious, it happens that you do not perform these three times, recite your deity's mantra twenty-one times. For high, middling, and low feats fast respectively for three days, two days, or one day. I have explained these points in accordance with what the *Susiddhi Tantra* says.

On these occasions [of effecting the achievement] it is not sufficient to invite the deity in front; the deity must be newly generated. According to the two masters [Varabodhi and Buddhaguhya], to achieve a maṇḍala [for this] or to generate a vase [as an inestimable mansion for the deity], and so forth, you should perform the ritual of self-generation of the six deities explained earlier and then when performing repetition, do whichever of the first two of the four-branched repetitions [observing the form of the letters at the heart of the deity in front or at your own heart] is appropriate. For the substance of the vase, the generation rite, and so on, it is sufficient to use the general procedure.

The *Susiddhi Tantra*[191] explains that if on the occasion of such yoga you have less hunger, become free from a disease, become of an unusual mind, become of especially great and steady magnificence, dream auspicious and true dreams, develop a greater liking for repetition, are little fatigued, smell fragrant odors [without depending on external substances], are intent on good qualities, or develop greater respect for the deity, these are signs of effectiveness in repetition-meditation.

The *Concentration Continuation Tantra*[192] says that nonfaith, indolence, being overcome[193] by hunger and thirst, excitement, great mental pain, doubt about the activity [which you are trying to achieve], not adhering to repetition and concentration, liking senseless talk, engaging in unsuitable actions, possession by an evil spirit, dreaming bad dreams, and so forth are causes of the deity's approaching elsewhere [that is, becoming farther away from yourself]. It says[194] that pacifying desire, hatred, haughtiness, deceit, and so forth as well as continuous abiding in repetition are causes of the deity's approaching. These should be understood [as applying] also during initial approximation.

If prior to achieving minor feats for your own and others' welfare—such as pacifying sickness—and prior to performing initiations, consecrations, and so on you complete the prerequisite meditative stabilization of the six deities and the number of repetitions through the approach of the four branches, it is very suitable even if you have not meditatively cultivated the concentrations of the three principles [abiding in fire, abiding in sound, and bestowing liberation at the end of sound]. Therefore, [insistence] on meditatively cultivating the concentrations of the three principles and on using all three objects of observation of repetition [the form of the letters in the heart of the deity in front and in one's own heart as well as the sounds] even on these occasions is a case of not distinguishing the boundaries [of when they are needed].

To say in conclusion:

> If one propounds to know the meaning of Action and Performance Tantras
> By knowing a portion of their meditations and repetitions
> Such as rites of fasting, bathing, and so forth, it is a source of laughter.
> Therefore, cherish arrangement of the tantra meanings into paths.
>
> This clear differentiation upon seeking the thought of the four general Action Tantras
> And in particular of the *Susiddhi* and *Concentration Continuation* tantras

According to the commentaries by the two Indian sages
Is the sole eye for viewing all the Action Tantras.

The second section of *The Stages of the Path to a Great Vajradhara: Revealing All Secret Essentials,* called "Stages of Progressing on the Path in Action Tantra," is concluded.

Performance Tantra

Outline

The stages of the path in Performance Tantra has four parts: (1) how to become a receptacle suitable for meditatively cultivating the path, (2) having become a receptacle, how to maintain purity of pledges and vows, (3) how to perform prior approximation while abiding in the pledges, and (4) how to achieve feats once the approximation is serviceable.

How to Become a Receptacle Suitable for Meditatively Cultivating the Path

One receives initiation in a maṇḍala such as that of Mahākaruṇāgarbhika and so forth as described in Performance Tantra and thereby becomes a receptacle for meditatively cultivating the path. Concerning this I have described mere entry into a maṇḍala and the modes of initiation for one who has entered in my *Explanation of the Root Infractions.*[195] Also, I will not write about the maṇḍalas and rites of initiation because I fear it would make this text too long; these should be known from the *Vairochanābhisambodhi Tantra* and Buddhaguhya's commentaries on it[196] as well as the *Vajrapāṇi Initiation Tantra,* and so forth.

Having Become a Receptacle, How to Maintain Purity of Pledges and Vows

You should act in accordance with the statement in the *Vairochanābhisambodhi Tantra*:[197]

> The pledges are to be taught to them:
> From today, child, you should not

Forsake the excellent doctrine
Or the mind of enlightenment
Even for the sake of your life henceforth.
You should not be miserly
Nor injure any sentient beings.
The Buddha explains these pledges
To you—a good system of conduct.
Protect these just as you
Would protect your own life.

and furthermore its statement to abide in the basis of training that is to abandon the ten nonvirtues [killing, stealing, sexual misconduct, lying, divisive talk, harsh speech, senseless chatter, covetousness, harmful intent, and wrong views]. Regarding other pledges, since those described in Action Tantra are mostly shared [with Performance Tantra] you should keep them (see 68–75).

The Great Vehicle vow that applies to both Action and Performance Tantra is, as the *Mañjushrī Root Tantra* (*mañjuśrīmūlatantra*) says, the Bodhisattva vow; hence, since root infractions are explained in Performance Tantra as they are in Asaṅga's *Grounds of Bodhisattvas* (*bodhisattvabhūmi*) and in the *Sūtra on Skill in Means,* I have explained these at length in my *Explanation of the Ethics Chapter.* Furthermore, in my *Explanation of the Root Infractions* I have extensively explained about how in Action and Performance Tantra it is not fitting to hold the vows of the five lineages [since these tantras do not involve the vajra master initiation] and have also described at length the rite for assuming the Bodhisattva vows, the point at which one incurs a root infraction with regard to them, and so forth; therefore, I will not elaborate [here].

How to Perform Prior Approximation While Abiding in the Pledges

Divisions of the Yoga for Prior Approximation

The *Vairochanābhisambodhi Tantra*[198] says:

> [O Vajrapāṇi,] Caretaker of the Secret, divine forms are of two types, thoroughly pure and thoroughly impure. About those, the thoroughly pure are entities of realization [of emptiness], devoid of all signs [that is, having the aspect of the ultimate]. The thoroughly impure are forms with signs—[that is, having the aspect of the conventional, a body with] colors and shapes. Concerning those, by means of the two types of divine forms two types of purposes are achieved; by means of the one with signs, [feats] having signs [common feats] arise, and by means of the one without signs feats having signs also arise [that is, the supreme feat of Buddhahood as well as common feats are attained].
>
> The excellent Victors assert that feats
> Having signs [arise] through that with signs.
> Through abiding in the signless
> Those having signs also are suitable to be
> achieved.
> Hence, you should rely in all
> Aspects on the signless.

As it says, [the yoga for prior approximation] is twofold—yoga with and without signs.

Yoga with signs is taken as deity meditation and repetition devoid of meditation on emptiness [in the sense that although it may be conjoined with the *force* of realizing emptiness, the mind of deity yoga itself is not realizing emptiness]. Yoga without signs is taken as deity meditation and repetition involving meditation on emptiness [in the sense that the mind of deity yoga itself actually realizes emptiness or, in other words, the wisdom itself appears in the form of a deity] and is not taken as simply meditation on emptiness. If yoga without signs did refer to just meditation on emptiness, it would be necessary to assert that one could be fully enlightened through emptiness yoga alone since the *Vairochanābhisambodhi Tantra* [as quoted above] says that both feats [supreme and common] are achieved through the signless.

When even the tantra teaches about thoroughly impure divine bodies, it calls them "forms with signs," referring not just to a form with a face and arms but to a specific form [that is, one not directly involving meditation on emptiness]. Though Buddhaguhya uses the convention "deity" even when he calls meditation on emptiness the "ultimate deity" [in Action Tantra on the first of the six deities (pp. 100–2)], here the terminology of "deity" is used within the context of dividing the deity's *form* itself into two types [one not directly involving and the other directly involving meditation on emptiness] and in the context of [indicating] which feats are achieved. Also, Chandrakīrti's *Brilliant Lamp* explains that this passage [from the *Vairochanābhisambodhi*] indicates [in a hidden way] the divine *bodies* of the two stages [of generation and of completion in Highest Yoga Tantra. Therefore, it is mistaken to think that yoga without signs refers to mere meditation on emptiness.]

[The yoga for prior approximation] is also divided into the two, mundane and supramundane yogas [which are other names for the yogas with and without signs]. The *Vairochanābhisambodhi*[199] says:

> I have explained [the yoga] having four branches
> By way of external and internal application.
> This moreover is the unsurpassed
> Of what have worldly imagination;
> Suppressed with the word of withdrawal,[200]
> The mind which has accorded with the deity
> Is taught as the supreme of whispered repetitions,
> Having imagination [of conventional phenomena].

> For the "mentally supramundane"
> Withdrawal [from external branches of repetition to the internal] and so forth are completely abandoned.
> [Oneself and the deity] are made undifferentiable in [terms of their empty] nature
> Through a mind creating oneness with the deity
> And apprehending nondifference.
> In no other way is [supramundane repetition] to be done.

The supramundane in this passage also is not taken as a non-contaminated [wisdom in the continuum of a Superior *directly* realizing emptiness] but is [a consciousness] having the aspect of selflessness [that is, realizing emptiness conceptually *or* directly] or a yoga conjoined with that [in which the wisdom itself manifests in form].

Subhagavajra's *Stages of the Great Vehicle Path* (*mahāyāna-pathakrama*)[201] says:

> About the actual paths Action Tantras, Performance Tantras, and Yoga Tantras speak of "means of achievement with signs and means of achievement without signs." The Great Yogas [Highest Yoga Tantras] speak of the "stage of generation and stage of completion." Those are the paths.

His description of the two stages as the system [only] of Highest Yoga Tantras and his using the terminology of the two yogas—with and without signs—for the lower tantra sets accord with this tantra [the *Vairochanābhisambodhi*] and are very good. I will explain the reasons later (pp. 195–96).

Yoga with Signs

This has two parts: the external four-branched repetition and the internal four-branched repetitions.

External Four-Branched Repetition

There do not appear to be as many deity meditations and repetitions that are made based on Performance Tantras as the many meditations and repetitions of deities that there are in evidence now based on Action Tantras, and if you know how to generate the yogas with and without signs in your continuum, the subsidiary branches of the path appear to be easier; hence, here I will not explain the others—preliminary protection of oneself and the place, offering to [exalted beings who are] bases of the amassing [of the accumulations of merit], worshipping and praising deities, and so forth—but will describe the stages of meditatively cultivating the two yogas as well as repetition.

First Branch: Self-Generation

Of the four branches the first branch, the base, is to generate yourself as a deity. The way to initially meditate on emptiness is to contemplate:

> The Buddhas understand that my own aggregates which depend on the great elements [earth, water, fire and wind] are ultimately like space and conventionally like reflections, and since there are none greater than the Buddhas, I also should realize this in just the way

> that they perceive it. It is like this: both myself and the deity to be meditated do not have inherent existence in the sense of being established by way of our own entity because of being dependent-arisings, like reflections.

Thinking thus, you should delineate that the two, yourself and the deity, are without inherent existence. Then, you must train thinking:

> The two emptinesses, which are the absence of inherent existence of the two, myself and the deity, are undifferentiable.

until firm ascertainment is eventually gained, and then generate yourself as a deity; the *Vairochanābhisambodhi* clearly says:

> Bodhisattvas practicing the Bodhisattva deeds from the approach of Secret Mantra should generate their body as a [divine] physical body in the following way:
>
> "There are none greater than the completely perfect Buddhas; the Ones-Gone-Thus completely and perfectly realize that my eyes, ears, nose, tongue, body, mind, and so forth are included in the four great elements and that even those [elements] are empty of their own nature, included within mere nominalities, similar and akin to space, unapprehendable [as inherently existent], arisen from causes and actions (*karma*), like reflections. Those [elements] also are continuously related as interdependent arisings. Whatever is dependently produced arises like a reflection. Therefore, because of being interdependently arisen, what the deity is I am; what I am the deity is."
>
> This is how you should physically generate your physical form as a divine body.

In the four tantra sets the mode of meditating on emptiness prior to deity meditation is necessarily like this; it is pithless to not delineate [emptiness] by way of the view [of the middle way] and then to merely utter a mantra such as *svabhāva* and so on [*Oṃ svabhāva-śuddhāḥ sarva-dharmāḥ svabhāva-śuddho 'haṃ* (Oṃ naturally pure are all phenomena, naturally pure am I)] and withdraw appearances [leaving a vacuity that is not understood as an absence of inherent existence]. Furthermore, Buddhaguhya's *Condensed Meaning of the "Vairochanābhisambodhi Tantra"* (*vairocanābhisambodhitantrapiṇḍārtha*) quotes a passage from the tantra stating that one should delineate the absence of inherent existence of the aggregates and so forth through the reasoning of the lack of their being one or many and thereupon perform deity yoga.

With respect to how to rise as a deity from within emptiness Buddhaguhya's *Condensed Meaning of the "Vairochanābhisambodhi Tantra"* says:

> The stage of your own conventional deity yoga is indicated here [in the *Tantra*] in two formats; about this, one is through the transformation of the aspect of your own mind, devoid of all appearance [and realizing emptiness], into the aspects of a moon disc and so forth, whereby appearance of yourself as your own deity is achieved.

He speaks of two modes [of rising as a deity from within emptiness, the first just described] in which a moon and so forth precede [appearing in physical form of a deity], and [a second way in which the deity] is generated all at once without those precursors; [Buddhaguhya later says that this second way] is moreover taught in the chapter on the deity-suchness and so forth in this tantra, but such is presently missing in the tantra as translated [into Tibetan].

According to the first [of the two ways], contemplate the letter *aṃ* on a thoroughly complete moon disc, which is [a manifestation of your] mind [realizing emptiness]. Make light spread out from and gather back into the syllable; then, through its transformation generate yourself as the great Vairochana with one face and two hands making the seal of meditative equipoise, with a body of golden color surrounded by interwoven flame, sitting on cushions of white lotus and moon, with head ornaments and plaited hair wound up on the top, and wearing light upper and lower garments. Perform the blessing [of important places of the divine body] into magnificence with mantras and hand configurations in either extensive or brief form. I will not write about these in detail (see pp. 103–4).

Second Base [Second Branch: Generation in Front]

Meditate on a One-Gone-Thus similar to yourself in front.

[Third and Fourth Branches: Mind (moon) and Sound (letters)]

Then, set the mantra series to be repeated on a moon at the heart of the deity in front.

Those are the four branches of repetition. In this way furthermore, the *Vairochanābhisambodhi Tantra*[202] says:

> Join the immutable [mantra letters] to the immutable
> [moon disc].
> Likewise, they move from the base [in front] to the base
> [yourself].
> Very restrained you should make
> A hundred thousand repetitions in mind.
> "The immutable" is the mind of enlightenment [appearing
> as a moon].
> The second ["immutable"] is called "sounds" [the forms of
> the letters on the moon].
> "Base" is to make the figure

Of one's deity as your own body.
The second base is to be known as a complete Buddha,
The supreme of the two-legged [imagined in front].
A māntrika contemplates
Abiding on a very pure moon disc.
The letters are well set in order
In the middle of that [moon disc].
Upon having suppressed [the wandering mind] with the
word of withdrawal,
Vitality and exertion are thoroughly purified.
"Vitality" is explained as wind;
"Exertion" is mindfulness [that is, distraction].
Having restrained those two,
Perform prior approximation well.

Concerning the two [words] "immutable"[203] [in the first line] there is no clear statement in Buddhaguhya's two commentaries on the *Vairochanābhisambodhi Tantra,* but in accordance with his commentary on the *Concentration Continuation Tantra* explained earlier (pp. 135–36) they are the moon and mantra series from among the four branches; the explanation that they are a moon [seat] and mantra at the time of deity generation [as when first imagining a moon seat, then a mantra on it, which transforms into the deity] is not the meaning.

The systems for (1) initially seeking stability regarding clear appearance of a divine body upon having restrained vitality and exertion [wind and distraction] and (2) then performing repetition within observing the letters are similar to the earlier explanations on the occasion of Action Tantra.

After the above passage, the *Vairochanābhisambodhi Tantra*[204] speaks of performing [repetition] for a month:

Then a māntrika, very restrained,
Should perform repetition for a month.
The prior practice of secret mantra

Is to put it from one base to the other.
All the Buddhas having great fame
Describe this as "prior practice."

"To put it from one base to the other" means that if you become tired from observing the mantra set on the moon at the heart [of the deity] in front, you should alternate with [observing it] at your own heart.

The [earlier] statement (p. 186) to perform repetition mentally is just an illustration; hence, both whispered and mental repetition are prescribed. The *Vairochanābhisambodhi*[205] says:

A supreme yogi should analyze
Which of the two aspects to do,
Repeating mentally or in whisper.

With respect to these two, you should first perform whispered repetition and then, when repeating mentally, stop vitality and exertion [breath and distraction], as earlier [explained in Action Tantra].

Internal Four-Branched Repetition

The first base is, from within emptiness, to generate [yourself as a deity] from any of the four—*a, ā, aṃ, aḥ*—as explained before; Buddhaguhya's *Condensed Meaning of the "Vairochanābhisambodhi Tantra"*[206] describes this as generating [yourself] as Shākyamuni. He says that you should meditate on [yourself as] Shākyamuni with a very pure and stable moon disc, like a [two-sided][207] mirror—[standing upright] at Shākyamuni's heart—meditating until you see your own body as a divine body.

The second base is to meditate on Vairochana—as described before [with one face and two hands making the seal of meditative equipoise, with a body of golden color surrounded by interwoven flame, sitting on cushions of white lotus and moon, with head ornaments and plaited hair wound up on the top, and wearing light upper and lower garments]—in the [upright] moon [at your heart imagined as Shākyamuni] as if dwelling in a cave. Contemplate the mantra as dwelling [standing around the edge facing inward] of a [flat] moon at his heart and perform repetition. [Your own mind meditated as the moon is the third branch, and the letters, the fourth branch.][208] It is said here also to repeat the mantra one hundred thousand times. The two repetitions [whispered and mental] and restraining vitality and exertion [breath and distraction] when repeating mentally are similarly needed here.

After "Describe this as 'prior practice,'" the *Vairochanābhisambodhi*[209] says:

> After that, offer even a few
> Flowers, incense, and so forth,
> And also dedicate these to enlightenment
> In order to become a Buddha.
> Māntrikas should perform repetition
> For a second month like this fearlessly.

Thus, it explains that one should perform the approximation for a month without mixing in offering flowers and so forth and for a month in connection with such. Also, the *Vairochanābhisambodhi*[210] says:

> These counts of secret mantra which I have mostly
> Prescribed as three hundred thousand
> Are taught as the number of repetitions
> For very pure māntrikas—
> Embodied beings free from ill-deeds.
> They are not to be done in any other way.

You should meditate in this way until, in dependence on holding the mind observing a divine body and in dependence on wind yoga, calm abiding is eventually gained.

Yoga without Signs

When you gain calm abiding observing the divine body, [moon, letters, sounds,] and so forth, you should meditate on emptiness; the *Vairochanābhisambodhi Tantra*[211] says, "In a grove, temple, cave, or place where your mind is isolated meditatively cultivate the [ultimate] mind of enlightenment, remaining until the mark [of success] arises." Buddhaguhya's *Condensed Meaning of the "Vairochanābhisambodhi Tantra"* explains that the mark [of success] is a firm mind as long as one wishes in the meditative stabilization realizing all phenomena as natureless.

Although a mode of meditating on emptiness is set forth prior to the four-branched repetition, it indicates how to take emptiness to mind *prior* to meditating on a deity; the stages of meditating *mainly* on emptiness [done at this point] are performed *after* deity yoga; Buddhaguhya's *Condensation*[212] says:

> The stages of the yoga for achieving repetition by way of familiarizing with the meditative stabilization of signlessness which has the character of the Truth Body of your own deity are as follows. As before, you should for a while previously actualize all the factors of the four branches of repetition, and so forth, and then analyze the imagined color, shape, and so on of your deity who is nondual with yourself, breaking them down into many particles.

How to meditate on signlessness is sets forth at length in this [*Vairochanābhisambodhi*] *Tantra*[213] itself:

> Caretaker of the Secret [Vajrapāṇi], concerning this a Bodhisattva practicing the Bodhisattva deeds by way of Secret Mantra who wishes to achieve the signless meditative stabilization should contemplate in this way: From where do signs [blue, yellow, and so forth] arise? Do they arise from my body, my mind, or my mentation? About that, the body is produced from actions (*karma*); it should be analyzed as naturally without activity like grass, wood, or dirt, as like an inert or external form, or like a mannequin. For, if someone belligerently angers at a mannequin and destroys it with fire, poison, a weapon, water, or a diamond or burns or cuts it, it does not have the least dislike; though it is offered various articles of gods and humans such as food, drink, baths, fragrant ointment, garlands, clothing, sandalwood, camphor, and so forth, it does not come to like that human. Why? A human who, out of unrealistic conceptions due to error aroused by his or her own pride, makes offering or does harm to a naturally empty form has a childish nature. Caretaker of the Secret, about the body you should cultivate recollection of the body in that way as empty of inherent existence.

Thus, it speaks of delineating and thereupon meditating on the body as empty of its own inherent existence, and with regard to how to individually investigate the mind, this [*Vairochanābhisambodhi Tantra*][214] also says:

> Caretaker of the Secret, furthermore you should contemplate the mind as without inherent existence, devoid of all signs [of blue, yellow, and so forth], and empty of inherent existence. Caretaker of the Secret, the mind does not have the three times [future, present, and past or production, abiding, and cessation]. You should contemplate it thinking thus, "That which is separate from

> the three times is inherently separate from signs." However, Caretaker of the Secret, childish common beings conceive of the mind as having signs; this is the same as an unreal conceptualization. That which is unreal is not to be known as "unproduced." Caretaker of the Secret, if Bodhisattvas who are practicing deeds by way of Secret Mantra have contemplated in this way, they will attain the meditative stabilization of signlessness. Caretaker of the Secret, when they dwell in the signless meditative stabilization, they approach and tend toward the secret mantra [feats] set forth by the One-Gone-Thus.

Thus, it sets forth how the mind does not inherently exist, that the conception of its true existence is only a mental superimposition, that if analysis of body and mind is done in this way, the meditative stabilization of signlessness is attained, and that when this meditative stabilization is attained, feats of mantra are attained. Buddhaguhya's *Condensed Meaning of the "Vairochanābhisambodhi"*[215] also says:

> In accordance with realization by way of whatever approach is suitable: Having manifested appearance in color and shape with yourself and the deity nondual,
>
> 1. analyzing [the divine body] by breaking it down into subtle particles, or by way of the reasoning of its not having been produced from the start and its not being produced,
> 2. or similarly through the yoga of turning your mind inward by way of the reasoning[216] [that is, technique] of withdrawing vitality [wind or currents of energy] (*srog slar sdud pa*),
> 3. or by way of not taking the appearance of color and shape to mind,
>
> actualize mere self-knowledge of the mind, free from

> your own body of divine form, without [dualistic] appearance, and repeat mentally whatever your knowledge mantra is.

You should meditate in accordance with its statement to meditate on the meaning of nonappearance devoid of the deity's color and shape from the approach of (1) completing analysis with the reasoning of the lack of being one or many or the diamond nodes,[217] or (2) setting the mind on the meaning [of emptiness] explained earlier (pp. 192–93) through withdrawing its running to the outside by means of the reasoning [that is, technique] of withdrawal of vitality [wind], or (3) not taking to mind the proliferative appearance [of the deity's body and so forth] within mindfulness of the view [of emptiness].[218]

These accord greatly with Kamalashīla's [three] works on the *Stages of Meditation*, the last of which says:

> The *Cloud of Jewels Superior Sūtra* also pronounces:
>
> > Those who are skilled in this way about faults take as their yoga meditation on emptiness in order to separate from all proliferations. Through much meditation on emptiness, when they thoroughly examine the nature of those places where the mind scatters and which it likes, they realize them as empty. When they also investigate what the mind is, they realize it as empty. When they also examine the nature of the mind by which it is realized, they realize it as empty. Through realizing such they enter into the yoga of signlessness.
>
> This indicates that those who do not investigate in this way will not enter into signlessness.

Implicit to the statement that one who analyzes by means of the wisdom of individual analysis will enter into the yoga of signlessness, it is being said that if one has abandoned the wisdom of individual investigation, one will not enter into the yoga of signlessness. In this tantra also it is said that one wishing to achieve the meditative stabilization of signlessness should analyze body and mind as not established in reality; hence, it also indicates that if one does not analyze with the wisdom investigating the suchness of things, the meditative stabilization of signlessness will not be produced.

Therefore, it is necessary to sustain the continuum of a consciousness ascertaining the meaning of the absence of inherent existence of all phenomena as delineated through the view [of emptiness]; (1) setting in nonconceptuality a mind not understanding the view or (2) despite having gained the view, sustaining only nonconceptuality at the time of meditation without sustaining ascertainment [of emptiness] by means of the view is not meditation on emptiness. As explained earlier (pp. 162–65), it is necessary to do it within alternating analytical meditation and stabilizing meditation since if you analyze too much by way of special insight, it is not suitable.

The Four Yogas

Thus, in Action and Performance Tantra there are four important yogas—deity and emptiness yogas, and wind and repetition yogas. About these, the two—the ultimate deity yoga and the conventional deity yoga—are the main means of achieving the two Bodies [Truth Body and Form Body]. Since repetition is a branch [of the process] of arousing the mind of the deity being meditated, it is included as a branch of conventional deity yoga. Since wind yoga is a branch [of the process] of making both deity yogas stable, it is included in both. Thereby, [the four] are included in the two yogas—[conventional and ultimate or] with and without signs.

Nevertheless, since it is explained that these do not have the stage of completion [which is found only in Highest Yoga Tantra], it is necessary (1) to know individually without confusion that the production of a blissful, clear, and nonconceptual meditative stabilization through the force of holding the winds inside and even the yoga of signlessness dependent on those are not the stage of completion and (2) to know individually without confusion the uncommon features of the stage of completion in Highest Yoga Tantra. For, if you do not know in detail just what features of the path exist in these lower tantra sets, you will not know the uncommon paths of the higher.

How to Achieve Feats Once the Approximation is Serviceable

(1) The achievement of the sword knowledge bearer and so forth in dependence on external substances such as a sword [for flying in space] and so on, (2) the achievement of activities such as pacification and increase and so forth through having meditated on discs of earth, water, fire, and wind in internal places in the body, and (3) the attainment of the meditative stabilization of not forgetting the altruistic mind of enlightenment upon performing the achievement [of the appearance] of Mañjushrī and so forth whereupon those Bodhisattvas eventually stroke one's head or say "Well done," after one has done repetition until such occurs are set forth in this *[Vairochanābhisambodhi] Tantra*. Many modes of achieving those and other such feats are set out.

Conclusion

Through the good arrangement of the meanings of all the two tantras [Action and Performance] into these four general structures[219] containing the paths (p. 64), if the tantras appear as advice for practice, then you will go among the count of those knowing the tantras. However, since otherwise one who knows only a bit of the path does not know the essential points of the general path, those with intelligence should strive at means whereby the texts of these two tantra sets dawn as advice for practice.

To say in conclusion:

> This description of the stages of the two yogas
> In accordance with the explanation by Buddhaguhya,
> scholar and adept,
> Of the meaning of the chief Performance Tantra, the
> *Vairochanābhisambodhi*,
> Is a door for easy entry to Performance Tantra.

The third section of *The Stages of the Path to a Great Vajradhara: Revealing All Secret Essentials,* called "Stages of Progressing on the Path in Performance Tantra," is concluded.

III

SUPPLEMENT

JEFFREY HOPKINS

EDITED BY

Elizabeth Napper

The Need for Common Feats

Since a follower of the Great Vehicle wishes to attain Buddhahood in order to help other beings, it is not sufficient merely to be liberated from cyclic existence; it is necessary to attain a state wherein the welfare of others can be accomplished effortlessly and spontaneously. This is done only with the Form Bodies of a Buddha—Complete Enjoyment and Emanation Bodies—and thus a Bodhisattva seeks the omniscience of Buddhahood.

Such omniscience is attained through removing the subtle obstructions that prevent simultaneous realization of all knowable objects—specifically, the appearance of objects as if existent in their own right and the consequent inability to realize the two truths, emptinesses and conventional objects, in direct cognition at the same time. In order to gain the capacity to overcome these obstructions the wisdom of a Bodhisattva must be enhanced. In the Sūtra, or Perfection, Vehicle a Bodhisattva does this through training in the six perfections—giving, ethics, patience, effort, concentration, and wisdom—in limitless forms over a "limitless" time, three periods of a countless number of great eons. ("Countless" refers to a one with fifty-nine zeros, and a "great eon" is composed of eighty intermediate ones—twenty each for formation of the world system, abiding of it, destruction, and vacuity.)[1] The practice of these deeds of giving and so forth empowers the mind so that eventually the wisdom realizing the emptiness of inherent existence can eradicate the obstructions to omniscience. That is the Sūtra mode of procedure.

The Mantra or Tantra path also has as its basis the generation of an altruistic aspiration to highest enlightenment and also involves the practice of the six perfections, but not for a limitless time in limitless varieties as is done in the Perfection Vehicle; rather, all four tantra sets make use of deity yoga, the special tantric means for amassing the collections of merit and wisdom quickly. Highest Yoga Tantra has, in addition, techniques for generating subtler minds realizing emptiness and for using the winds, or currents of energy, that are the mounts of these subtler minds as the substantial cause of an actual divine body. Through this enhancement of wisdom the obstructions to omniscience are quickly removed and Buddhahood is attained.

In the three lower tantras—Action, Performance, and Yoga—deity yoga is used to bring about the speedy achievement of many common feats and to directly come under the care of Buddhas and high Bodhisattvas, receiving their blessings, and so forth. This faster progress is achieved through a threefold process known as prior approximation, effecting the achievement of feats, and using the feats in the performance of activities for the welfare of others.

The initial period of deity yoga is called prior approximation because one is accustoming to a deity through becoming closer and closer to its state, whereupon the deity grants the feat, either directly or in the sense of bestowing a capacity to the mind. Actually effecting the achievement of feats is done by way of carrying out prescribed burnt offerings or repetition of mantra, and so forth, after the approximation has been completed. These feats are then used for the welfare of others in the third stage, which involves activities of (1) pacification such as overcoming plague or relieving others of demons, (2) increase of lifespan, intelligence, wealth, and so forth, (3) control of resources, persons harmful to others' welfare, and so forth, and (4) ferocity, such as expelling or confusing harmful beings.

These feats—as well as the capacity to understand all treatises immediately upon reading them, clairvoyance, and so forth—are attained through cultivation of deity yoga, itself a means for amassing the collections of merit and wisdom quickly, and the use of feats for the benefit of others amasses even more merit. Through this speedy and profound process the merit necessary for the achievement of Buddhahood is accumulated in less than the three periods of countless great eons required in the Sūtra Vehicle, whereby the path to Buddhahood is shortened.

Ngagwang Paldan's *Presentation of the Grounds and Paths of Mantra*[2] says:

> The attainment of the supreme [state of Buddhahood] by means of the three lower tantra sets depends on prior achievement of worldly feats.... Thus, Tsongkhapa says, "Initially, one maintains purely the pledges and vows that are the sources of feats. Then one strives at the yogas with and without signs, and when capacity is attained one effects the achievement of common and uncommon feats whereby progress is made on the path. This mode of procedure should be known for the three lower tantras [Action, Performance, and Yoga]."
>
> There is a reason why one must first achieve common feats in order to achieve the supreme through the paths of the three lower tantra sets, for as Shāntideva's *Engaging in the Bodhisattva Deeds* (*bodhicaryāvatāra,* IX. lab) says:
>
> All these branches [of giving, ethics, and so
> forth] were spoken
> By the Sage for the sake of wisdom.
>
> It is the system of both Great Vehicles [Perfection and Mantra Vehicles] that the factors of method enhance the wisdom realizing emptiness. In the Perfection Vehicle this wisdom is caused to possess the capacity to abandon the obstructions to omniscience through training for a limitless time in limitless varieties of giving and so forth. ... However, the three lower tantras do not say that one trains for a limitless time in limitless varieties of giving and so forth as in the Perfection Vehicle, nor do they set forth a means of generating a special subject [that is, a

> subtler consciousness] that realizes emptiness, as is done in Highest Mantra [Highest Yoga Tantra]. Therefore, the realization of emptiness must be enhanced through skill in means, such as many common feats and being blessed into magnificence under the direct care of Buddhas and higher Bodhisattvas. . . .
>
> The mere rough corpus of the path—altruistic mind generation which is the basis of the [Bodhisattva] deeds and training in the six perfections which are the deeds—is common [to the Perfection and Mantra Vehicles] but the training in limitless varieties of giving and so forth is not shared with Mantra.

In Highest Yoga Tantra techniques are used to generate special minds—called the minds of vivid white appearance, vivid red increase, vivid black attainment, and clear light,[3] respectively more and more subtle—which are used to realize emptiness. The techniques revolve around using in the path the bliss arising from the desire for male-female union. Thus, in Highest Yoga Tantra the usage of desire in the path is for the sake of enhancing the wisdom realizing emptiness by way of actually generating subtler consciousnesses that realize emptiness.

In the lower tantras, although desire is used in the path to enhance the wisdom so that it can gain the capacity to overcome the obstructions to omniscience, it is not used to manifest subtler consciousness. Nevertheless, the bliss consciousness that—in the practice of Action Tantra—arises upon the mutual gazing of the meditated god and goddess is used to realize emptiness; however, it is not a subtler consciousness, as in Highest Yoga. Due to this difference between Highest Yoga Tantra and the three lower ones, the feature of the latter's path being faster than the Perfection Vehicle is not described as arising from using desire in the path but from the attainment of common feats. In Highest Yoga Tantra, on the other hand, the feature of achieving Buddhahood in one short lifetime of this degenerate era is through using desire in the path to generate subtler levels of consciousness.

Tsongkhapa explains that, therefore, the attainment of Buddhahood in one short lifetime is a distinguishing feature of Highest Yoga and that it is mistaken to hold that such can be done through the paths of the three lower tantras alone without eventually using the paths of Highest Yoga. Ngagwang Paldan's *Presentation of the Grounds and Paths of Mantra*[4] says:

> The three lower tantras do involve using in the path the bliss that arises upon looking at, smiling at, and holding hands or embracing a meditated Knowledge Woman [consort]; however, this is not done for the sake of generating a special subject [that is, subtle consciousness] realizing emptiness, for such is a distinguishing feature only of Highest Yoga Tantra. Nonetheless, most of [Tsongkhapa's] followers explain that this does not mean that the bliss [consciousness] that arises upon looking, smiling, and so forth does not realize emptiness. . . . [Still] Tsongkhapa says that the faster speed of the path [in the lower three tantras] comes by way of common feats and so forth. He does not say anywhere that it comes from a more powerful mind realizing emptiness by way of using desire in the path . . .
>
> [Although the three lower tantras present a path that is faster than the Perfection Vehicle] Tsongkhapa's *Great Exposition of Secret Mantra* says, "The feature of speed in which complete enlightenment [is attained] without depending on the passage of countless eons is a distinguishing trait of Highest Yoga. Therefore, the attainment of such by the trainees of the lower tantra sets is in dependence on their entering the two stages of Highest Yoga; their own paths alone are not sufficient. Hence, do not hold that all features of speed in Mantra are only to become fully enlightened in one lifetime of

> this era of disputation or without depending on countless eons [of practice]."

In Action Tantra the special techniques involved in the four-branched repetition and the concentrations of abiding in fire, of abiding in sound, and on the end of sound make it possible to pass from the path of accumulation to the path of seeing—which usually takes one period of countless great eons—in as little as several years.

The Complete Meditation

Action Tantras are of two types, general and specific. General tantras present the path and surrounding activities in a manner that is suitable for all three Action Tantra lineages—One-Gone-Thus, lotus, and vajra. Specific tantras, on the other hand, present meditations and so forth within the framework of a particular deity and lineage.

It is from the four general Action Tantras—*General Secret Tantra, Questions of Subāhu Tantra, Susiddhi Tantra*, and *Concentration Continuation Tantra*—that Tsongkhapa draws his explanation of the general meditation of the Action class. He briefly cites the *General Secret Tantra* in connection with initiation, the main topic of that tantra, and cites the *Questions of Subāhu Tantra* only a few times—with regard to how to repeat mantra, the qualities of calm abiding, and achieving feats. His presentation is structured around copious reference to the *Concentration Continuation Tantra* with Buddhaguhya's commentaries and the *Susiddhi Tantra* with Varabodhi's commentary. The former does not detail the preliminary rites, pledges, and so forth, which Tsongkhapa takes from the *Susiddhi Tantra* and Varabodhi's formulation of it into a *Means of Achievement* (*sgrub thabs, sādhana*).

Thus, the presentation of Action Tantra in the *Great Exposition of Secret Mantra* is a general one, in the sense of supplying a mode of procedure applicable to all deities in that class. It is laid out in the order of practice, to be used as a framework for practicing a particular deity.

The body of the path is subsumed under three headings—prior approximation, effecting the achievement of feats, and activities (*bsnyen sgrub las gsum*):

Concentration with Repetition

Approximation occurs before effecting the achievement of feats and thus is said to be *prior*. It is accomplished through concentration (*dhyāna*), which is divided into two types, with repetition and not relying on repetition, structured around a progression from the coarse to the subtle:

- meditative stabilization observing a divine body
- meditative stabilization observing a divine speech mantra
  - observing the form or sound of letters and performing whispered repetition
  - observing the form or the sound of letters and performing mental repetition
  - one's own mind realizing the suchness of self appears in the aspect of blazing fire and mantra sounds
  - one's own mind appears in the aspect of the mantra sounds
- meditative stabilization observing a divine mind, that is, observing suchness.

Concentration with repetition refers to meditation that eventually involves repetition but does not necessarily do so at all times. Repetition is done in two ways: the coarser is to whisper, and the subtler to repeat the mantra mentally. Repetition is performed within continuous and intense concentration on oneself as a deity and a similar deity in front of oneself. It is called the four-branched repetition because it requires maintenance of four factors: imagination of (1) oneself as a deity, (2) a deity in front, (3) a moon disc either at the heart of the deity in front or one's own heart, and (4) the written letters of the mantra, which are set upright around the edge of the moon disc facing inward.

Whereas the generation of oneself as a deity is done from within meditation on emptiness, the generation in front is a matter of inviting a deity to come. Therefore, the preliminaries of the four-branched repetition involve extensive preparation for the visit of a deity, who is treated like a guest. As Tsongkhapa says (p. 109), it is more convenient to generate the deity in front first and oneself as a deity second because the latter involves one-pointed observation of your own divine body within stoppage of the breath and thus it would be distracting to do the many activities related with inviting the deity in front.

The generation, or imagination, of oneself as a deity begins with meditation on emptiness, called the suchness of self; this is also called the ultimate deity even though it does not have the face, arms, and so forth of a deity. In brief, after one has identified well the sense of a solidly existent I, reasoning is used to refute its inherent, or concrete, existence. The late Gelugpa scholar and yogi Ngagwang Rabtan said that often a yogi will spend months in merely the first step of identifying the concrete sense of I that is to be refuted by the view of selflessness. With that sense of I as the target, one applies the reasoning that reveals the falseness of this vivid, seemingly true appearance. Rather than deciding that reasoning is unsuitable to reveal reality because it cannot substantiate the mode of appearance of phenomena, reasoning is used as the tool that reveals the falsity of this concrete mode of appearance, thereby establishing the absence of inherent existence as the actual mode of being of persons and other phenomena. The vacuity that is the absence, or negative, of inherent existence appearing to such an analytical consciousness is an emptiness, and since an actual wisdom is undifferentiably fused with it, even if yogis have not achieved such a profound state they imagine that they have, pretending or believing that their mind has become of the entity of emptiness in nonconceptual meditative equipoise. This emptiness is understood as being the ultimate nature both of oneself and of the deity being meditated and thus is called the ultimate deity.

In the next steps this wisdom is used as the basis of emanation, first appearing as a moon over which the sounds of the mantra of the deity resound, then as the forms of mantra letters standing upright on the moon, and then as the form of the deity itself. These steps are part of concentration with repetition, but as they do not involve any whispered or mental repetition, even the manifestation of wisdom as the sounds of the mantra above the moon does not constitute "repetition." Once the form of the deity has appeared, during this phase of meditation the mind is mainly held to one's own body imagined as a deity, occasionally putting more emphasis on the deity in front but without losing the appearance of one's own divine body.

Until a meditative stabilization observing the divine body becomes firm, the function of repetition is merely that of resting or revivifying the mind. However, when it has become firm, one passes to a subtler cultivation of meditative stabilization observing a divine speech mantra. This is of four varieties (see p. 208); the first involves performing whispered repetition within observing the form of the letters either in the heart of the deity in front or in one's own heart and then observing the sound of the letters.

When whispered or mental repetition is performed within observing the deity in front with a moon at the heart on which the mantra letters stand, one is as if reading the letters—repeating the mantra neither swiftly nor slowly, such that only oneself can hear it. This meditation is said to have three objects of observation: (1) the deity in front, (2) the moon at his/her heart, and (3) the letters of the mantra that stand along the rim of the moon disc. Still, during this period one does not lose the appearance of one's own body as a divine body. This is possible because of the previous cultivation of self-generation.

Gradually, as the mind stays more and more on its object, one desists from whispered repetition and, holding the breath, repeats the mantra mentally. During exhalation, one views one's own divine body but without losing the appearance of the deity in front.

When it is necessary to leave the session, one proceeds as if backwards through the process of observation, passing from the sound to the form of the letters, to the moon in the heart of the deity in front, to the deity in front, to one's own divine body, to the letters on the moon at one's own heart, to the sounds above the moon, to the moon disc, to the pride of the sameness of the nature of oneself and the deity, and finally to the suchness of self. One remains in equipoise on the emptiness of inherent existence and then rises in a divine body like an illusion. Within such divine pride, one goes about daily activities, maintaining a lesser form of deity yoga so that the periods between sessions and the actual meditative sessions will be mutually supportive.

The next phase of the concentration with repetition involves inhaling into one's own heart the moon disc together with the letters that are in the heart of the deity in front. Whispered repetition is performed, but when the mind becomes steady, one holds the breath and recites the mantra mentally, as if one's mind is in the center of the disc and is reading the letters of the mantra that are on it. With exhalation the moon and letters move to the deity's heart, and then with inhalation return to one's own.

In the next phase the sounds of the mantra become the object of observation, but this does not mean that the deity in front, one's own divine body, the moon, or the form of the letters disappear. Rather, one is focusing on the sounds of the letters, which, initially, are being whispered. Then, one stops the breath, whereupon it is impossible to engage in whispered repetition, and mental repetition is done.

When this meditative stabilization becomes firm, the concentration of the four-branched repetition is complete, after which one offers the virtue of the repetition to the Supramundane Victor for the sake of achieving whatever feat is being sought. One asks the deity to put up with omissions in the conduct of the rite and then requests the guest to depart, asking the guest to come again.

Concentration Not Relying on Repetition

When one has attained capacity in concentration with repetition, one passes on to the subtler concentration of abiding in fire. This concentration is called an abiding in fire because the sounds are imagined as dwelling in a tongue of fire at the heart of one's divine body. This also is a meditation observing a divine speech mantra, but repetition is not involved because in this case one's own mind appears in the aspect of the sounds of the mantra, not as if oneself is reciting, but as if hearing another's repetition. The internal sign of success is that the mantra sounds reverberate continuously, the former sounds not ceasing during the latter, like the continual ringing of a bell.

When this concentration of abiding in fire becomes firm, one is not affected by hunger or thirst and has developed a meditative stabilization, but still has not generated actual calm abiding. To do this, one passes to cultivation of the concentration of abiding in sound. A small divine body is imagined within the flame that is on the moon disc at the heart of one's own divine body. Then, one stops the breath and ceases distraction, "leaving off" concentration on the small divine body and so forth and concentrating on only the mantra sounds. As in the concentration of abiding in fire, the sounds do not appear as if recited by oneself but by another.

Though one is said to leave the observation of the small divine body and so forth, those do not disappear. The steadiness of mind is such that within appearance of the small divine body, flame, moon, and so forth, one can take as the main object of observation just the mantra sounds in the sense of focusing on them. Then, when exhaling, one's own divine body is observed, loosening the concentration slightly. Because the mantra sounds in the concentration of abiding in fire and in sound are free of the aspect of one's own recitation, these concentrations are said to not rely on repetition.

When the concentration of abiding in sound becomes firm, a fully qualified calm abiding is attained; within mental and physical pliancy and bliss, one is able to remain on whatever object one chooses as long as one likes. With the attainment of calm abiding, the cultivation of meditative stabilization observing a divine speech mantra is complete.

Then one passes to an even subtler cultivation of a meditative stabilization observing a divine mind, that is to say, observing suchness—the emptiness of inherent existence. This is the concentration bestowing liberation at the end of sound. Realization of emptiness was cultivated earlier at the point of the ultimate deity in self-generation and is involved in all subsequent steps in that the mind realizing emptiness was believingly used as the basis of emanation of the various divine appearances. Also, since māntrikas—those who have attained the path of accumulation of the Vajra Vehicle—are the sharpest among Bodhisattvas, they have conceptually realized emptiness prior to entering the Mantra path. However, they have not yet realized emptiness with a mind of calm abiding and special insight. Since the four-branched repetition and the concentrations of abiding in fire and in sound are for the sake of achieving calm abiding, during that process one does not engage in analytical meditation with respect to emptiness; rather, one mainly engages in stabilizing meditation with respect to a divine body or speech mantra, for analysis would cause the mind to become unstable. Now, however, with the completion of the concentration of abiding in sound, calm abiding has been attained and analytical and stabilizing meditation can be alternated—the object of observation now being the emptiness of inherent existence.

Despite the many statements in the text that all other objects are abandoned, the mantra sounds, divine body, and so forth—as Tsongkhapa points out—do not necessarily disappear in the concentration bestowing liberation at the end of sound. In terms of ascertainment, just emptiness is being ascertained, but the mantra sounds, divine body, and so forth may *appear* to that consciousness. It is a feature of the Mantra Vehicle (and some say of the Sūtra Vehicle also) that the phenomenon being understood to be empty can also appear to a conceptual consciousness realizing that emptiness. Ngagwang Paldan's *Presentation of the Grounds and Paths of Mantra*[5] says:

> If the mind realizing emptiness is powerful, then the yoga with signs [that is, with appearance of a deity and so forth] which follows it will be conjoined with it [that

> is, will be affected by the force of the realization of emptiness]. Tsongkhapa's *Small Exposition of the Stages of the Path* says:
>
> > If the wisdom realizing emptiness is strong, then when one gives gifts, makes obeisance, circumambulates, and so forth, the mind that observes those, though not realizing emptiness, will be in possession of the power of that mind [realizing emptiness]. There is no contradiction in this. For instance, if at the beginning of a session one initially establishes a firm altruistic aspiration for enlightenment, then, when set in meditative stabilization on emptiness, it will be conjoined with the force of that altruistic aspiration, which nevertheless is not actually present.
>
> That is the mode of nonseparation of method and wisdom in the Sūtra system, but in the Mantra system it is not merely that. The nonseparation of method and wisdom in the Mantra system is taken as an undifferentiability of method and wisdom which are a simultaneous composite, in the entity of one consciousness, of the two—vast deity yoga and the profound wisdom realizing the absence of inherent existence.

Thus, the difference between the concentration bestowing liberation at the end of sound and all those preceding is that the earlier deity yoga was merely conjoined with the *force* of realizing emptiness whereas here in the concentration on the end of sound, the one consciousness that appears as the mantra sounds, divine body, and so forth, also actually realizes emptiness.

When through alternating analytical and stabilizing meditation the capacity of the mind increases to the point where analysis itself induces calm abiding, a union of calm abiding and special insight with emptiness as the object is attained. This marks the beginning of the Action Tantra path of preparation. It leads to direct realization of emptiness at the beginning of the path of seeing, at which time merely emptiness appears, a divine body no longer does, for only a Buddha can *directly* realize emptiness and conventional phenomena at the same time.

Through the power of the special techniques involved in the concentrations with repetition and not relying on repetition, a Bodhisattva is able to pass from the path of accumulation to the path of seeing much faster than in the Perfection Vehicle, where it takes one period of countless eons. This is enhanced by the feats attained upon successful completion of the concentration on the end of sound; at that point one can come under the direct care of Buddhas and high Bodhisattvas and utilize special talents such as knowing all treatises immediately upon reading them, clairvoyance, and long life, thereby hastening direct realization of emptiness.

The deity yoga of Action Tantra, found in the concentrations with repetition and not relying on repetition, incorporates these special techniques for the generation of meditative stabilization that is a union of calm abiding and special insight. The manifestation of wisdom as a divine body, divine speech mantra, and divine mind provides means for speedily accumulating the collections of merit and wisdom in order to actualize quickly the Form and Truth Bodies of a Buddha—all in order to help others.

Presentation of the Meditation as a Practice Text

Let us utilize the three headings of the body of the path—prior approximation, effecting the achievement of feats, and activities (*bsnyen sgrub las gsum*)—as an overall framework to render Tsongkhapa's brilliant amalgamation of sources into a practice text, a *Means of Achievement* (*sgrub thabs, sādhana*), containing within it the interlocking layers of vocabulary that he has mined from Indian tantras and commentaries. In this construction from

Tsongkhapa's explanation, the chosen deity is Avalokiteshvara, and the lotus lineage is used for illustration. Since the text covers many levels of progress, like stages of the path texts it may be utilized in reflective meditation (*shar sgom*) in which each level is caused to imaginatively dawn to the mind, or it may be utilized only for the level appropriate to the practitioner. (The framework and instructions are in regular type; the recitations and descriptions of meditative reflections are in bold type.)

Means of Achievement for Action Tantra Deity Yoga

I. Prior Approximation: Approaching the State of a Deity

YOGA WITH SIGNS

A. Concentration with repetition

Meditative Stabilization of Exalted Body

1. Preliminaries to the four-branched repetition

What to do initially in your place of dwelling

Daily, when you rise from bed in the early morning for the first session and at the beginning of other sessions, construct the pledge seal of the lotus lineage (seal 2) and, holding it at your heart, say:

Oṃ padma-udbhavaye svāhā.

Make homage to the Buddhas and Bodhisattvas: putting your palms together, observe all the Buddhas in the ten directions and bow down at their feet, saying:

Oṃ sarva-tathāgata kāya-vāk-citta-vajra-praṇamena sarva-tathāgata-vajra-pāda-vandanaṃ karomi.

Offering yourself, offer your body, saying:

If until I am in the essence of enlightenments, I totally and thoroughly offer myself at all times to all Buddhas and Bodhisattvas abiding in the ten directions, may the great Buddhas and Bodhisattvas please take hold of me. Please bestow upon me the unsurpassed feat of Buddhahood.

Go for refuge and generate an altruistic intention to become enlightened:

To Buddha, Doctrine, and Supreme Community
I go for refuge until enlightenment.
To achieve the welfare of myself and others
I will generate the mind of enlightenment.

Listen, O Buddhas and Bodhisattvas
Abiding in the ten directions,
I now for the sake of perfect enlightenment
Will generate the mind of enlightenment.

Create protection by making the seal (seal 4) of the Fierce Unobscured One (*mnol ba med pa*), saying the mantra:

Oṃ vajra-krodha mahābālā hana daha paca vidhvaṃsaya ucchuṣma-krodha hūṃ phaṭ.

(Create protection with this mantra also when eating, drinking, urinating, and defecating.)

Reflecting on purity, think:

The two syllables—*ma,* the entity of Vairochana, on a moon at my heart and *ha,* the entity of Achala, at my head—with interconnecting flames—are stirred up.

and say:

Oṃ svabhāva-śuddhāḥ sarva-dharmāḥ svabhāva-śuddho 'haṃ. (*Oṃ* naturally pure are all phenomena; naturally pure am I.)

and imagine:

All phenomena have become naturally pure.

Then, leaving the house, brush your teeth and so forth. Collect and remove the dirt and dust in the temple and so forth.

When you enter the place of practice, visualize the deities vividly, make homage, bowing down at their feet, saying:

Oṃ sarva-tathāgata kāya-vāk-citta-vajra-praṇamena sarva-tathāgata-vajra-pāda-vandanaṃ karomi.

Repeat this engagement in the pledges:

Oṃ viraja viraja, mahāvajri sata sata, sarate sarate, trayi trayi, virdhamani saṃbhañjani taramati siddha-agretaṃ svāhā.

Homage to the Three Jewels. Homage to the Bodhisattva, the great being, the Superior Avalokiteshvara.
May I cure all illness
Of all sentient beings
Through their seeing, hearing,
Touching, or remembering me.

Go for refuge and generate an altruistic intention to become enlightened, as before, saying:

To Buddha, Doctrine, and Supreme Community
I go for refuge until enlightenment.
To achieve the welfare of myself and others
I will generate the mind of enlightenment.

Listen, O Buddhas and Bodhisattvas
Abiding in the ten directions,
I now for the sake of perfect enlightenment
Will generate the mind of enlightenment.

2. Actual concentration with repetition

a. Concentration on the four branches of repetition

First branch: Other-base[6]

Imagining a deity in front of yourself

Imagine the ground for a divine residence:

In front is a ground of many precious substances covered with grains of gold.

Bless it into magnificence by reciting once:

Oṃ calavī hūṃ svāhā.

Imagine:

On top of it is an ocean, white like milk, adorned with flowers such as lotus and utpala. Flocks of birds as if made of jewels fly overhead.

Bless these into magnificence by reciting once:

Oṃ vimāla-dhaha hūṃ.

Imagine Mount Meru with lotus and divine residence:

In the middle is the great square Mount Meru adorned on all four sides with stairs, made respectively of gold, silver, sapphire, and topaz. The mountain is covered with well-grown wish-granting trees, themselves adorned with thousands of flapping victory banners. On top of the mountain is a huge lotus; its stalk, rising out of the center of Mount Meru, is adorned with jewels, petals made of jewels, a gold corolla, and topaz anthers with silver lines surrounding the top at its center. From the lotus stalk hundreds, thousands, tens of thousands, and millions of lotus latticeworks emerge. The syllable *bhrūṃ,* standing upright in the middle of the lotus, transforms into an empty inestimable mansion. In the middle of the palace is another lotus, the deity's seat.

With seal 19 bless the imagined residence into magnificence by reciting a hundred times:

Namaḥ sarvatathāgatānāṃ sarvathā udgate spharaṇahimaṃ gaganakhaṃ svāhā.

Imagine a canopy over the divine residence:

Instantaneously, a canopy appears over the residence.

Inviting the deity

You have previously prepared an oblation; the substance of the vessel (gold, silver, stone, wood, and so forth) and the contents (barley and milk, sesame and yogurt, cow urine and rice, and so forth) are determined by the feat that you are seeking to receive from the deity after the meditations are completed. Infuse the oblation with incense, and bless it into a magnificent state by reciting the appropriate mantra seven times.

Oṃ namo mahā-śrīyāyai, sau me siddhi siddha sādhaya, śivi śivaṃkari, abhaha, sarva-artha-sādhani svāhā.

Facing the front where a painting, or the like, of the deity is placed, bow down, saying the mantra:

Oṃ sarva-tathāgata kāya-vāk-citta-vajra-praṇamena sarva-tathāgata-vajra-pāda-vandanaṃ karomi.

Then, kneeling, invite the deity through making the seal of invitation (seal 20), which is a beckoning gesture, saying:

Due to my faith and your compassionate pledges,
Come here, come here, O Supramundane Victor.
Accepting this oblation of mine,
Be pleased with me through this offering.
Ārolik, ehyehi.

Assuming the same posture as Avalokiteshvara—that is, sitting—hold up the oblation at the level of your head and offer it, saying:

Oṃ avalokiteśvara arghaṃ pratīccha svāhā.

If the proper ingredients have not been obtained, beg the deity's pardon:

Whatever even slightly has been done wrongly
Out of the obscuration in my mind,
Please, O Protector, bear with it all
Since you are the refuge of all the embodied.

Whatever has been done here
Due to nonacquisition, lack of thorough knowledge,
Or not having the capacity,
It is right for the Chief to bear with it all.

Then:

The Supreme Superior, the Great Compassionate One, Avalokiteshvara—with white body bedecked with various jewel adornments, having one face with an affectionate smiling aspect and two eyes, with four arms, the two upper hands holding a wish-granting jewel at the heart, the other right hand holding a pearl rosary, and the other left hand holding a white lotus, with an antelope skin draped over the left shoulder, sitting in the adamantine cross-legged posture on a lotus seat—arrives together with his inestimable mansion, which fuses with the imagined mansion.

Offer a seat while reciting:

It is good that the compassionate Supramundane Victor has come.
I am meritorious and fortunate.
Taking my oblation,
Please pay heed and grant my request.

From compassion for myself and transmigrators
As long as I make offering
May the Supramundane Victor please remain here
Through your powers of magical creation.

Displaying the pledge vajra seal (seal 24), recite once:

Śaṃkare samaye svāhā.

Make seal 26, and say the essence-mantra for the lotus lineage:

Ārolik.

Make the great pledge seal of the lotus lineage (seal 2) and revolve it to protect against obstructors. Dispel obstructors from the articles of offering, saying:

To Buddha, Doctrine, and Supreme Community,
I go for refuge until enlightenment.
To achieve the welfare of myself and others
I will generate the mind of enlightenment.

Listen, O Buddhas and Bodhisattvas
Abiding in the ten directions,
I now for the sake of perfect enlightenment
Will generate the mind of enlightenment.

and repeating into scented water:

Namo ratnatrayāya, namaṣcaṇḍa-vajrapāṇaye, mahāyakṣasena-pataye, namo vajra-krodhāya, tadyathā oṃ hulu hulu tiṣṭha tiṣṭha bandha bandha hana hana amṛte hūṃ phaṭ

and sprinkle the flowers to clear away obstructors. Putting scented water in the left hand, repeat the mantra for the lotus lineage into the water and dispel obstructors with it:

Ārolik.

With the seal of generating magnificence (seal 14), spread magnificence on top of the offerings and say the appropriate mantra for generating magnificence:

Oṃ divya divya dhipaya, aveśa mahāśrīyaye svāhā. (Lotus lineage)

With the oblation seal (seal 28), offer oblation, saying:

You have come blissfully, Supramundane Victor.
Come here and please be seated.
Receiving my oblation also,
Please take pleasure mentally from this.
I have respect for you.
Oṃ sarva-tathāgata-avalokiteśvara-saparivāra arghaṃ pratīccha svāhā.

With the footbath seal (seal 29), offer a footbath, saying:

You have come blissfully, Supramundane Victor.
Come here and please be seated.
Receiving my footbath also,
Please take pleasure mentally from this.
I have respect for you.
Oṃ sarva-tathāgata-avalokiteśvara-saparivāra pravara-satkaraṃ pratīccha svāhā.

With the seal of washing the body (seal 30), imagine washing the deity's body with great clouds of perfumed water that have risen from many precious gold vases and so forth filled with fragrant perfumes; say:

You have come blissfully, Supramundane Victor.
Come here and please be seated.
Receiving my bath also,
Please take pleasure mentally from this.
I have respect for you.
Oṃ sarva-tathāgata-avalokiteśvara-saparivāra sarvadevatā-acinta-amṛta svāhā.

Mentally offer clothing and adornments; offer music, and mentally raise up melodies of praise.

With the perfume seal (seal 31), offer perfume, saying:

With faith I offer these perfumes

Of wholesome divine substances
Arisen from the clean, most clean.
Receiving them, be pleased with me.
Oṃ sarva-tathāgata-avalokiteśvara-saparivāra āhara āhara sarvavidyādhari pūjite svāhā.

With the flower seal (seal 32), offer flowers, saying:

With faith I offer these flowers
Of auspicious divine substance,
Grown from the clean, most clean.
Receiving them, be pleased with me.
Oṃ sarva-tathāgata-avalokiteśvara-saparivāra āhara āhara sarva-vidyādhari pūjite svāhā.

With the incense seal (seal 33), offer incense, saying:

With faith I offer divine substances
Made with perfume,
Pleasant essences of the forest.
Receiving them, be pleased with me.
Oṃ sarva-tathāgata-avalokiteśvara-saparivāra āhara āhara sarvavidyādhari pūjite svāhā.

With the seal of divine food (seal 34), offer food, saying:

With faith I offer
These foods of mantra,
Pleasant medicinal essences.
Receiving them, be pleased with me.
Oṃ sarva-tathāgata-avalokiteśvara-saparivāra āhara āhara sarvavidyādhari pūjite svāhā.

With the lamp seal (seal 35), offer lamps, saying:

With faith I offer these dispellers
Of darkness, conquering harmers,
Auspicious and virtuous.
I beg you to receive these lamps.
Oṃ sarva-tathāgata-avalokiteśvara-saparivāra ālokāya ālokāya vidhādhare pūjite svāhā.

Repeat one hundred times the mantra of blessing the place into magnificence:

Namaḥ sarvatathāgatānāṃ sarvathā udgate spharaṇahimaṃ gaganakhaṃ svāhā.

Praise the Three Jewels—Buddha, his doctrine, and the spiritual community:

Homage to the One-Gone-Thus,
Protector with great compassion,
Omniscient teacher,
Oceanic field of merit and attainments.

Homage to the pacifying doctrine,
Through purity separating from desire,
Through virtue liberating from bad transmigrations,
In all ways the supreme ultimate.

Respectful homage to the spiritual community,
Liberated, teaching the path of liberation,
Completely dwelling in the precepts,
Excellent field of merit, endowed with attainments.

Praise the lords of the three lineages—Mañjushrī, who is the physical manifestation of the wisdom of all Buddhas; Avalokiteshvara, who is the physical manifestation of the compassion of all Buddhas; and Vajrapāṇi, who is the physical manifestation of the power of all Buddhas:

Homage also to Mañjushrī,
Bearer of the appearance of a youth,
Vividly adorned with the lamp of wisdom,
Dispeller of the three worlds' darkness.

Homage to the always merciful,
Whose name is Avalokiteshvara,
Composite of all excellent qualities,
Strongly praised by all Buddhas.

Homage to Vajrapāṇi,
Powerful and fierce,

Virtuous king of knowledge-mantra,
Tamer of the hard to tame.

Make praises specifically of Avalokiteshvara, and repeat one hundred times the mantra of bringing forth praise:

Namaḥ sarva-buddha-bodhisattvānāṃ, sarvatra saṃkurumita avijñā-rāśini namo stute svāhā.

Disclose ill deeds with an attitude of contrition and future restraint:

Ones-Gone-Thus residing
In all directions of the worlds,
Foe Destroyers, and Bodhisattvas,
I ask you to heed me.

Whatever ill deeds
I have committed in any lifetime,
Or, disturbed by the power of desire,
Stupidity, or anger in cyclic existence
In former lives or in this life,
Whatever ill deeds I have done,
Asked others to do, or admired even a little,
Even slight ones unconscientiously done
With body, speech, or mind
To Buddha, doctrine, or spiritual community,
Or gurus, father and mother,
Foe Destroyers, Bodhisattvas,
Or any object of giving,
Or to other sentient beings—
Educated or uneducated—
Having mentally collected all these,
I bow down in great respect
To the perfect Buddhas and their children
Manifest before me now
And disclose individually
And repeatedly my mistakes
With pressed palms and saddened mind.

Just as the perfect Buddhas know
The ill deeds that I have committed,
I make individual disclosure.
Henceforth I will not do such.

Take refuge in Buddha, his doctrine, and the spiritual community with strong intent:

So that the sufferings of beings might be pacified
I respectfully go for true refuge
To Buddha, Doctrine, and Spiritual Community
As long as I remain alive.

Admire your own and others' virtues:

Set in equipoise, I take admiration
In the varieties of practical implementation of doctrine.

Entreat the Buddhas to remain teaching and supplicate them not to withdraw physical appearance so beneficial to the world:

To generate nonconceptual pristine wisdom
I entreat you to turn the wheel of doctrine
And not to pass away from sorrow
Until trainees are satisfied.

Make prayer-wishes:

Just as the earlier Buddha-children
Made prayer-wishes,
I also with a virtuous mind

Plant prayer-wishes in that way.
May all beings have happiness,
Peace, and freedom from disease.
May I be capable in all activities
And also possess all good qualities.

May I be wealthy, generous,
Intelligent, and patient,
Having faith in virtue, memory
Of former births in all lives, and empathy.

Cultivate the four immeasurables—compassion, love, joy, and the equanimity that is devoid of the conceptions of subject and object as inherently existent:

May all sentient beings be free from all suffering.
May all sentient beings be endowed with all happiness.
May all sentient beings be blissful with the bliss of Buddhahood.
May all sentient beings pass from sorrow with the unsurpassed nirvāṇa of a Buddha.

Generate an altruistic intention to become enlightened such that it definitely suffuses your mental continuum:

Foundational Step: Equality

1. From their own point of view, friends, enemies, and neutral beings equally want happiness and do not want suffering.

2. From my own point of view, each and every one of them has been my friend limitless times over beginningless cyclic existence and will definitely help me again in the future; each has equally been my enemy; and each has equally been neutral.

3. Thus from whatever side it is considered, my own or others, there is no point in exaggerating feelings of intimacy or alienation. I should not value one person as basically good and another as bad, even though their present actions may be good or bad, helpful or harmful. There is no reason to be nice at heart to one person and not nice to another. Though it is true that people are friends or enemies temporarily—helpful or harmful—it is a mistake to use this fluid state as the basis for an inflexible attraction or hatred.

First Step: Recognizing Friends

1. My births in cyclic existence have no beginning.

2. When I was born from a womb as an animal or human, or when I was born from an egg, I required a mother. Since my births are innumerable, I must have had innumerable

mothers over the course of those many lifetimes. The implication is that every living being has been my mother at some time. See whether there is a reason why any sentient being has not been my mother; such a conclusion is impossible.

3. The times I took birth from a womb or an egg are unlimited in number, and therefore my mothers are also unlimited in number.

4. Each sentient being has to have been my mother many times.

Second Step: Appreciating Kindness

Visualize your prime nurturer, vividly in front, and think:

> **This person was my mother many times over the continuum of lives; in just this present lifetime she has bestowed on me a body that supports an auspicious life in which I am able to progress spiritually. She sustained me in her womb for nine months, during which she could not behave as she wished but had to pay special attention to this burden that she carried in her body, making it difficult to move about. Even though my movements would cause her pain, she would take delight in them, thinking how strong her child was, rather than becoming angry and concentrating on her pain. Her sense of closeness and dearness was great.**

If you use as a model a person other than your mother, recall in detail the kindnesses he or she extended.

Having understood the kindness of your prime nurturer of this lifetime, extend this understanding gradually to other friends, then neutral persons, and, finally, enemies.

Third Step: Returning Kindness

Think:

> **If my mother (or best friend) of this lifetime was blind and, not in her right mind, was proceeding along the edge of a frightful cliff without a guide, and if I, her own child, did not**

pay attention and take on the task of helping her, it would be awful.

Extend the example:

All sentient beings throughout space have been my mother and have protected me with great kindness; they do not know what in their behavior to discard and what to adopt in order to promote their own long-term interests. Without a spiritual guide, they are walking along the edge of a cliff of frightful sufferings in cyclic existence. If, knowing this, I did not consider their welfare but only my own freedom, it would be awful.

In response to being cared for by others in this and other lifetimes, develop a determination to help them in whatever way is appropriate:

I will do whatever I can for these beings—my own nurturing friends—stricken by such suffering.

Commit to their welfare.

Fourth Step: Love

Starting with your best friend, think:

This person wants happiness but is bereft. How nice it would be if she or he could be imbued with happiness and all the causes of happiness!

Continue the same meditation with respect to more and more friends until this wish for happiness and all the causes of happiness is equally strong for all of them, and then consider neutral beings and finally enemies.

Then intensify the feeling, starting with friends, with:

This person wants happiness but is bereft. May she or he be imbued with happiness and all the causes of happiness!

Extend the same wish to neutral beings, and enemies.

Then intensify the feeling, starting with friends, with:

I will do whatever I can to cause her or him to be imbued with happiness and all the causes of happiness!

Extend the same wish to neutral beings, and enemies.

Fifth Step: Compassion

Bring to mind a friend who has obvious pain, and think:

> **Like me, this person wants happiness and does not want suffering, yet is stricken with such pain. If this person could only be free from suffering and the causes of suffering!**

Visualize a friend who, even though not blatantly suffering, will suffer in the future due to substantial counterproductive actions of the kind that we all have committed over the course of beginningless time. Think:

> **Like me, this person wants happiness and does not want suffering, yet is stricken with such pain. If this person could only be free from suffering and the causes of suffering!**

Slowly extend this meditation person by person, first with more friends, then with neutral persons, and finally with enemies, eventually including all sentient beings throughout space.

Then intensify the feeling, starting with friends, then neutral persons, and then enemies:

> **Like me, this person wants happiness and does not want suffering, yet is stricken with such pain. May this person be free from suffering and the causes of suffering!**

Extend the same wish to neutral beings, and enemies.

Then intensify the feeling, starting with friends, then neutral persons, and then enemies:

> **Like me, this person wants happiness and does not want suffering, yet is stricken with such pain. I will help this person be free from suffering and all the causes of suffering!**

Extend the same wish to neutral beings, and enemies.

Sixth Step: Total Commitment

1. **Afflictive emotions do not dwell in the nature of the mind; therefore, they can be removed.**
2. **Since afflictive emotions can be separated from the mind, it is realistic for me to work to achieve enlightenment and to help others do the same.**
3. **Even if I have to do it alone, I will free all sentient beings**

from suffering and the causes of suffering, and join all sentient beings with happiness and its causes.

Seventh Step: Seeking Altruistic Enlightenment

Analyze whether in your present state you have the capacity to bring about the welfare of all beings by freeing them from suffering and joining them with happiness.

> **Though I can help others on a limited level, I cannot yet do so on a vast level. In addition to giving food, clothing, and shelter it is necessary to educate people so that they can take care of their own lives. Teaching what should be adopted and discarded is crucial, and therefore I must know their dispositions and interests and have full knowledge of beneficial practices. Thus it is necessary for me to achieve enlightenment, in which the obstacles keeping me from realizing everything knowable are completely removed and I gain total realization of the nature of persons and things.**

Think:

> **I will attain Buddhahood in order to liberate stricken transmigrating beings.**

and say:

> **To pacify the suffering**
> **Of limitless realms of sentient beings,**
> **Release them from bad transmigrations,**
> **Liberate them from afflictive emotions,**
> **And protect them completely**
> **From the varieties of sufferings**
> **When the discomforts of cyclic existence crowd in,**
> **I will generate an altruistic intention to become enlightened.**
>
> **May I always be a refuge**
> **For all destitute sentient beings,**
> **A protector of the protectorless,**
> **A support of those without support,**

A refuge for the unprotected,
Maker of the miserable happy.

May I cause the pacification
Of all sentient beings' afflictive emotions.
May whatever virtuous actions
I have accumulated in this and other lives
Assume the aspects of the collections
That are called merit and wisdom.

May whatever effort I make
By way of the six perfections
Be of benefit to all beings
Without there being any exception.

Making effort until enlightenment,
I will strive at actions temporarily
And limitlessly over lives so that, in short,
All the afflictive emotions of all sentient beings
May be pacified and they be freed.

Second branch: Self-base

Imagining Yourself as a Deity: Meditation of the Six Deities

1. Ultimate Deity (also called Emptiness Deity or Suchness Deity): meditate on yourself and the deity as the same in being empty of inherent existence.

Ascertain what is being negated—inherent existence:

Imagine, for instance, that someone criticizes you for something you actually have not done, saying, "You ruined such-and-such," pointing a finger at you.

Watch your reaction. How does the "I" appear to your mind?

In what way are you apprehending it?

Notice how that "I" seems to stand by itself, self-instituting, established by way of its own character.

Ascertain the entailment of emptiness:

Analyze whether the "I" that is inherently self-established in the context of the mind-body complex could have a way of existing other than being part of or separate from mind and body.

Take other phenomena, such as a cup and a table, or a house and a mountain, as examples. See that there is no third category of existence. They are either the same or different.

Decide that if the "I" inherently exists as it seems to, then it must be either one with or separate from mind and body.

Ascertain that the "I" and the aggregates are not inherently the same by considering the consequences if the "I" is the same as mind-body and if the "I" is established in and of itself in accordance with how it appears to your mind:

Since mind and body are plural, a person's selves also would be plural!

Since I am just one, mind and body also would be one!

Ascertain that the "I" and the aggregates are not inherently different by considering the consequences if the "I" is inherently different from mind-body and if the "I" is established in and of itself in accordance with how it appears to your mind:

I and mind-body would have to be completely separate!

In that case, I would have to be findable after clearing away mind and body!

I would not have the characteristics of being produced, abiding, and disintegrating!

I would have to be just a figment of the imagination or permanent!

I would not have any physical or mental characteristics!

Not finding yourself either of these ways, realize the absence of inherent existence of the "I" in space-like meditative equipoise.

Reflect on the sameness of yourself and the deity in terms of your final nature:

Just as my own suchness is ultimately free from all the proliferations of inherent existence, so also is the deity's suchness. Hence, in nonconceptual perception of the final mode of abiding of phenomena, the suchness of myself and of the deity are undifferentiable, like a mixture of water and milk.

2. Sound Deity (also called tone deity)
From within emptiness my wisdom realizing the ultimate deity manifests as the tones of the mantra resounding in space.[7]
Oṃ maṇi padme hūṃ.

3. Letter Deity
My mind having the aspect of realizing the undifferentiable suchness of myself and the deity becomes a moon disc. The mantra tones resounding in space are set upright on the edge of the moon disc in the aspect of written letters, like very pure mercury adhering to or completely mixing with grains of gold. (The letters are not just color and shape, but are fused with their respective sounds.)

4. Form Deity
The moon and mantra letters transform such that variegated rays of light are emitted from the moon and mantra letters. From the points of the light rays innumerable forms of the deity emerge, pervading the entire sphere of space. Through emanating great clouds of offerings they make splendid offerings to all the Buddhas and Bodhisattvas. Also, they emanate great clouds from which a rain of ambrosia descends, extinguishing the fires of the sufferings of all transmigrators, hell-beings, and so forth, as well as satisfying beings with whatever they need—giving a good body to those who need it, coolness to those suffering from heat, the warmth of the sun to those suffering from cold, food and drink to the hun-

gry and thirsty—emanating to each just what he or she needs, providing beings with the basis for practicing the spiritual path as well as teachers to instruct them in the four truths, the two truths, and so forth, whereby they ascend the five paths and ten Bodhisattva grounds and attain the final happiness of Buddhahood.

Then, the divine bodies dissolve back into the rays of light with all their magnificent qualities of body, speech, and mind and return and enter the moon disc and mantra letters, whereupon I emerge in the full form of Avalokiteshvara, the Supreme Superior, the Great Compassionate One, with white body bedecked with various jewel adornments, having one face with an affectionate smiling aspect and two eyes, with four arms—the two upper hands holding a wish-granting jewel at the heart, the other right hand holding a pearl rosary, and the other left hand holding a white lotus—with an antelope skin draped over the left shoulder, sitting in the adamantine cross-legged posture on a lotus seat.

5. Seal Deity

Construct the pledge seal of the lotus lineage (seal 2) and bless into a magnificent state the heart, point between the brows, the neck, and the shoulders[8] through touching them with the seal and repeating the pledge mantra:

Oṃ padma-udbhavaye svāhā.

With the oblation seal (seal 28), offer oblation to yourself as the deity, saying:

Arghaṃ pratīccha svāhā.

With the footbath seal (seal 29), offer a footbath, saying:

Oṃ pravarasatkaraṃ pratīccha svāhā.

With the seal of washing the body (seal 30), imagine washing the deity's body with great clouds of perfumed water that have risen from many precious gold vases and so forth filled with fragrant perfumes; say:

Oṃ sarva-devatā-acinta-amṛta svāhā.

Mentally offer clothing and adornments; offer music, and mentally raise up melodies of praise.

With the perfume seal (seal 31), offer perfume, saying:

Āhara āhara sarva-vidyādhari pūjite svāhā.

With the flower seal (seal 32), offer flowers, saying:

Āhara āhara sarva-vidyādhari pūjite svāhā.

With the incense seal (seal 33), offer incense, saying:

Āhara āhara sarva-vidyādhari pūjite svāhā.

With the seal of divine food (seal 34), offer food, saying:

Āhara āhara sarva-vidyādhari pūjite svāhā.

With the lamp seal (seal 35), offer lamps, saying:

Ālokāya ālokāya vidhādhare pūjite svāhā.

Offer praise:

Homage to the always merciful,
Whose name is Avalokiteshvara,
Composite of all excellent qualities,
Strongly praised by all Buddhas.

6. Sign Deity

Within observing just that deity that has been generated, develop clear appearance of your divine body and develop pride in being that deity.

To do this:

Stop the exhalation and inhalation of breath; withdraw inside movements of the breath throughout the body like a turtle's retracting its limbs and like drinking water drawn up with the tongue by means of the upwards-moving wind. Also, withdraw inside the usual intense movement of the nonequipoised mind out through the senses. Nevertheless, leave your eyes a little open, raise your face a little, and set yourself in one-pointed meditative equipoise, observing your own body clarified as a deity. Like a person dwelling in a cave and looking outside, you are as if inside the divine body observing it from within.

Hold your breath as much as you can, all the while observing one aspect of the divine body.

Then, let the breath out gently; relax, viewing your general body clarified as a deity.

Again hold your breath and observe the same one aspect of your divine body. Do this until you gain the capacity to stop—by means of the clear appearance of the deity and by means of the pride of being a deity—the pride of ordinariness. Both clear appearance and divine pride are necessary.

Resting

Ceasing visualizing your divine body, observe the letters on the moon disc in space (which is the second part of the third deity, the "letter deity").

Ceasing visualizing the letters on the moon, observe the moon disc in space (which is the first part of the "letter deity").

Ceasing visualizing the moon disc, observe the sounds of the mantra reverberating in space (which is the second deity, the "sound deity").

Ceasing observing the sounds of the mantra, observe the pride of the sameness of the nature of yourself and the deity (which is the last part of the first deity, the "ultimate deity").

Ceasing observing the pride of the sameness of the nature of yourself and the deity, observe the suchness of self, your own emptiness of inherent existence (which is the first part of the "ultimate deity").

Remain in meditative equipoise on your own emptiness.

All at once rise in a divine body, which is the same as that visualized earlier.

Between sessions

Between sessions remain within deity yoga, albeit not as complete as before, going about daily activities.

Meditative Stabilization of Exalted Speech

Third branch: Moon

A moon disc appears at the heart of the deity in front.

Fourth branch: Sound

The written letters of the mantra are set upright and facing inward around the edge of the moon disc at the heart of the deity in front.

Rays of light are emitted from the moon and mantra letters. From the points of the light rays innumerable forms of the deity emerge, pervading the entire sphere of space. Through emanating great clouds of offerings they make splendid offerings to all the Buddhas and Bodhisattvas. Also, they emanate great clouds from which a rain of ambrosia descends, extinguishing the fires of the sufferings of all transmigrators, hell-beings, and so forth, as well as satisfying beings with whatever they need—giving a good body to those who need it, coolness to those suffering from heat, the warmth of the sun to those suffering from cold, food and drink to the hungry and thirsty—emanating to each just what he or she needs, providing beings with the basis for practicing the spiritual path as well as teachers to instruct them in the four truths, the two truths, and so forth, whereby they ascend the five paths and ten Bodhisattva grounds and attain the final happiness of Buddhahood.

b. *Repetition in dependence upon the four branches (deity in front, yourself as a deity, moon, and letters)*

(1) Repeat mantra within observing the form of the letters[9]

(a) Repeat mantra within observing the form of the letters at the heart of the deity in front

Whispered repetition

Focusing on the three—the front deity, moon, and letters—repeat mantra in whisper, as if reading the letters, while exhaling.

While inhaling, switch to observing yourself as a deity without repetition.

Repeat the above.

Mental repetition

Holding your breath after inhalation and focusing on the three—the front deity, moon, and letters—repeat mantra mentally as if listening to your own recitation.

While exhaling, switch to observing yourself as a deity without repetition.

Repeat the above.

Resting

Stop repeating mantra.

Ceasing visualizing the forms of the mantra letters, observe the moon on which they stood at the heart in the deity in front (which is the moon branch).

Ceasing visualizing the moon, observe the deity in front (which is the branch called "other-base").

Ceasing visualizing the deity in front, observe your own divine body (which is the branch called "self-base" and, within it, the sixth deity, the sign deity, as well as the fourth deity, the "form deity").

Ceasing visualizing your divine body, observe the letters on the moon disc in space (which is the second part of the third deity, the "letter deity").

Ceasing visualizing the letters on the moon, observe the moon disc in space (which is the first part of the "letter deity").

Ceasing visualizing the moon disc, observe the sounds of the mantra reverberating in space (which is the second deity, the "sound deity").

Ceasing observing the sounds of the mantra, observe the pride of the sameness of the nature of yourself and the deity (which is the last part of the first deity, the "ultimate deity").

Ceasing observing the pride of the sameness of the nature

of yourself and the deity, observe the suchness of self, your own emptiness of inherent existence (which is the first part of the "ultimate deity").

Remain in meditative equipoise on your own emptiness.

All at once rise in a divine body, which is the same as that visualized earlier.

Between sessions

Between sessions remain within deity yoga, albeit not as complete as before, going about daily activities.

(b) Repeat mantra within observing the form of the letters at your own heart

Whispered repetition

Inhale—into your own heart from the heart of the deity in front—the moon disc together with the mantra letters standing at its edge.

Perform whispered repetition, focusing on the moon and letters.

At the end of exhaling, emit the moon and letters back to the deity in front, focusing on moon and letters, without repetition.

Repeat the above.

Mental repetition

Inhale—into your own heart from the heart of the deity in front—the moon disc together with the mantra letters standing at its edge without repetition.

Stop your breath and recite mantra mentally, focusing on moon and letters, as if your mind is in the center of the moon disc and is reading the letters of the mantra standing on the edge of the moon disc facing inward.

When exhaling, stop repetition of mantra, and move the moon and letters with your breath to the deity's heart—focusing on the moon and letters.

With inhalation, repeat the above.

(2) Repeat mantra within observing the sound of the letters

Whispered repetition

Within retaining visualization of the deity in front and yourself as a deity with the moon and the mantra letters on the moon at your heart, repeat mantra in whisper, focusing on just the sounds.

Mental repetition

Within retaining visualization of the deity in front and yourself as a deity with the moon and the mantra letters on the moon at your heart, repeat mantra mentally while stopping breath and distraction, focusing on just the sounds.

Resting: Observe the divine body, then return to the sounds of the letters.

c. Concluding the concentration of the four-branched repetition

With the vase seal (seal 36) offer the virtue of the session for the sake of feats:

I offer this virtuous root of mine to the Supramundane Victor as a cause of such-and-such feat. O Protector, please bestow such-and-such feat.

Arrange whatever offerings have been newly acquired, and clear away obstructors in the flowers and so forth through, repeating into scented water either the mantra of Kuṇḍali:

Namo ratnatrayāya, namaṣcaṇḍa-vajrapāṇaye, mahāyakṣasena-pataye, namo vajra-krodhāya, tadyathā oṃ hulu hulu tiṣṭha tiṣṭha bandha bandha hana hana amṛte hūṃ phaṭ.

or the mantra of all activities of the lotus lineage:

Oṃ namo mahā-śrīyāyai, sau me siddhi siddha sādhaya, śivi śivaṃkari, abhaha, sarva-artha-sādhani svāhā.

and putting scented water in left hand, repeat into the water the lineage essence:

Ārolik.

and sprinkle the flowers and so forth. From the seal of dispelling obstructors (seal 10), construct the seal of generating magnificence (seal 14), and with it distribute magnificence on top of the perfume, flowers, and so forth and repeat the mantra of generating magnificence:

Oṃ divya divya dhipaya, aveśa mahāśrīye svāhā.

thinking that thereby:

The offerings turn into perfect divine substances.

Then, bless them into magnificence with the mantra of Kuṇḍali:

Namo ratnatrayāya, namaṣcaṇḍa-vajrapāṇaye, mahāyakṣasena-pataye, namo vajra-krodhāya, tadyathā oṃ hulu hulu tiṣṭha tiṣṭha bandha bandha hana hana amṛte hūṃ phaṭ.

and repeat the essence mantra of the lotus lineage:

Ārolik.

With the oblation seal (seal 28), offer oblation, saying:

You have come blissfully, Supramundane Victor.
Come here and please be seated.
Receiving my oblation also,
Please take pleasure mentally from this.
I have respect for you.
Arghaṃ pratīccha svāhā.

With the footbath seal (seal 29), offer a footbath, saying:

You have come blissfully, Supramundane Victor.
Come here and please be seated.
Receiving my footbath also,
Please take pleasure mentally from this.
I have respect for you.
Oṃ pravarasatkaraṃ pratīccha svāhā.

With the seal of washing the body (seal 30), imagine washing the deity's body with great clouds of perfumed water that have risen from many precious gold vases and so forth filled with fragrant perfumes; say:

You have come blissfully, Supramundane Victor.
Come here and please be seated.
Receiving my bath also,
Please take pleasure mentally from this.

I have respect for you.
Oṃ sarva-devatā-acinta-amṛta svāhā.

Mentally offer clothing and adornments; offer music, and mentally raise up melodies of praise.

With the perfume seal (seal 31), offer perfume, saying:

With faith I offer these perfumes
Of wholesome divine substances
Arisen from the clean, most clean.
Receiving them, be pleased with me.
Āhara āhara sarva-vidyādhari pūjite svāhā.

With the flower seal (seal 32), offer flowers, saying:

With faith I offer these flowers
Of auspicious divine substance,
Grown from the clean, most clean.
Receiving them, be pleased with me.
Āhara āhara sarva-vidyādhari pūjite svāhā.

With the incense seal (seal 33), offer incense, saying:

With faith I offer divine substances
Made with perfume,
Pleasant essences of the forest.
Receiving them, be pleased with me.
Āhara āhara sarva-vidyādhari pūjite svāhā.

With the seal of divine food (seal 34), offer food, saying:

With faith I offer
These foods of mantra,
Pleasant medicinal essences.
Receiving them, be pleased with me.
Āhara āhara sarva-vidyādhari pūjite svāhā.

With the lamp seal (seal 35), offer lamps, saying:

With faith I offer these dispellers
Of darkness, conquering harmers,
Auspicious and virtuous.
I beg you to receive these lamps.
Ālokāya ālokāya vidhādhare pūjite svāhā.

Praise the Three Jewels—Buddha, his doctrine, and the spiritual community:

Homage to the One-Gone-Thus,
Protector with great compassion,
Omniscient teacher,
Oceanic field of merit and attainments.

Homage to the pacifying doctrine,
Through purity separating from desire,
Through virtue liberating from bad transmigrations,
In all ways the supreme ultimate.

Respectful homage to the spiritual community,
Liberated, teaching the path of liberation,
Completely dwelling in the precepts,
Excellent field of merit, endowed with attainments.

Praise the lords of the three lineages—Mañjushrī, who is the physical manifestation of the wisdom of all Buddhas; Avalokiteshvara, who is the physical manifestation of the compassion of all Buddhas; and Vajrapāṇi, who is the physical manifestation of the power of all Buddhas:

Homage also to Mañjushrī,
Bearer of the appearance of a youth,
Vividly adorned with the lamp of wisdom,
Dispeller of the three worlds' darkness.

Homage to the always merciful,
Whose name is Avalokiteshvara,
Composite of all excellent qualities,
Strongly praised by all Buddhas.

Homage to Vajrapāṇi,
Powerful and fierce,
Virtuous king of knowledge-mantra,
Tamer of the hard to tame.

Ask for forbearance for not having the circumstances to perform the rite exactly according to the tantra:

Whatever even slightly has been done wrongly
Out of the obscuration in my mind,
Please, O Protector, bear with it all
Since you are the refuge of all the embodied.

Whatever has been done here
Due to nonacquisition, lack of thorough knowledge,
Or not having the capacity,
It is right for the Chief to bear with it all.

Request Avalokiteshvara to depart together with his inestimable mansion, saying:

***Oṃ* may you bestow yogic feats**
Concordant with effecting the welfare of all sentient beings.
Having gone to a Buddha Land,
Please may you come again.

From the seal of invitation (seal 20), make the seal of requesting departure (seal 37), and say:

***Ārolik gaccha.* Together with his inestimable mansion he has gone to his natural abode.**

Free the directions and intermediate directions that were bound earlier by making the seal of unequal limbs (seal 38), circling it from the left, and saying:

Oṃ hulu hulu caṇḍali-mataṃ givi svāhā.

Between sessions

Between sessions remain within deity yoga, albeit not as complete as before, going about daily activities.

Continuation of Meditative Stabilization of Exalted Speech

B. Concentration Not Relying on Repetition

1. Concentration of Abiding in Fire

(Because mantra is heard as if recited by someone else, it is said to be concentration not relying on repetition.)

1. Contemplate the emptiness of inherent existence of yourself and the deity through the six deities.
2. While visualizing yourself in the form of Avalokiteshvara and conceiving of yourself to be Avalokiteshvara, imagine a tiny moon at your heart with a blazing tongue of fire, like the flame of a butter lamp.
3. Your mind of wisdom realizing emptiness appears as the mantra sounds in the flame at your heart, resounding continuously like bells. Within stopping breath and distraction, your mind is as if dwelling inside the tongue of flame and itself is appearing in that flame as the sounds, as if you were listening to recitation by someone else or the letters were sounding of their own accord. Observe mainly the flame and sounds. Because your mind of wisdom itself is appearing as the mantra sounds, the sounds of the mantra and your own final nature are completely mixed like water and milk.
4. Exhaling, observe your own larger divine body.

Repeat steps 3 and 4.

2. Concentration of Abiding in Sound

(Because mantra is heard as if recited by someone else, it is said to be concentration not relying on repetition.)

1. While visualizing yourself in the form of a deity and conceiving of yourself to be a deity with a flame at the heart, imagine a tiny deity within the flame.
2. Imagine a moon disc at the heart of the tiny deity.
3. Imagine a flame on the moon disc at the heart of the tiny deity.
4. When this visualization becomes firm, your own mind appears as the mantra sounds within the flame at the heart of the tiny deity. Within stopping breath and distraction, your mind is as if dwelling inside the tongue of flame and itself is appearing in that flame as the sounds, as if listening to recitation by someone else or resounding of their own accord. Observe mainly the sounds of the mantra. Because your

mind of wisdom itself is appearing as the mantra sounds, the sounds of the mantra and your own final nature are completely mixed like water and milk.[10]

5. Exhaling, observe your own larger divine body.

Repeat steps 4 and 5. (When resting, observe the written syllables.)

Gradually, calm abiding, which is a state of meditative stabilization conjoined with the bliss of mental and physical pliancy, is achieved. The final stages of achieving calm abiding are:

1. The "winds" (currents of energy) involved in unhealthy physical states are calmed and leave the body through the top of the head, where a tingly sensation is felt.

   Then, a *mental pliancy,* which is a pacification of unhealthy states making the mind heavy and preventing its usage in virtue according to will, is generated; this makes the mind serviceable.

2. Through its force, a "wind" of serviceability moves throughout the body, inducing a *physical pliancy* that causes separation from physical states of roughness and heaviness, whereupon you are able to use the body at will in virtuous actions without any sense of hardship. Your body is light like cotton and is as if filled with this serviceable wind.

3. Experiencing this special internal sense of smoothness, you have a *bliss of physical pliancy.*

4. Due to the mental consciousness paying attention to this bliss accompanying the body consciousness, a *bliss of mental pliancy* is generated. Your body seems to have dissolved, and nothing but the object of meditative observation appears.

5. Your mind is so buoyantly joyous that it now seems almost unable to remain on its object, but the excessive buoyancy is gradually removed, and you attain an *immovable pliancy,*

remaining stably and joyously on the object of observation. This is calm abiding.

YOGA WITHOUT SIGNS

Meditative Stabilization of Exalted Mind

3. Concentration Bestowing Liberation at the End of Sound

1. Focus not on appearance in a divine body, whispered repetition, mental repetition, or the concentrations of abiding in fire and abiding in sound, but on the emptiness of inherent existence. Although there are still divine appearances to the appearance factor of your consciousness, they no longer appear to the ascertainment factor, which is concerned only with the emptiness of inherent existence, which is now the focus. Because of the previous training, these other factors remain appearing without effort, and you simultaneously and explicitly realize their absence of being established from their own side.

2. Alternate analytical and stabilizing meditation on the emptiness of inherent existence in order to make them of equal strength.

3. Gradually the power of analysis itself is able to induce physical and mental pliancies similar to those of calm abiding, but to a greater degree. Thereby, special insight, which is a union of calm abiding and special insight, is attained.

II. Effecting the achievement of yogic feats

Feats are in three categories:

1. *pacification,* such as avoiding untimely death, illnesses, epidemics, harmful influences, and contagion;
2. *increase,* such as enhancing lifespan, youthfulness, magnificence, power, qualities of realization, and resources;
3. *ferocity* such as killing, expelling, or confusing harmful beings.

These feats—which also include clairvoyance, invisibility, the capacity to understand all treatises immediately upon reading them, swift footedness, and empowering pills for youthfulness, and so forth—are sought in order to enhance the power of the very yoga that comprises prior approximation. Thus, although the triad of prior approximation, effecting achievement of feats, and engaging in altruistic activities suggests a movement from the first to the last, the yoga that constitutes the first phase is the most important. The feats that allow a practitioner to perform special activities for the benefit of others bring about merit further enhancing the capacity of this same yoga so that Buddhahood can be achieved.

III. Activities

Use the yogic feats of pacification, increase, and ferocity for your own and others' temporary and final aims.

Correlation with the Paths

The five paths—accumulation, preparation, seeing, meditation and no more learning—are presented for the Mantra Vehicle just as they are for the Perfection Vehicle. In Action Tantra persons who have trained in the three principal aspects of the path—the intention definitely to leave cyclic existence, the altruistic mind of enlightenment induced by love and compassion, and the correct view of emptiness—first enter into a maṇḍala of any of the three lineages and receive initiation. Then, when they have cultivated the aspiration to enlightenment for the sake of others such that it manifests spontaneously and nonartificially outside of meditation as it would in intense meditation, they have attained the Action Tantra path of accumulation. It marks becoming a tantric Bodhisattva and is specifically the thought to attain Buddhahood by way of the Action Tantra path for the sake of others' welfare.

During the path of accumulation Bodhisattvas achieve calm abiding by way of the four-branched repetition and the concentrations of abiding in fire and abiding in sound. They also train in the concentration bestowing liberation at the end of sound through alternating analytical and stabilizing meditation with respect to the emptiness of inherent existence. Then when they generate a consciousness of special insight realizing emptiness, they have passed to the Action Tantra path of preparation.

On the four levels of that path—heat, peak, forbearance, and supreme mundane qualities—the sense of duality between the wisdom and its object, emptiness, gradually diminishes. The path of seeing occurs with the initial, direct, totally nondualistic realization of emptiness, gained through cultivating the concentration bestowing liberation at the end of sound. It acts as the antidote to the artificial afflictive obstructions, that is to say, the conception of inherent existence and its attendant afflictions as fortified by false teachings and scriptures.

The path of meditation begins with the form of the concentration on the end of sound that is able to act as an antidote to the big of the big innate afflictions and ranges until just before achieving full enlightenment. During this period yogis pass through nine of the ten Bodhisattva grounds, gradually purifying the mind of the nine degrees of innate afflictions and the four degrees of the obstructions to omniscience:

First ground—the path of seeing.

Second ground—from attaining the antidote to the big of the big innate afflictions.

Third ground—from attaining the antidote to the middling of the big innate afflictions.

Fourth ground—from attaining the antidote to the small of the big innate afflictions.

Fifth, sixth, and seventh grounds—from attaining the antidote respectively to the big of the middling, middling of the middling, and small of the middling innate afflictions.

Eighth ground—from attaining simultaneously the antidotes to the big of the small, middling of the small, and small of the small innate afflictions. The big obstructions to omniscience are also abandoned during a second phase of the eighth ground.

Ninth ground—from attaining the antidote to the middling obstructions to omniscience.

Tenth ground—from attaining the antidote to the coarse of the small obstructions to omniscience. During a second phase of the tenth ground the antidote to the subtle of the small obstructions to omniscience is attained, at which point one has the pristine wisdom, the end of the continuum as a sentient being with obstructions yet to be removed. Immediately after this one becomes a Buddha.

The afflictive obstructions—comprised of the ignorance conceiving inherent existence and the other afflictions such as desire, hatred, enmity, and jealousy that it induces—prevent liberation from cyclic existence. These obstructions are removed gradually by means of the concentration bestowing liberation at the end of sound over the first seven Bodhisattva grounds. Then, on the eighth, ninth and tenth grounds, the concentration bestowing liberation at the end of sound, enhanced by the factors of method, eliminates the obstructions to omniscience—not the conception but the *appearance* of inherent existence. The final path, that of no more learning, is comprised of the states of one who has become a Buddha through the Action Tantra path.

About these, Ngagwang Paldan's *Presentation of the Grounds and Paths of Mantra*[11] says:

> With regard to the way of positing the Action Tantra paths as the five paths and ten grounds, the Action Tantra path of accumulation is comprised of the paths—once pure initiation has been attained—ranging from the point at which nonartificial experience is developed with respect to a mind promising "I will attain Buddhahood by way of the Action Tantra path" through to but not including the attainment of the special insight realizing emptiness through the force of having cultivated the concentration bestowing liberation at the end of sound. The Action Tantra path of preparation is comprised of the paths ranging from that special insight through to but not including direct realization of emptiness through the force of having cultivated the concentration on the end of sound. The Action Tantra path of seeing is comprised of the paths ranging from direct realization of emptiness by that concentration through to but not including generation of the actual antidote to the big of the big afflictions to be abandoned by the path of meditation. The Action Tantra path of meditation is comprised of the paths ranging from the concentration

on the end of sound that has become the actual antidote to the big of the big afflictions to be abandoned by the path of meditation through to the point of being about to become fully enlightened by the paths of Action Tantra. The Action Tantra path of no-more-learning is comprised of the paths of one who has become a Buddha through the paths of this tantra.

From among those, the path of seeing is the first ground. The second ground begins with attaining the actual antidote to the big of the big afflictions to be abandoned by the path of meditation. The third ground begins with attaining the actual antidote to the middling of the big afflictions, and the fourth ground with the actual antidote to the small of the big. The fifth, sixth, and seventh grounds are posited from attaining the antidotes respectively to the big, middling, and small of the middling afflictions. The eighth ground is from the simultaneous attainment of the actual antidote to the triple cycle of small afflictions. Also, on the eighth ground the big obstructions to omniscience are abandoned, and then the ninth ground begins with attaining the actual antidote to the middling obstructions to omniscience. The tenth ground is from attaining the actual antidote to the coarse of the small obstructions to omniscience. Then the actual antidote to the subtle of the small obstructions to omniscience is posited as the pristine wisdom the end of the continuum.

These and other such topics must be asserted in accordance with the way of the Sūtra system Consequentialists because a mode of abandoning the two obstructions in the three lower tantra sets that is different from the Perfection Vehicle is not explained in any reliable text and such is not established by reasoning.

Thus, although the four-branched repetition and the concentrations are used as means for attaining common feats that enhance the path, these also comprise the very body of the path leading to Buddhahood, for the concentration on the end of sound itself, as it progresses in capacity, removes the obstructions to liberation and to omniscience. The feats gained through the concentration on the end of sound—which is the culmination of deity yoga—bestow powers through which vast merit is achieved. That merit, in turn, further empowers the concentration on the end of sound so that it can overcome the obstructions to omniscience, whereupon the welfare of others is furthered as it could not be otherwise.

Since Bodhisattvas' aim is to help others, they seek to enhance the wisdom realizing emptiness so that it can remove the subtlest of obstructions to omniscience. This enhancement is done through deity yoga itself as well as the special feats and activities that are at a practitioner's disposal upon completing the concentrations of deity yoga, that is to say, upon attaining the concentration bestowing liberation at the end of sound. In this context the objective of deity yoga and of the powers gained through it is the removal of obstructions, thereby allowing progression over the grounds and paths and issuing forth the ability to manifest in form in accordance with the needs of trainees.

Appendix 1

Lineages of Action Tantras and Performance Tantras

A translation from Paṇchen Sönam Dragpa's *General Presentation of the Tantra Sets: Captivating the Minds of the Fortune*[1]

Inner Divisions of Action Tantra

This has two parts: the divisions of the individual lineages and the general division of the three lineages.

Divisions of the Individual Lineages in Action Tantra

This has three parts: the One-Gone-Thus, lotus, and vajra lineages.

Divisions of the One-Gone-Thus Lineage

[The tantras of] the One-Gone-Thus lineage have eight [divisions]:

1. tantras of the principal of the One-Gone-Thus lineage,
2. tantras of the lord of the One-Gone-Thus lineage,
3. tantras of the mothers of the One-Gone-Thus lineage,
4. tantras of the crown protrusion of the One-Gone-Thus lineage,
5. tantras of the group of fierce males and females of the One-Gone-Thus lineage,
6. tantras of the group of messengers of the One-Gone-Thus lineage,

7. tantras of the group of Bodhisattvas of the One-Gone-Thus lineage,
8. tantras of the groups of serpents and harm-bestowers (*yakṣa*) of the One-Gone-Thus lineage.

Tantras of the Principal of the One-Gone-Thus Lineage

The principal of the One-Gone-Thus lineage is the Teacher Shākyamuni. Without being requested by his retinue, he set forth [the rite of][2] the hundred letters, as well as its benefits. Requested, he set forth the *Royal Tantra Stating the Three Pledges* (*trisamayavyūharāja,* P134), which teaches the maṇḍala in which the Teacher himself acts as the principal. The *[Sūtra of] Excellent Golden Light* (*suvarṇaprabhāsottamasūtrendrarāja*) in three versions—great, middling, and small (P174-6)—the subject matter of which accords in part [with the above tantras], is included in the set of [tantras of the principal of the One-Gone-Thus lineage]. The assertions by one that these are in the sūtra class and by another that they are common to sūtra and tantra are not reasonable because these set forth means of achieving Shrīmahādevi and the four great kings as well as how to draw their maṇḍalas.

Tantras of the Lord of the One-Gone-Thus Lineage

The lord of the One-Gone-Thus lineage is Mañjushrī; there is an extensive *Mañjushrī Root Tantra* (*mañjuśrīmūlatantra,* P162) of thirty-six chapters, which teaches the modes of the twelve deeds and so forth, and there is a more condensed *Achievement of Mañjushrī as a Sole Hero* (*siddhaikavīramahātantrarāja,* P163) of four chapters. The first chapter teaches how—by way of Buddhas and Bodhisattvas—to analyze dreams, how to apply the activity of protecting from lightning, and the means of achieving the nine Jambhala deities. In the fourth chapter there is a teaching of a compendium of initiations depending on Tārā Kurukulle and the mode of the circle of protection of the male and female circles of harm-bestowers facing [each other], and so forth.

Some [mistakenly make reference to] the *Means of Achievement of the Heart of the Perfection of Wisdom Sūtra* (*prajñāpāramitāhṛdayasādhana*) [which describes] generation of oneself as the Teacher Shākyamuni from within the emptiness of having gathered the environments and beings into clear light. Also the *Means of Achievement* (P3464) [which is a commentary on the above],[3] said to be by Nāgārjuna, in which the Great Mother is surrounded by the sons—the Buddhas of the ten directions, and the *Permission Rite of the Eight Clear Realizations,* said to be by Pa-dam-pa (*pha dam pa*) [Bodhidharma?], and so forth are just cases of name-borrowing [by spurious authors].

Although some include the two rites of the Medicine Guru—longer and shorter—in the sūtra class, these are reasonably Action Tantras because Ratnakīrti [in his *Sarvadhāraṇīmaṇḍalavidhi,* P3957][4] proves them to be Action Tantras "due to their involving assumption [of a day] of purification and renewal, and so forth" and since they speak of four-sided, four-doored maṇḍalas, and so forth.

Tantras of Mothers of the One-Gone-Thus Lineage

The mothers of the One-Gone-Thus lineage are Mārīchi and the five guards (*rakṣa*). [The tantras] are the *Retention of Mārīchi* (*mārīcināmadhāraṇī,* P182) as well as its rite [the *Imagination of Mārīchi* (*māyāmārīcijātatantrād uddhitaṃ kalparāja,* P183) and so forth]. In the *Illusory Imagination of Mārīchi* (*māyāmārīcimaṇḍalavidhi mārīcijātadvādaśasahasra-uddhitaṃ kalpahṛdayasaptaśata*) there clearly are presentations of the [stages of] generation and completion as well as of channels, winds, and drops [which are topics found exclusively in Highest Yoga Tantra]; therefore, it is said that [this text] likely is an adulteration in which Highest Yoga and Action Tantra are confused.

The five guards are Pratisarā, Mahāmayūrī, Shitavati, Mantranudharini, and Sahasrapramardani.[5] Ratnākarashānti (P3947) presents the rites of their maṇḍalas and their activities in detail. There also are *Means of Achievement* [of the five] individually and in common by Jetāri.[6]

Tantras of the Crown Protrusions of the One-Gone-Thus Lineage

These are Vijaya Uṣhṇīsha, Sitatāpatra Uṣhṇīsha, Vimāla Uṣhṇīsha, and Jvala Uṣhṇīsha (Victorious, White Umbrella, Stainless, and Blazing Crown Protrusions). With respect to the first, there is the *Retention of Uṣhṇīsha Vijaya Purifying All Bad Migrations* (*sarvadurgatipariśodhanī-uṣṇīśavijayanāmadhāraṇī*, P198) together with [the rite] of applying its activities. This was requested of Vijaya by Shakra, the King of Gods, for the sake of the Devaputra Very Steady [who had foreseen rebirth in bad migrations].[7] There is also an *Imagination of Vijaya* (*sarvatathāgatoṣṇīśav ijayanāmadhāraṇīkalpa,* P200), which teaches how to make a victory reliquary (*rnam rgyal gyi mchod rten*), how to make imprinted holy objects (*sāccha*) to put inside it, and so forth.[8]

Sitatāpatra Uṣhṇīsha has four [tantras], the *Unconquerable by Others* (*sarvatathāgatoṣṇīśasitātapatrānāma-aparā jitāpratyaṃgiramahāvidyārajñī,* P202), the *Paramasiddhi* (*tathāgatoṣṇīśasitātapatre aparājitāmahāpratyamgirāparamasiddhināmadhāraṇī,* P203), and the two *Lessers* without introduction that appeared in lands of gods [*tathāgatoṣṇīśasitātapatre aparājitānāmadhāraṇī,* P204, P205].[9] Among these, the first two, except for being different translations, are the same, the *Paramasiddhi* being the better translation. Its commentary by Shuramgamavarma has explanations of secret maṇḍala, knowledge mantra, essence mantra, and quintessential mantra.

There are about fourteen miscellaneous texts by Chandragomin, which include a *Maṇḍala Rite, Rite of Food Offering* (P3904), *Rite of the Circle of Protection* (P3906), *Rite of Burnt Offering* (P3922), and so forth. There are also rites of maṇḍala by Vajrāsana (P3929), Tikṣhṇavajra (P3926), and Vajrankusha.[10] Although there are maṇḍala rites by Padmankusha (P3932) and Varmavajra (P3927), they are not correct because the maintaining of the vows of the five lineages [which occurs only in Yoga and Highest Yoga Tantra] and so forth appear frequently in them. Also, there are a rite written by a Tibetan who borrowed Chandragomin's name, a [work on] the creation of food-offering figures for practice that is said to be from India, and a rite by Porog Gönpo Dorjay (*pho rog mgon po rdo rje*), which is the system of explanation initially in Tibet.

With respect to Vimāla Uṣhṇīsha, there are [tantras] teaching how to create a maṇḍala of perfumed water and the creation of the one hundred and eight reliquaries. Regarding these, there are a general compendium and individual compendia by the master Sahajalalita.

With respect to Blazing Uṣhṇīsha, there is, for instance, the first chapter of the *Mañjushrī Root Tantra* treated separately.

The "Black Uṣhṇīsha" is unquestionably made up by a nonhuman of Tibet.

Tantras of the Group of Fierce Males and Females of the One-Gone-Thus Lineage

These are the two, the *Secret Imagination Conquering the Three Worlds* (*krodhavijayayakalpaguhyatantra*, P291) and the *Retention of the Goddess Chundi* (*cundidevīdhāraṇī*, P188).

Tantras of the Group of Messengers of the One-Gone-Thus Lineage

These are the *Retention of Parṇashavari* (*parṇaśavarināmadhāraṇī*, P186), the *Imagination of Parṇashavari*, and so forth.

Tantras of the Group of Bodhisattvas of the One-Gone-Thus Lineage

These are, for instance, the *One Hundred and Eight Names of Avalokiteshvara* (*avalokiteśvarāṣṭottaraśatakanāmadhāraṇīmantraśita*, P320) set out separately.

Tantras of the Groups of Serpents and Harm-Bestowers of the One-Gone-Thus Lineage

These are, for instance, the *Tantra Giving Rise to Wealth* and the *Tantra Issuing Forth Ambrosia* (*amṛtabhavanāmadhāraṇī*, P354), which teaches a water-offering.

Divisions of the Lotus Lineage

The lotus lineage has five divisions [comprised of the tantras of]:

1. the principal of the lotus lineage,
2. the lord of the lotus lineage,
3. the mother of the lotus lineage,
4. the fierce males and females of the lotus lineage,
5. the group of messengers.

Tantras of the Principal of the Lotus Lineage

The principal of the lotus lineage is Amitāyus. With respect to his tantras, there are the two that arose in lands of gods and that are corrupt[11] and the *Deathless Drum Sound Tantra* that is pure.

Tantras of the Lord of the Lotus Lineage

The lord of the lotus lineage is Avalokiteshvara. The three [texts] of the *Tantra of the Lotus-Netted Avalokiteshvara* (*avalokiteśvarapadmajalamūlatantrarāja*) in twelve thousand stanzas were not translated into Tibetan, but the shorter one (P364) in one thousand stanzas teaches two maṇḍalas of 1,227 deities among whom Avalokiteshvara acts as the main [figure]. There are also the beginning of a translation of the *Imagination of the Eleven-Faced [Avalokiteshvara]* and longer and shorter *Lion's Roar Retentions* (*avalokiteśvarasiṃhanādanāmadhāraṇī*, P386, and *siṃhanādatantra*, P385).

Tantras of the Mother of the Lotus Lineage

The mother of the lotus lineage is Ārya-tārā; with respect to her tantras, the third chapter of the thirty-five chapters [of the *Tantra of the Various Arisings from Tara, the Mother of All Ones-Gone-Thus* (*sarvatathāgatamātanitā-ārevisvakarmabhavatantra,* P390)], which teaches one hundred and eight maṇḍalas and the currently [popular] *Twenty-One Homages* (*ekaviṃśatistotra,* P77) are the same.

Objection: Those are not the same because the third chapter of that [text] must be taken as an Action Tantra, whereas Chandragomin[12] commented on the *Twenty-One Homages* as Highest Yoga.

Answer: That reason is indefinite because the *Expression of the Names of Mañjushrī* (*mañjuśrījñānasattvasya paramārthanāmasaṃgīti,* P2), for instance, (1) in Kalkī Puṇḍarīka's (*rigs ldan pad ma dkar po*) great commentary [*Stainless Light* (*Vimālaprabhā,* P2064)] is commented on in accordance with Kālachakra; (2) in Āryadeva's *Lamp Compendium of Practice* (*caryāmelakapradīpa,* P2668) is commented on in accordance with *Guhyasamāja;* and (3) by the masters Vīlasavajra (*sgeg pa'i rdo rje*) and Mañjushrīkīrti[13] (P3357) is commented on in accordance with Yoga [Tantra].

Tantras of the Fierce Males and Females of the Lotus Lineage

The Fierce One of the lotus lineage is Hayagrīva; the extensive tantra of Hayagrīva was not translated into Tibetan; the abbreviated is this *Hayagrīva Tantra* ([?] *avalokiteśvarahayagrīvadhāraṇī,* P379, 531).

Tantras of the Group of Messengers of the Lotus Lineage

These are the *Mahālakṣhmi Sūtra* (*mahāśrīyasūtra,* P399) and so forth.

Divisions of the Vajra Lineage

The vajra lineage also has five [divisions like the lotus lineage].

Tantras of the Principal of the Vajra Lineage

The principal of the vajra lineage is the One-Gone-Thus Akṣhobhya. There is a *Vajra-akṣhobhya Tantra* (*sarvakarmāvaraṇaviśodhanīnāmadhāraṇī,* P401), which teaches the maṇḍala purifying bad migrations.

Tantras of the Lord of the Vajra Lineage

The lord is Vajrapāṇi. There are the three tantras of Vajrapāṇi—root, explanatory, and continuation. Also, there are the *Vajrapāṇi Taming of Elementals Tantra* (*bhūtaḍāmara*, P404) and the *Vajravidāraṇā Tantra* (*vajravidāraṇānāmadhāraṇī,* P406). With respect to the *Vajravidāraṇā* the translators made it into twenty-one stanzas and said it was spoken on the vajra seat [at Bodh Gaya]. The system of the paṇḍita Buddhaguhya [however] is that the vajra seat is the place [where Buddha] tamed the demons and became enlightened and is not a place where he turned the wheel of doctrine; hence, he does not assert that the *Vajravidāraṇā Tantra* was spoken there. Well then, where was it spoken? It was spoken in a cave in the Vajra Mountain to the southeast of Meru, an area of Knowledge Mantra Bearers. With respect to the manner in which it was spoken, King Ajātashatru had killed his father King Bimbisāra and was being called by the name "Perverse Heart." At that time, since the nonvirtues were being widely committed in the world, great famine arose, whereupon four great kings made a request [to Buddha]. The Supramundane Victor spoke to Vajrapāṇi, who emanated the body of Vidāraṇa and spoke. The Supramundane Victor, having said "Good," spoke [this tantra], which has one hundred and eight chapters together with this [section by Vajrapāṇi].

Tantras of the Mother of the Vajra Lineage

There is the *Tantra of Blazing Flames* (*vajrājitānala-pramohaṇīnāmadhāraṇī,* P408).

Tantras of the Fierce Ones of the Vajra Lineage

There is the *Amṛtakuṇḍali Tantra* (*kuṇḍalyamṛtahṛdayacaturthanāmadhāraṇī,* P755).

Tantras of the Groups of Messengers of the Vajra Lineage

There are the *Great Power Great Vehicle Sūtra* (*mahābalanāmamahāyānasūtra,* P416) and the *Vajratunda Tantra* (*vajratundanāmanāgasamaya,* P411). It should be known that the *Vajra Hook* ([?] *lohatuṇḍanāmadhāraṇī,* P413, 414) and the *Vajra Garuda Wing Tantra* are fakes.

General Division of the Three Lineages

[The Action Tantras of the three lineages in general] are the *General Secret Tantra, Susiddhi Tantra, Questions of Subāhu Tantra,* and *Concentration Continuation Tantra.* The first of these teaches the maṇḍala rites of Action Tantra in general, ranging from the rite for the place [where initiation will be conferred] through the bestowal of initiation and also sets forth the three thousand five hundred maṇḍalas related with the three lineages.

The *Susiddhi Tantra* teaches the approximation and achievement related with the fierce Susiddhi, the detail of his activities, and those topics in the presentation of initiation in the *General Secret Tantra* that needed supplement. The *Questions of Subāhu Tantra* teaches the measure of [having completed] approximation of the deities indicated in the *General Secret Tantra* and the *Susiddhi Tantra* as well as how to achieve the limitless activities.

The Action Tantra the *Concentration Continuation* teaches the mode of progressing on the paths in Action Tantra in general—the concentrations of the four branches of repetition, abiding in fire, abiding in sound, and bestowing liberation at the end of sound as well as what to do before and after those, rites for [achieving] feats, rites of burnt offering, how to practice, in what sort of place, and so forth. . . .

Presentation of Performance Tantra

There are Performance Tantras of the One-Gone-Thus lineage, Performance Tantras of the lotus lineage, and Performance Tantras of the vajra lineage. The first [a Performance Tantra of the One-Gone-Thus lineage] is, for instance, the *Vairochanābhisambodhi*. The second [a Performance Tantra of the lotus lineage] is, for instance, the *Extensive Tantra of Hayagrīva,* but it was not translated into Tibetan. The third [Performance Tantras of the vajra lineage] are the *Vajrapāṇi Initiation Tantra,* and so forth.

Appendix 2:

Structure of the Presentation

An illustration in tabular form of the structure of Tsongkhapa's *Great Exposition of Secret Mantra,* continued from *Tantra in Tibet.*

- Uncommon Stages of the Path in the Vajra Vehicle
  - Stages of the Path in Action and Performance Tantras (p. 41)
    - Analysis of Whether Action and Performance Have Self-Generation and Entry of a Wisdom-Being (p. 43)
      - Masters' [Varying] Assertions (p. 45)
      - Correct Position (p. 50)
    - Individual Explanations of the Stages of the Path (p. 61)
      - General Structure (p. 61)
      - Actual Stages (p. 65)
        - In Action Tantra (p. 67)
          - How to Become a Receptacle Suitable for Cultivating the Path (p. 67)
          - How to Maintain Purity of Pledges and Vows (p. 68)
          - How to Perform Prior Approximation (p.77)
            - Reasons for Prior Approximation (p. 77)
            - Its Stages (p. 79)
              - Concentration with Repetition (p. 79)
                - How to Perform the Preliminaries (p. 79)
                  - What to do Initially in the Place of Dwelling (p. 79)
                  - How to Bathe Outside and Enter the Place of Practice (p. 83)
                  - Having Enrobed and Sat on the Cushion, Blessing the Offerings (p. 90)
                  - Protecting Oneself and the Place (p. 94)
                - Actual Concentration of the Four-Branched Repetition (p. 99)
                  - Concentrations of the Branches of Repetition (p. 99)
                    - Generating Oneself as a Deity (p. 100)
                    - Offering and so forth to the Wisdom-Being Invited in Front (p. 111)
                      - Generation of the Residence (p. 111)
                      - Inviting the Resident Deity and Asking the Deity to Sit (p. 113)
                      - Displaying Seals (p. 116)
                      - Offering and Praising (p. 118)
                      - Discolosure and So Forth (p. 127)
                - How to Conclude (p. 144)
          - How Feats Are Achieved (p. 167)

→(the present translation ends at this point)

- Performance Tantra (p. 177)
  - How to Become a Receptable Suitable for Cultivating the Path (p. 177)
  - How to Maintain Purity of Pledges and Vows (p. 177)
  - How to Perform Prior Approximation (p. 179)
    - Divisions of the Yoga (p. 179)
    - Meaning of the Divisions (p. 183)
      - Yoga with Signs (p. 183)
        - External Four-Branched Repetition (p. 183)
        - Internal Four-Branched Repetition (p. 188)
      - Yoga without Signs (p. 191)
  - How to Achieve Feats (p. 196)

- Concentration Not Relying on Repetition (p. 149)
  - Concentrations of Abiding in Fire and in Sound (p. 149)
  - Concentration on the End of Sound (p. 154)
    - Stages of Leaving the State of Sound (p. 154)
    - The Actual Concentration (p. 160)

- How to Perform Repetition in Dependence on the Branches (p. 133)
  - How to Assemble the Rosary and Count (p. 133)
  - How to Perform Repetition Observing What Objects (p. 135)
    - Repetition Observing the Form of Letters (p. 135)
      - Repetition Observing the Form of Letters at the Heart of a Deity in Front (p. 135)
      - Repetition Observing the Form of Letters at Your Own Heart (p. 138)
    - Repetitions Observing the Sound of Letters (p. 139)
  - How to Reinstate the Repetition if Unfavorable Conditions Arise (p. 142)

- Cultivating the Four Immeasurables (p. 129)

List of Abbreviations

"Dharma" refers to the *sde dge* edition of the Tibetan canon published by Dharma Press: the *Nying-ma Edition of the sDe-dge bKa'-'gyur and bsTan-'gyur* (Oakland, CA: Dharma, 1980).

"Karmapa *sde dge*" refers to the *sde dge mtshal par bka' 'gyur: A Facsimile Edition of the 18th Century Redaction of Si tu chos kyi 'byung gnas Prepared under the Direction of H H. the 16th rgyal dbang karma pa* (Delhi: Delhi Karmapae Chodhey Gyalwae Sungrab Partun Khang, 1977).

"P," standing for "Peking edition," refers to the *Tibetan Tripiṭaka* (Tokyo-Kyoto: Tibetan Tripiṭaka Research Foundation, 1955–1962).

"Toh" refers to the *Complete Catalogue of the Tibetan Buddhist Canons,* edited by Prof. Hukuji Ui (Sendai, Japan: Tohoku University, 1934), and *A Catalogue of the Tohuku University Collection of Tibetan Works on Buddhism,* edited by Prof. Yensho Kanakura (Sendai, Japan: Tohoku University, 1953).

"Tokyo *sde dge*" refers to the *sDe dge Tibetan Tripiṭaka—bsTan ḫgyur preserved at the Faculty of Letters, University of Tokyo,* edited by Z. Yamaguchi, et al. (Tokyo: Tokyo University Press, 1977–1984).

Notes

Preface

1. *legs grub kyi rgyud, susiddhitantra;* P431, vol. 9.
2. *bsam gtan phyi ma rim par phye pa, dhyānottarapaṭalakrama;* P430, vol. 9.
3. In Tibetan, his name is usually *byang chub mchog,* but Duldzin Dragpa Gyaltshan's *Presentation of the General Rites of Action and Performance Tantra* gives it as *ye shes mchog.* Varabodhi's commentary is *legs par grub par byed pa'i sgrub pa'i thabs bsdus pa, susiddhikarasādhanasaṃgraha;* P3890, vol. 79.
4. *sangs rgyas gsang ba.* His commentary is *bsam gtan phyi ma rim par phye ba rgya cher bshad pa, dhyānottarapaṭalaṭīkā;* P3495, vol. 78.
5. *sgrub thabs, sādhana.*
6. *Condensed Meaning of the "Vairochanābhisambodhi Tantra," vairocanābhisambodhitantrapiṇḍārtha, rnam par snang mdzad mngon par rdzogs par byang chub pa'i rgyud kyi bsdus pa'i don;* P3486, vol. 77; Buddhaguhya also wrote a longer *Explanation* of the same tantra, *vairocanābhisambodhivikurvitādhiṣṭhānamahātantrabhāṣya, rnam par snang mdzad mngon par byang chub pa rnam par sprul pa'i byin gyis brlabs kyi rgyud chen po'i bshad pa;* P3487, vol.77, p. 110, *rgyud 'grel, ngu* 76b.8–337a.3; *sde dge* 2663, *rgyud, nyu* 65a.3–260b.7, likely the same as *vairocanābhisambodhivikurvitādhiṣṭhānamahātantravṛtti, rnam par snang mdzad mngon par byang chub pa rnam par sprul pa'i byin gyis brlabs kyi rgyud chen po'i 'grel pa;* P3490, vol.77, p. 229, *rgyud 'grel, cu* 1–230a.5; *sde dge* 2663, *rgyud, nyu* 261a.1–*tu* 116a.7.
7. I have written at length on the process of Action Tantra meditation in *Tantric Techniques* especially in chapters 4–7 in the light of Carl Jung's psychoanalytic teachings as laid out in chapter 3, titled "Jung's Warnings Against Inflation" (Ithaca, NY: Snow Lion Publications, 2008).

II: The Great Exposition of Secret Mantra 2 and 3

1. For the most part Tsongkhapa is reworking Butön Rinchendrub's (*bu ston*) encyclopedic presentation of this issue in his *Extensive General Presentation of the Tantra Sets, Collected Works*, Part 15 ba (New Delhi, International Academy of Indian Culture, 1969), 86.6–88.7. Butön here tends to side with those who say that Action Tantra does not involve generation of oneself as a deity, but earlier when presenting the path of Action Tantra (54.5–61.7), he follows Buddhaguhya's assertion of the opposite, repeatedly and explicitly describing self-generation in Action Tantra. Tsongkhapa step by step takes apart Butön's later argument against self-generation in Action Tantra. Then in the later sections Tsongkhapa uses Buddhaguhya's commentary on the *Concentration Continuation Tantra,* as Butön did, to present the path of self-generation in Action Tantra, though in much greater detail than his predecessor. Thus Tsongkhapa's presentation is both in dependence on and in contradistinction to that of Butön, whose seeming contradiction is explained only in the encyclopedic nature of Butön's work.
2. Butön's *Extensive General Presentation of the Tantra Sets* mentions this text (86.7).
3. P3495, vol. 78, 69.5.7–70.1.2.
4. Stanza 5ab:
   གསང་སྔགས་བསམ་གཏན་ཞེས་བྱ་བ།། མཆོག་ཏུ་གསང་བ་ཡང་དག་གསུངས།།
   P430, vol. 9, 53.2.8.
5. P3495, vol. 78, 70.5.1–4.
6. *vajravidāraṇā-nāma-dhāraṇi,* Toh. 750.
7. P431, vol. 9, 64.1.2. This is cited in Varabodhi's *Clear Realization of Susiddhi* (P3890, vol. 79, 272.1.7). For Tsongkhapa's commentary see p. 141. Instead of *ma gtang ba* the Peking edition reads *ma gtogs pa* as does Yeshay Gyaltshan, 504.2.
8. P3495, vol. 78, 70.5.8–71.1.3.
9. An ichneumon is a small squirrel-like animal called a "jewel-bag" because it spits forth jewels; it is held in the hand of this deity as a hand-symbol. At the end of the stanza there is a gap in the quoted text. The latter part of the quote is found in Butön's *Extensive General Presentation of the Tantra Sets*, 86.7.
10. Tsongkhapa's own opinion, as given on pp. 50–51, is that the *Vairochanābhisambodhi* is clearly a Performance Tantra.
11. P3890, vol. 79, 270, 1.4–6. This is cited in Butön's *Extensive General*

Presentation of the Tantra Sets (87.4), which confirms *bstan to* rather than *bstan te*. The Sanskrit of *"Clear Realization of Susiddhi"* has been constructed in order to accord with the Tibetan, using *abhisamaya* (*mngon rtogs*) rather than *sādhana-saṃgraha*. Butön refers to the *Daśatattva* as the *Daśatattvāvatāra*, 87.5.

12. P2758.
13. See *Tantra in Tibet*, pp. 144–47.
14. See Butön's encyclopedic presentation of this issue in his *Extensive General Presentation of the Tantra Sets, Collected Works,* Part 15 ba (New Delhi, International Academy of Indian Culture, 1969), 86.6–88.7. The reference here is to where Butön sides with those who say that Action Tantra does not involve generation of oneself as a deity; Tsongkhapa step by step takes apart Butön's argument against self-generation in Action Tantra. In later sections Tsongkhapa uses Buddhaguhya's commentary on the *Concentration Continuation Tantra,* as Butön does, to present the path of self-generation in Action Tantra, though in much greater detail than his predecessor. Thus Tsongkhapa's presentation is both in contradistinction to and in dependence on that of Butön.
15. *dge slong ma dpal mo*.
16. The text (88.5) reads *sambhuṭa*.
17. P430, vol. 9, 55.3.4. Buddhaguhya's commentary is P3495, vol. 78, 73.2.7.
18. Khaydrub Geleg Palsang (Lessing and Wayman, *Mkhas-Grub Rje's Fundamentals of the Buddhist Tantras,* 136.18). It is also said that it is titled *Dhyānottara* because of presenting the latter concentrations—those following the initial practices explained earlier in the *Vajroṣhṇīṣha*. See Buddhaguhya (P3495, vol. 78, 73.2.5).
19. P3495, vol. 78, 73.3.3; the citation from the tantra is chapter 5; P126, vol. 5, 252.1.5. Tsongkhapa also makes a longer citation of this in the Performance Tantra section (68b.5), using a different translation that also contains six omitted lines; see p. 186 for that as well as a note discussing the implications that in Sanskrit a term for both "letter" and "immutable" is *akṣara* and how this affects the translation of *yi ge* as "immutable" in what here is the first line.
20. P3504, vol. 78, 140.3.6. Butön's *Extensive General Presentation of the Tantra Sets* quotes this (56.2) and mentions it again (87.3).
21. P3333, vol. 71, 135.5.1.
22. Both Paṇchen Sönam Dragpa (*General Presentation of the Tantra Sets,* 22b.2–4) and Khaydrub Geleg Palsang (Lessing and Wayman, *Mkhas-*

Grub Rje's Fundamentals of the Buddhist Tantras, 166.18–28) cite texts mentioned in the first hypothesis as reasons why there is self-generation in Action Tantra, but this does not contradict Tsongkhapa's point that there are explanatory *illustrations* from Highest Yoga in some of the texts found in these collections.

23. Correcting *skyod* to *spyod.*
24. To have lineage means to have the lot of being a suitable vessel for the teaching.
25. Stanza 34:
    དུས་གསུམ་དུ་ནི་ཕྲ་མོ་འདི།། གསང་སྔགས་སྒྲུབ་ལ་བརྟེན་པ་ཡིས།། ཚངས་པ་རྟག་ཏུ་རིག་བྱ་བ།། ཡན་ལག་བཅུ་ཡི་ཆོ་གའི་ལས།།

    P430, vol. 9, 53.5.2.
26. *Commentary on the "Concentration Continuation Tantra,"* P3495, vol. 78, 80.5.7–81.1.8.
27. Tsongkhapa literally says "the three, knowledge mantra and so forth" to stand for these three, thereby putting the middle term of the reference at the head.
28. Correcting *'jug* to *mjug.*
29. *rtsa ltung gi rnam bshad / gsang sngags kyi tshul khrims kyi rnam bshad dngos grub kyi snye ma zhes bya ba,* P6188, vol. 160. For a complete translation, see Gareth Sparham, *Tantric Ethics: An Explanation of the Precepts for Buddhist Vajrayāna Practice* (Boston: Wisdom Publications, 2005).
30. This material is taken from Khaydrub Geleg Palsang (Lessing and Wayman, *Mkhas-Grub Rje's Fundamentals of the Buddhist Tantras,* 144.21ff, 148.8, and 140.7); the last sentence is also found in Ngagwang Paldan's *Presentation of the Grounds and Paths of Mantra* (*rgyud smad par khang* edition), 2b.2.
31. Khaydrub Geleg Palsang (Lessing and Wayman, *Mkhas-Grub Rje's Fundamentals of the Buddhist Tantras,* 154.7).
32. P431, vol. 9, 56.1.1–3.4. This is quoted in Ratnākarashānti's *Precious Lamp, Commentary on the Difficult Points of the "Kṛṣhṇayamāri Tantra,"* P2782, vol. 66, 259.2.8–5.7.
33. *Tīrthika,* non-Buddhist practitioners who are called Forders because of propounding a ford to liberation.
34. This is specifically a pastry cooked in sesame oil (*snum 'khur*) according to Pabongkha (*Miscellaneous Notes from Jo-nay Pandita's Explanation of the "Great Exposition of Secret Mantra,"* 650.3).
35. Pabongkha (*Miscellaneous Notes from Jo-nay Pandita's Explanation of the*

"Great Exposition of Secret Mantra," 650.3) says *cung peng ni skyur rtsis snyal ba phyis sman zhes grags pa de yin.*

36. This is most likely the meat, blood, fat, and so forth that demons eat.
37. The Delhi edition (103.2) reads *byi byad,* whereas the *Susiddhi Tantra* itself (P431, vol. 9, 56.2.5) and Butön read *bya byed,* which is unlikely. The translation is uncertain.
38. *lo ma,* as confirmed by the Delhi edition (103.3) and the *Susiddhi Tantra* (P431, vol. 9, 56.2.5).
39. Food that increases desire.
40. The *Susiddhi Tantra* (P431, vol. 9, 56.2.8) reads *'jol nyog,* which has the same meaning.
41. The term *sad* means *nyams sad pa,* test, experiment.
42. P431, vol. 9, 56.5.1.
43. The first fifteen days of the first month in the lunar year.
44. P431, vol. 9, 57.2.2–5.
45. Most likely the vows of individual emancipation and the ethics of abandoning the ten nonvirtues.
46. Probably self-entry.
47. P2782, vol. 66, 260.3.2–6.
48. "And so forth" includes having a special purpose or taking into account the customs of one's area.
49. Stanza 5:
    གསང་སྔགས་བསམ་གཏན་ཞེས་བྱ་བ།། མཆོག་ཏུ་གསང་བ་ཡང་དག་གསུངས།། དྲང་སྲོང་དཀའ་ཐུབ་ཆེན་པོ་ཡང་།། དེ་དག་མེད་ན་མི་འགྲུབ་བོ།།

    P430, vol. 9, 53.2.8; Buddhaguhya's commentary is P3495, vol. 78, 69.1.1–70.1.7. "Sages" (*ṛṣi, drang srong*), according to Pabongkha (*Miscellaneous Notes from Jo-nay Pandita's Explanation of the "Great Exposition of Secret Mantra,"* 650.4), are those whose body, speech, and mind have been straightened or, according to Buddhaguhya (70.1.5), restrained.
50. The five clairvoyances are the clairvoyances of the divine eye, divine ear, memory of former lifetimes, knowing others' minds, and magical emanation.
51. "Secret mantra" here means a deity.
52. Correcting *'jug* to *mjug.*
53. This section follows Varabodhi's *Clear Realization of Susiddhi,* P3890, vol. 79, 268.1.1ff. With respect to the mantras that text reads *tathāgatodbhavāya, padmodbhavāya,* and *vajrodbhavāya*; it repeats *kāyavākcitta* after the second *sarva-tathāgata.* In general, the mantras have been left unedited, with only occasional variants cited in the notes. The

smaller section headings are added from Varabodhi's *Clear Realization of Susiddhi*.

54. Pabongkha (*Miscellaneous Notes from Jo-nay Pandita's Explanation of the "Great Exposition of Secret Mantra,"* 650.5) identifies *mnol ba med pa* as *sme ba brtsegs pa: Bhurkumkūta.*
55. The text reads *śuddha* and *dharmā,* which were changed to accord with Duldzin Dragpa Gyaltshan (*Presentation of the General Rites of Action and Performance Tantra,* 5b.6).
56. Duldzin Dragpa Gyaltshan's *Presentation of the General Rites of Action and Performance Tantra,* 2a.6.
57. Duldzin Dragpa Gyaltshan (*Presentation of the General Rites of Action and Performance Tantra,* 2a.6) inserts here the pledge seal and secret mantra of the lineage, which Tsongkhapa mentions on the next page as preceding picking up earth.
58. This section follows Varabodhi's *Clear Realization of Susiddhi,* P3890, vol. 79, 268.2.6ff.
59. Duldzin Dragpa Gyaltshan's *Presentation of the General Rites of Action and Performance Tantra,* reads *vasudhe;* Varabodhi's *Clear Realization of Susiddhi* reads *vaisudhe.*
60. Varabodhi's *Clear Realization of Susiddhi* reads *om hūṃ khakīli.*
61. Varabodhi's *Clear Realization of Susiddhi* reads *oṃ hana dhuna matha vidh[v]aṃsaya udsaraya phaṭ.*
62. Duldzin Dragpa Gyaltshan's *Presentation of the General Rites of Action and Performance Tantra,* 3a.3.
63. Duldzin Dragpa Gyaltshan (*Presentation of the General Rites of Action and Performance Tantra,* 3b.3) describes how to do an actual ablution: "Squat, stop talking, and put your two hands between your knees. Bend a little the middle and ring fingers of the right hand with the palm turned upwards, and hold this toward your mouth. Wipe the mouth many times with water [in which] anthers [have been soaked], and having touched the two ear-holes, two eyes, nose, mouth, hands, navel, and head two or three times, drink three gulps of the water, wiping the lips twice."
64. Duldzin Dragpa Gyaltshan's *Presentation of the General Rites of Action and Performance Tantra,* 3a.5.
65. Duldzin Dragpa Gyaltshan (*Presentation of the General Rites of Action and Performance Tantra,* 3b.2) refers to the group of deities.
66. Duldzin Dragpa Gyaltshan (*Presentation of the General Rites of Action and Performance Tantra,* 3b.3) specifies the mantra, for example, *oṃ sarva-tathāgata-uṣṇīśa-sitātāpatre hūṃ phaṭ svāhā.*

67. Duldzin Dragpa Gyaltshan (*Presentation of the General Rites of Action and Performance Tantra,* 3b.3) describes how to do an actual ablution: "Squat, stop talking, and put your two hands between your knees. Bend a little the middle and ring fingers of the right hand with the palm turned upwards, and hold this toward your mouth. Wipe the mouth many times with water [in which] anthers [have been soaked], and having touched the two ear-holes, two eyes, nose, mouth, hands, navel, and head two or three times, drink three gulps of the water, wiping the lips twice."
68. Duldzin Dragpa Gyaltshan's *Presentation of the General Rites of Action and Performance Tantra,* makes this clear (3b.5).
69. This section is from Varabodhi's *Clear Realization of Susiddhi,* P3890, vol. 79, 269.3.2.
70. Duldzin Dragpa Gyaltshan's *Presentation of the General Rites of Action and Performance Tantra,* 4a.1.
71. *ngan sel;* literally, "clearing away the bad," *poa cynosuroides.*
72. The lucky posture is like that of Maitreya, sitting on a "chair." The lotus posture is with the soles of the feet touching; the vajra cross-legged is the one usually called the lotus posture in the "West."
73. This is a conjecture based on Duldzin Dragpa Gyaltshan's *Presentation of the General Rites of Action and Performance Tantra,* (4a.5) not mentioning "image"; the identifications of the reference and the mantra are his (4a.5).
74. Duldzin Dragpa Gyaltshan's *Presentation of the General Rites of Action and Performance Tantra,* 4a.3.
75. In both the Delhi edition and Varabodhi's *Clear Realization of Susiddhi* the mantra reads this way; the Dharamsala edition was obviously miscopied.
76. This sentence has been moved in translation for the sake of clarity since it refers to the circlet; it appears in the text after the second *Susiddhi Tantra* quotation.
77. The long *ā* also appears in Duldzin Dragpa Gyaltshan's *Presentation of the General Rites of Action and Performance Tantra.* These are the essence mantras of the three lineages, the appropriate one is to be repeated.
78. This sentence is omitted in Duldzin Dragpa Gyaltshan's *Presentation of the General Rites of Action and Performance Tantra.*
79. According to Lati Rinpoche, obstructors range from the external such as war and plague, to the internal such as sleep and sickness, and the secret such as unserviceability of the mind in the direction of virtue.
80. Correcting *bab* to *bag pas.*

81. This section follows Varabodhi's *Clear Realization of Susiddhi,* P3890, vol. 79, 268.5.7–269.1.3.
82. This section follows Varabodhi's *Clear Realization of Susiddhi,* P3890, vol. 79, 269.1.8ff.
83. According to Lati Rinpoche, this means to cause them to dissolve into the Truth Body.
84. Duldzin Dragpa Gyaltshan refers to the upper demonic gods (*steng gi lha'i gdon rnams, Presentation of the General Rites of Action and Performance Tantra,* 5a.1).
85. The reading *de ni,* rather than the occasional misreading *de nas,* is confirmed by Duldzin Dragpa Gyaltshan (*Presentation of the General Rites of Action and Performance Tantra,* 5a.2) *zhes pa rigs gsum gyi rig pa'i rgyal po'i sngags brjod pas,* identifying the above as the secret mantra of the knowledge kings rather than referring to something else.
86. The fence is made of big vajras standing on end, with small ones filling in between.
87. Duldzin Dragpa Gyaltshan (*Presentation of the General Rites of Action and Performance Tantra,* 5a.5) mentions only the dagger seal (seal 15); he identifies the Kīlikīla mantra as that on p. 95, not the one on p. 86.
88. *Kara kara* has been added from the Delhi edition and Varabodhi's *Clear Realization of Susiddhi.*
89. Stanza 8:
    ལྷ་ཡི་སྐུ་ཡི་གནས་དེ་ལ།། དང་པོ་ཁོ་ནར་མཆོད་ནས་ནི།། རྣལ་འབྱོར་གནས་བཅས་ཤེས་རབ་ཅན།། བདེར་གཤེགས་མདུན་དུ་བསམས་ནས་ནི།།

    P430, vol. 9, 53.2.3. Buddhaguhya's commentary is P3495, vol. 78, 71.3.3–4.6. In his citation of the commentary Tsongkhapa is paraphrasing 71.3.3–5.
90. *la* reads *las* in Buddhaguhya's commentary, P3495, vol. 78, 71.3.4.
91. Nevertheless, Tsongkhapa's explanation of the process of imagining oneself as a deity also draws heavily from Buddhaguhya's depiction.
92. This and the next paragraph paraphrase Buddhaguhya's commentary, P3495, vol. 79, 269.4.7–5.3.
93. Stanza 9:
    ཕྱི་ནས་ཡན་ལག་རྣམ་གྲོལ་བ།། མི་འབྱེད་འབྱེད་པ་རྣམ་པར་སྦྱངས།། ཐུ་བ་མི་གཡོ་གསལ་བ་སྟེ།། བློ་ཡི་དབྱིད་པ་མདུན་ན་གནས།།

    P430, vol. 9, 53.3.2.
94. This bracketed paragraph is drawn from Buddhaguhya's commentary, P3495, vol. 78, 71.4.6–72.2.5. Tsongkhapa is now primarily following Buddhaguhya's commentary, the section on the six deities being

71.4.6–72.4.3.

95. P3890, vol. 79, 269.5.3–8.
96. One rises not in the sense of getting up from the meditation but of ceasing to use the suchness of self as the *main* object of meditation. At this point Tsongkhapa does not mention imagining the sounds of the mantra as reverberating above a moon disc; neither do Buddhaguhya (P3495, vol. 78, 72.3.7), Duldzin Dragpa Gyaltshan (*Presentation of the General Rites of Action and Performance Tantra,* 5b.3), nor Khaydrub (Lessing and Wayman, *Mkhas-Grub Rje's Fundamentals of the Buddhist Tantras,* 160.3); however, later when explaining how to rest (p. 137) Tsongkhapa, in going through the reverse process, puts the dissolution of the moon disc after the sound deity, suggesting that a moon disc appears prior to or at least simultaneous with the mantra sounds. In cases where the text is not clear on procedure, lamas often advise practitioners to do whatever is more appealing. In the introduction the Dalai Lama describes manifestation of a moon disc at this point, but on another occasion he explained the sound deity as solely the reverberation of the mantra sounds in the sphere of emptiness.
97. For the example see Yeshay Gyaltshan's *Illumination of the Meaning of Action Tantra,* 487.3.
98. P3890, vol. 79, 270.1.1.
99. P3890, vol. 79, 270.1.1–4.
100. Khaydrub Geleg Palsang (Lessing and Wayman, *Mkhas-Grub Rje's Fundamentals of the Buddhist Tantras,* 160.22).
101. P3890, vol. 79, 270.1.7.
102. P3495, vol. 78, 71.1.1 (the first and second sides on this page have been transposed) and 72.4.3. Based on Bo-dong's *General Presentation of Action Tantra, Collected Works,* vol. 24 (New Delhi, Tibet House, 1971), 320.5, it can be conjectured that the sign deity is so called because of being like the arising of a sign upon being impressed with a seal.
103. P3495, vol. 78, 72.2.5ff.
104. Stanza 10ab:
    བདག་ཉིད་འདི་འདྲར་བྱས་ནས་ནི།། སྔགས་ཀྱི་རྣམ་པར་ཤེས་པས་བསྒོམ།།
    P430, vol. 9, 53.3.3.
105. Buddhaguhya's *Commentary on the "Vidāraṇa Tantra,"* P3504, vol. 78, 140.3.6.
106. The text has "letter" before "sound," which is usually taken as merely for the sake of euphony; however, Paṇchen Sönam Dragpa takes it literally (*General Presentation of the Tantra Sets,* 23b.1).

107. See the Supplement in the third volume, *Yoga Tantra,* of this series for a separate chapter on the Five Manifest Enlightenments drawn from Khaydrub's *Extensive Explanation of the Format of the General Tantra Sets.*
108. P3495, vol. 78, 72.4.3. The Delhi edition correctly reads *re shig spyi'i gsang sngags;* the Dharamsala edition omits *spyi'i.*
109. This section follows Buddhaguhya, P3495, vol. 78, 72.4.8ff.
110. Stanza 10bcd:
    སྔགས་ཀྱི་རྣམ་པར་ཤེས་པས་བསྒོམས།། བསྡམས་ནས་ཉིད་དེ་འཛིན་ལ་གནས།། སྲོག་དང་རྩོལ་བ་རབ་ཏུ་བསྡམས།།
    P430, vol. 9, 53.3.3. Buddhaguhya's commentary is P3495, vol. 78, 72.2.8.
111. This most likely means to meditate *at least* through to the form deity since normally one would proceed through to the sign deity.
112. About this, Paṇchen Sönam Dragpa (*General Presentation of the Tantra Sets,* 23b.6–24a.5) says:

    > The *prāṇāyāma* explained here [in Action Tantra] and in Highest Yoga are similar in name but not in meaning, time, purpose, or mode. They differ in meaning, for in the *Guhyasamāja* of Highest Yoga *prāṇa* is explained as wind and *āyāma* as lengthening, whereby it refers to a life-lengthening wind. In the *Kālachakra* [also Highest Yoga] *prāṇa* is explained as wind and *āyāma* as stopping the movement of winds in the right and left channels as well as causing them to enter the central channel. Here [in Action Tantra] *prāṇa* is explained as wind, *āyāma* as conceptuality, and binding as stopping the passing outwards of wind and conceptuality and binding them inside.
    >
    > [Highest Yoga and Action Tantra] differ with respect to the time [of practicing *prāṇāyāma*] because in Highest Yoga it is only during the stage of completion, whereas here it is only during [the yoga] with signs. The purpose differs because in Highest Yoga it is for the sake of gathering the winds in the central channel, whereas here it is for the sake of generating clear appearance of a deity through the force of eliminating the movement of conceptuality to objects by stopping the movement of wind to the outside. The mode [of practice] differs because in Highest Yoga the mind is held on an object of observation such as the upper or lower points of the central channel, whereas here the mind is held on the clear appearance of a deity without letting

> conceptuality operate on objects through the force of stopping the movement of wind outside and binding it inside.

It needs to be analyzed whether in Action Tantra "binding as stopping the passing outwards of wind and conceptuality and binding them inside" would be limited only to yoga with signs since from time to time in the practice of yoga without signs this process is required. See, for instance, Tsongkhapa's citation, in the section on yoga without signs in Performance Tantra, of Buddhaguhya's explanation "of the yoga of turning your mind inside by way of the reasoning [that is, technique] of withdrawing vitality [wind or currents of energy] (*srog slar sdud pa*)" and Tsongkhapa's explanation of this as "setting the mind on the meaning [of emptiness] explained earlier (pp. 192–93) through withdrawing its running to the outside by means of the reasoning [that is, technique] of withdrawal of vitality [wind]." That Tsongkhapa just above says "here it is said that it should be done simultaneously with holding the mind on the divine body" likely does not indicate that in Action Tantra wind yoga is limited to yoga with signs but is in reference to a particular situation when wind yoga is employed.

113. This section follows Varabodhi's *Clear Realization of Susiddhi,* P3890, vol. 79, 270.1.7ff.
114. Duldzin Dragpa Gyaltshan's *Presentation of the General Rites of Action and Performance Tantra* has *sarvathā kham udgate.*
115. P3890, vol. 79, 272.2.7.
116. This section for the most part follows Varabodhi's *Clear Realization of Susiddhi,* P3890, vol. 79, 270.2.8ff.
117. Duldzin Dragpa Gyaltshan (*Presentation of the General Rites of Action and Performance Tantra,* 8b.1) reads *ehyehi* throughout.
118. P431, vol. 9, 61.5.5. The next sentence refers to the same, 61.4.2.
119. Stanza 33:
    གསང་སྔགས་ལ་སོགས་དང་ལྡན་པའི།། རིག་སྔགས་ཁྲོ་བོ་མང་པོ་ཀུན།། རྒྱལ་བའི་སྐུ་ལ་མངོན་ཕྱོགས་
    པར།། བསམ་གཏན་ངོམས་ཕྱིར་རྟག་ཏུ་གནས།།

    P430, vol. 9, 53.5.2.
120. P3495, vol. 78, 80.5.4.
121. The two stanzas are found in Duldzin Dragpa Gyaltshan's *Presentation of the General Rites of Action and Performance Tantra,* 9b.5.
122. This section follows Varabodhi's *Clear Realization of Susiddhi,* P3890, vol. 79, 270.4.8–271.1.1.
123. This section follows Varabodhi's *Clear Realization of Susiddhi,* P3890, vol. 79, 271.1.2–4.4.

124. The recitation as well as the offering of the footbath do not appear in Varabodhi's *Clear Realization of Susiddhi* but are in the *Susiddhi Tantra* itself (P431, vol. 9, 62.1.3).
125. According to Duldzin Dragpa Gyaltshan (*Presentation of the General Rites of Action and Performance Tantra,* 10a.6), for Sitatāpatra the mantra to be put at the head of each offering mantra is *oṃ sarva-tathāgata uṣṇīśa-sitātapatre saparivāra.* For the footbath Duldzin Dragpa Gyaltshan's *Presentation of the General Rites of Action and Performance Tantra* reads *oṃ pravara-satkāraṃ padyaṃ pratīccha svāhā.*
126. Duldzin Dragpa Gyaltshan's *Presentation of the General Rites of Action and Performance Tantra,* 10b.2.
127. Duldzin Dragpa Gyaltshan (*Presentation of the General Rites of Action and Performance Tantra,* 10b.3) describes how to do these.
128. Duldzin Dragpa Gyaltshan (*Presentation of the General Rites of Action and Performance Tantra,* 11a.6) has *vidhyādhara* and continues with an offering of pleasant sounds.
129. Varabodhi's *Clear Realization of Susiddhi* (P3890, vol. 79, 271.4.4) mentions praising and gives the mantra found at the end of this section but not the actual offering verses, which are found in the *Susiddhi Tantra* (P431, vol. 9, 62.5.7).
130. Correcting *gzhi* to *zhing* in accordance with the *Susiddhi Tantra* (P431, vol. 9, 62.5.7) and Yeshay Gyaltshan (469.1).
131. The titles of the sub-sections are taken from Varabodhi's *Clear Realization of Susiddhi* (P3890, vol. 79, 271.4.5) and Khaydrub Geleg Palsang (Lessing and Wayman, *Mkhas-Grub Rje's Fundamentals of the Buddhist Tantras,* 184.26). Tsongkhapa has taken the text from the *Susiddhi Tantra* (P431, vol. 9, 63.1.3–3.2).
132. Not being omniscient, one does not know all one's ill-deeds, but the Buddhas do, and thus one discloses ill-deeds in accordance with what they know.
133. This and the next stanza are not in the Peking *Susiddhi Tantra.*
134. In this section the introductory prose is from Varabodhi's *Clear Realization of Susiddhi* (P3890, vol. 79, 271.4.7–8), and the stanzas are from the *Susiddhi Tantra* (P431, vol. 9, 63.2.2–7).
135. Reading *bzlas brjod kyi yan lag bzhi'i* ***nang nas gzhi'i*** *yan lag yin te* in accordance with TBRC W20510-4934-3, p. 90. In the first line of the stanza from the *Concentration Continuation Tantra* cited above, "Flow to the bases, mind, and sound," (*sgra dang sems dang gzhi la gzhol*) only three terms are given for the four branches, "basis," which indicates both

generation of oneself as a deity and generation of the deity in front and hence two branches (and thus has been translated by the plural "bases" in the stanza), "mind," which indicates a flat moon disc in the heart of the deity in front, and "sound," which indicates the letters of the mantra standing around the edge of the moon facing inward. Therefore, the term "basis" (or "bases") is a term that indicates two of the four branches of repetition.

136. This section, except for the first two sentences, is a combination of the *Susiddhi Tantra* (P431, vol. 9, 63.3.3–7) and Varabodhi's *Clear Realization of Susiddhi* (P3890, vol. 79, 271.5.2–272.1.1).

137. P431, vol. 9, 63.3.7.

138. According to Duldzin Dragpa Gyaltshan (*Presentation of the General Rites of Action and Performance Tantra,* 13b.4) one does this by reciting *oṃ gurusarva-tathāgata-kāya-vāk-citta-praṇamena sarva-tathāgata-vajra-pāda-vandanaṃ karomi.*

139. The Delhi edition reads *jatanajeya* whereas the *Susiddhi Tantra* reads *jatanajaya.*

140. These sections are parts of the intensive meditation and are not prescriptions for repetitition of mantra when tired, as is obvious both from their content and from the fact that they contain subsections prescribing what to do when tired.

141. Stanza 11:
སྒྲ་དང་སེམས་དང་གཞི་ལ་གཞོལ།། གསང་སྔགས་མི་འགྱུར་གཞི་ལ་གནས།། ཡན་ལག་མ་ཉམས་གསང་སྔགས་བཟླས།། ངལ་ན་བདག་ལ་ངལ་སོས་ཤིག །

P430, vol. 9, 53.3.4; the commentary is P3495, vol. 78, 73.4.1.

142. The bracketed material in this paragraph is drawn from Khaydrub Geleg Palsang (Lessing and Wayman, *Mkhas-Grub Rje's Fundamentals of the Buddhist Tantras,* 188.2).

143. This section follows Buddhaguhya's commentary, P3495, vol. 78, 74.1.4–8.

144. Stanza 12:
མི་འགྱུར་བ་དང་ཡི་གེར་ལྡན།། གཞི་ལས་གཞིར་གྱུར་དེ་བཞིན་ཏེ། རང་སྔགས་ཕྱིར་ནི་གང་བརྟགས་པ།། ཡིད་ཀྱི་དག་པ་བསམ་པར་བྱ།།

P430, vol. 9, 53.3.4; the explanation is drawn from Buddhaguhya's commentary, P3495, vol. 78, 74.2.6ff.

145. In Sanskrit the term for both "letter" and "immutable" is *akṣara* "immutable," since letters immutably indicate specific sounds; thus the stanza plays on the double meaning of the term.

146. Stanzas 13–14:

སླར་སྡུད་པ་ཡིས་བཀུག་ནས་ནི།། སྲོག་དང་རྩོལ་བ་བསྡམས་པའི་ཡིད།། གསང་སྔགས་རིག་པ་སྔགས་ལ་སྦྱར།། ཡིད་ཀྱི་བཟླས་བརྗོད་བརྩམས་པར་བྱ།། འདི་ཉིད་ཀྱི་ནི་ཚིག་ཡིས།། ཡང་ན་ཤུབ་ཕུར་བྱ་ཡང་རུང་།། སྔགས་རིག་དངོས་གྲུབ་འདོད་པ་ཡིས།། བཟླས་བརྗོད་གཞན་དུ་མི་བྱའོ།།

P430, vol. 9, 53.3.5. Buddhaguhya's commentary is P3495, vol. 78, 74.4.7–75.2.6; his commentary on the first line is:

> [The *Concentration Continuation*] says, "Having again bound the mind through withdrawal"; the drawing back again of the unequipoised mind moving, as it likes, back and forth to whatsoever [objects] by way of the eyes and so forth, in the manner of withdrawing the winds of the entire body and the placement of it inside one's own body is withdrawal (*slar sdud pa*). [Thus, the above phrase from the tantra] is the same as saying, "Having through that withdrawal bound and contracted [the mind] and directed it inside."
> (*slar bsdud pa yis bsdams nas ni zhes bya ba gsungs te/ mnyam par ma bzhag pa'i yid rang dgar 'byung ba mig la sogs pa'i sgo nas ji ltar srid par phan tshun du rab tu rgyu ba lus thams cad kyi rlung bsdu ba'i tshul gyis slar bkug la rang gi lus kyi nang du 'jug pa ni slar sdud pa ste/ slar bsdud pa des bsdams shing gcum la nang du phyogs par byas nas zhes bya ba'i tha tshig ste*)

147. The rite of observing the sounds of a mantra.
148. Buddhaguhya (P3495, vol. 78, 75.1.2) indicates the importance of mental repetition: "Since mental repetition is a cause of subtle meditative stabilization, one should always perform it; however, if one wants to perform whispered repetition, then one should do it with this application [observing the sounds of the mantra]."
149. P3495, vol. 78, 75.2.3.
150. P3890, vol. 79, 272.1.1.
151. The remainder of this section is drawn from the *Susiddhi Tantra* (P431, vol. 9, 63.4.4–64.1.5).
152. *stūpa,* often a monument to an event in the life of Shākyamuni Buddha.
153. P431, vol. 9, 63.4.6.
154. The first two paragraphs of this section are drawn from the *Susiddhi Tantra* (P431, vol. 9, 54.1.4–4.8); the remainder is drawn from Varabodhi's *Clear Realization of Susiddhi* (P3890, vol. 79, 272.4.7–5.4).
155. P3890, vol. 79, 272.5.2.
156. P3890, vol. 79, 272.5.4.
157. This section is mainly from Varabodhi's *Clear Realization of Susiddhi* (P3890, 272.2.4–4.2).

158. In the *Susiddhi Tantra* this is found at P431, vol. 9, 64.1.8–2.2.
159. P3890, vol. 79, 272.4.2. Duldzin Dragpa Gyaltshan (*Presentation of the General Rites of Action and Performance Tantra,* 16b.6) identifies this as a purification of the faults of yawning, sneezing, and so forth.
160. Stanza 17:
    གསང་སྔགས་མེ་གནས་དངོས་གྲུབ་སྟེར།། སྒྲ་གནས་རྣལ་འབྱོར་སྟེར་བར་དྲན།། སྒྲ་མཐར་ཐར་པ་སྟེར་བ་ཉིད།། འདི་དག་དེ་ཉིད་གསུམ་པོ་ཡིན།།

    P430, vol. 9, 53.3.8; Buddhaguhya's commentary is P3495, vol. 78, 75.5.1ff.
161. Stanzas 18–20:
    མི་འབྱེད་ལས་བྱུང་དངོས་པོ་རྣམས།། བློ་ཅན་གྱིས་ནི་བདག་ལ་བསྔམས།། སྔགས་པ་ཡན་ལག་འདས་ལ་གནས།། ཞེན་པ་མེད་པར་བསམ་གཏན་བྱ།། སྒྲ་ཞེས་བྱ་བ་འཕྲེང་བར་སྦྱར།། ཡི་གེ་བརྒྱུས་པ་མི་འགྱུར་རྣམས།། དྲིལ་བུའི་སྒྲ་བཞིན་མ་ཆད་པར།། ཡིད་ལ་ཞེན་པར་སེམས་པ་ན།། མེ་ཡི་ནང་གནས་ཞི་བ་སྟེ།། ཚིག་རྣམས་དག་པ་ཡན་ལག་ལྡན།། སྲོག་དང་རྩོལ་བ་བཀག་པའི་བདག ། གཉིད་སྤངས་ནས་ནི་རྣམ་པར་བསམ།།

    P430, vol. 9, 53.3.8; Buddhaguhya's commentary is P3495, vol. 78, 75.5.8ff., from which the bracketed material is taken.
162. Pabongkha's *Miscellaneous Notes from Jo nay Pandita's Explanation of the "Great Exposition of Secret Mantra,"* 63.5.
163. P3495, vol. 78, 77.1.7.
164. Ibid.
165. Stanzas 21–22:
    སྙིང་གར་གནས་པ་ཟླ་བ་ནི།། དྲི་མེད་ཟླ་བའི་དཀྱིལ་འཁོར་ཏེ།། དེ་ནང་རབ་ཏུ་ཞི་བ་ཡི།། མེ་ལྕེ་རབ་ཏུ་འོད་བཟང་བ།། མི་འགྱུར་གཞི་ནི་དེར་བཞག་ནས།། བདེ་བར་འདུག་ནས་སྒྲ་བསམ་མམ།། མི་འགྱུར་བ་ལ་ཡི་གེ་བཞག ། སྒྲ་ཉིད་འབའ་ཞིག་བསམ་པར་བྱ།།

    P430, vol. 9, 53.4.2; Buddhaguhya's commentary is P3495, vol. 78, 77.2.1–5.4.
166. Stanza 24:
    ལྟོས་བཅས་ཡན་ལག་གྱུར་པར་སྣང་།། སྒྲ་ཞེས་བྱ་དང་ཡིད་ཀྱིས་དང་།། ཚིག་རྣམས་དག་པ་རིག་སྔགས་དབང་།། ཡན་ལག་སྤང་བ་རྒྱལ་བས་མཆེན།།

    P430, vol. 9, 53.4.4; Buddhaguhya's commentary is P3495, vol. 78, 78.1.3–5.8.
167. P3495, vol. 78, 78.1.6.
168. P3495, vol. 78, 78.5.4.
169. Correcting *dmigs pa'i* to *dmigs pas.*
170. P3495, vol. 78, 78.5.2.
171. Correcting *bskyed* to *bskyod.*
172. For a discussion of these see Gedün Lodrö, *Calm Abiding and Special Insight,* trans. and ed. by Jeffrey Hopkins (Ithaca, NY: Snow Lion Publications, 1998), chaps. five and six; and Jeffrey Hopkins, *Meditation on*

Emptiness (London: Wisdom Publications, 1983; rev. ed., Boston: Wisdom Publications, 1996), Part One, chapters eight and nine.

173. Often the term "view" refers to emptiness that is called the "objective view," or "object viewed" (*yul gyi lta ba*), but here it refers to the consciousness realizing emptiness, the "subjective view," or "viewing subject" (*yul can gyi lta ba*).

174. The reference is to Stanza 9 of the *Concentration Continuation Tantra:*

> Afterwards, freed from the limbs
> [Your own suchness is] not discriminated [by others]—
> Thoroughly devoid of discrimination, and subtle.
> Unmoving and clear, mental analysis remains in its presence.

175. P3495, vol. 78, 72.1.5.

176. P3495, vol. 78, 72.1.7.

177. P3495, vol. 78, 72.2.1. With respect to the word "observation" in the first sentence the Peking edition reads *yan lag med pa* ***dmigs pa*** but the Cone edition reads *yan lag med pa* ***dmigs pa med pa,*** which is being followed here.

178. Khaydrub Geleg Palsang (Lessing and Wayman, *Mkhas-Grub Rje's Fundamentals of the Buddhist Tantras,* 200.13).

179. The feats described in this chapter are common feats, not the uncommon temporary feats of attaining the paths or the final feat of attaining Buddhahood (which are described in the Supplement at the end of this book). In the three lower tantras Buddhahood must be achieved through enhancement of the path by way of common feats; thus, these are explained here.

180. P431, vol. 9, 63.4.8.

181. Stanza 15:
རིག་སྔགས་དེ་ཉིད་མ་ལུས་དང་།། བདག་གི་དེ་ཉིད་ཆོག་དང་།། བཟླས་བརྗོད་དེ་ཉིད་མཆོག་ཤེས་ན།། མིས་ཉི་དངོས་གྲུབ་ཐོབ་པར་འགྱུར།།
P430, vol. 9, 53.3.6.

182. This section is drawn from the *Susiddhi Tantra,* P431, vol. 9, 60.3.3–61.2.5.

183. This section is drawn from the *Susiddhi Tantra,* P431, vol. 9, 69.3.3.

184. This section is drawn from the *Susiddhi Tantra,* P431, vol. 9, 59.5.5–60.3.5 and 69.2.6; however, the *Susiddhi Tantra* has the times for pacifying and increasing activities reversed.

185. cancri.

186. This section is drawn from the *Susiddhi Tantra,* P431, vol. 9, 55.4.4–45.1.1.

187. This section is drawn from the *Susiddhi Tantra,* P431, vol. 9, 59.5.7–60.3.8. The lotus cross-legged posture may be the lotus posture in which the soles of the two feet are together in front of oneself. The lucky posture is said to be that of Maitreya, sitting on a throne with the feet flat on the floor.
188. The first half of this sentence is in the *Susiddhi Tantra,* P431, vol. 9, 61.3.3.
189. This section is drawn from the *Susiddhi Tantra,* P431, vol. 9, 61.1.6–3.2.
190. This section is drawn from the *Susiddhi Tantra,* P431, vol. 9, 65.2.1–4.1.
191. P431, vol. 9, 64.3.4.
192. Paraphrasing *Concentration Continuation Tantra* stanzas 35–38; P430, vol. 9, 53.5.3–6.
193. Correcting *zin* to *zil* in accordance with the Delhi edition.
194. Paraphrasing *Concentration Continuation Tantra* stanza 39.
195. *rtsa ltung gi rnam bshad / gsang sngags kyi tshul khrims kyi rnam bshad dngos grub kyi snye ma zhes bya ba,* P6188, vol. 160. For a complete translation, see Gareth Sparham, *Tantric Ethics: An Explanation of the Precepts for Buddhist Vajrayāna Practice* (Boston: Wisdom Publications, 2005).
196. These are Buddhaguhya's *Condensed Meaning* (P3486, vol. 77) and *Explanation* (P3487, vol. 77) or *Commentary* (P3490, vol. 77), the last two appearing to be different translations of the same text.
197. P126, vol. 5, 249.3.8; this is quoted in part in Buddhaguhya's *Condensed Meaning of the "Vairochanābhisambodhi Tantra,"* P3486, vol. 77, 101.5.6, 103.3.6, and 272.3.1.
198. This is quoted in Buddhaguhya's *Condensed Meaning of the "Vairochanābhisambodhi Tantra,"* P3486, vol. 77, 104.5.4 and 106.3.5, and his *Commentary,* P3487, vol. 77, 284.5.6; the tantra itself is P126, vol. 5, 255.5.7–256.1.3, chapter 9.
199. Chapter 9; P126, vol. 5, 256.2.7–256.3.1. The part on supramundane yoga is cited in Buddhaguhya's *Condensed Meaning of the "Vairochanābhisambodhi Tantra,"* P3486, vol. 77, 106.4.6. Buddhaguhya's *Commentary on the "Vairochanābhisambodhi Tantra"* cites the first eight lines and the last six lines as two separate units, identifying that they explain the mundane and supramundane repetitions respectively, P3490, vol.77, 286.1.3–286.2.5; Dharma, vol. 59, text 2663A, 1438.4–1439.5:

    > [The passage beginning with] "I have explained [the yoga] having four branches/ By way of external and internal application"

through to "Is taught as the supreme of whispered repetitions [Involving observation (of conventional phenomena)]," says that—from between the brief indications earlier of those that have the nature of the ultimate and the conventional—the four branches of conventional repetition, that is to say, three external branches and one internal branch, which I have explained, are worldly repetition and furthermore are supreme among repetitions involving imagination. When Buddhaguhya speaks of "the four branches of conventional repetition, three external branches and one internal branch," he likely is making a condensation of the more usual mode of four branches each for external and internal repetition, abbreviating the total of eight branches into three for external repetition and one for internal repetition.

"Suppressed with the word of withdrawal" is as [explained] earlier. "The mind which has accorded with the deity" says that the mind is to observe [or imagine] this one-pointedly.

[The passage beginning with] "For the 'mentally supramundane'" through to "In no other way is [supramundane yoga] to be done" comments in detail on the ultimate repetition explained earlier. In that, "Withdrawal [from external branches of repetition to the internal] and so forth are completely abandoned" says that since the supramundane repetition does not apprehend the nature of a thoroughly impure deity, there is no withdrawal from the branches of external repetition to internal repetition.

"Oneness with the deity" says that the form of the deity and one's own form are taken as one. "And apprehending nondifference" says that since it is possible for different forms to operate in one place, the taking of the two—the deity and oneself—to be one is not such but is to take the two—the deity and oneself—to be nondifferent. Also, since it is possible for the nondifference of the two—the deity and oneself—to be in terms of physical nature, in order to dispel [that possibility, the text] says, "are made undifferentiable in [terms of their empty] nature through the mind." It is not that [their] form and so forth are to be made into one; rather, both minds are to be made undifferentiable in the nature of emptiness.

"In no other way is [supramundane repetition] to be done" says that supramundane repetition is not be done in a way other

than like this. In brief, apprehending the suchness of the sounds that are one's essence [mantra], one breaks down one's own form in emptiness and thereupon realizes that just as one's own form [is understood] as empty, so all phenomena also are the same in [their] nature of emptiness. Since, in that way all phenomena are undifferentiable in [their] nature of emptiness, one realizes that the natures of oneself and of the deity also are undifferentiable in the character of emptiness, and thereupon staying in one-pointed meditative stabilization on emptiness, one mentally makes repetition.
(*phyi dang nang gi sbyor ba yis// yan lag bzhi pa ngas bshad pa// zhes pa nas/ shub ste bzlas brjod byed pa'i mchog / ces pa'i bar gyis ni gong du don dam pa dang kun rdzob kyi rang bzhin mdor bstan pa de las kun rdzob kyi bzlas pa phyi'i yan lag gsum dang nang gi yan lag gcig ste bzhir ngas bshad pa de ni 'jig rten gyi bzlas pa ni yin la/ de yang dmigs pa dang bcas pa'i bzlas pa'i nang na mchog go zhes pa'o// slar sdud pa yi tshig gis non// zhes pa ni snga ma bzhin no// lha yi rjes su song ba'i yid// ces pa ni 'di la sems rtse gcig du dmigs par bya'o zhes pa'o/ yid kyi 'jig rten 'das zhes bya// zhes pa nas/ gzhan du bya ba ma yin no// zhes pa'i bar gyis ni gong du bshad pa'i don dam pa'i bzlas pa de zhib tu 'grel pa ste/ de la/ slar sdud la sogs rnam par spangs// shes pa 'jig rten las 'das pa'i bzlas pa de yong su ma dag pa'i lha'i rang bzhin la dmigs pa ma yin pas phyi rol kyi bzlas pa'i yan lag las nang gi yan lag tu bsdu ba med do zhes pa'o// lha dang gcig tu byed pa dang/ zhes pa ni lha'i gzugs dang bdag gi gzugs gcig tu byed pa'o// tha dad ma yin 'dzin pa yi// zhes pa ni lha dang bdag gnyis gcig tu bya ba yang gzugs tha dad pa gnas gcig tu 'jug pa yang srid* [reading *srid* for *sred* in accordance with Dharma 1439.2] *pas de lta bu ma yin gyi// lha dang bdag gnyis tha mi dad par bya'o zhes pa'o// lha dang bdag gnyis tha mi dad pa yang gzugs kyi rang bzhin du tha mi* [reading *mi* for *ma* in accordance with Dharma 1439.2] *dad pa srid pas de bsal ba'i phyir/ yid kyi* [Dharma 1439.3 reads *kyis*] *rang bzhin dbyer med bya// zhes gsungs pa yin te/ gzugs la sogs pa gcig tu bya ba ni ma yin gyi yid gnyis pa stong pa nyid kyi rang bzhin du dbyer med par bya'o zhes pa'o// gzhan du bya ba ma yin no zhes pa ni 'jig rten las 'das pa'i bzlas pa de tshul 'di 'dra ba las gzhan du mi bya'o zhes pa ste mdor na rang gi snying po gang yin pa'i sgra'i de kho na nyid la dmigs nas bdag nyid kyi gzugs stong pa nyid du bshig ste shigs*

nas kyang ji ltar bdag gi gzugs stong pa nyid du phyi nang gi chos thams cad kyang stong pa'i rang bzhin du gcig par rtog par bya ste/ de ltar chos thams cad stong pa'i rang bzhin du dbyer med pas bdag dang lha'i rang bzhin kyang stong pa'i mtshan nyid du dbyer med par rtog par byas la/ stong pa'i ting nge 'dzin rtse gcig pa la gnas nas yid la bzlas par bya'o zhes pa'o)

200. This meaning of *slar sdud pa* ("withdrawal") as "meditative withdrawal of the mind from sense objects" is similar to the meaning of the grammatical term *slar bsdu* as a full stop, a terminator; in the context of meditation, it is a stoppage of external distraction and "drawing back" inside. For Buddhaguhya's explanation of *slar sdud pa* as "withdrawing vitality (currents of energy)" (*srog slar sdud pa*) see the citation (p. 193) from his *Condensed Meaning of the "Vairochanābhisambodhi Tantra"*; also, for his explanation of *slar sdud pa* as "withdrawal from the branches of external repetition to internal repetition" (*phyi rol kyi bzlas pa'i yan lag las nang gi yan lag tu bsdu ba*), see the citation from his *Commentary on the "Vairochanābhisambodhi Tantra"* in the previous note. In these, *slar sdud pa* means "withdrawal."
201. P4540, vol. 81, 193.5.7–194.1.1.
202. Chapter 5; P126, vol. 5, 252.1.5; cited in Buddhaguhya's *Condensed Meaning of the "Vairochanābhisambodhi Tantra,"* P3486, vol. 77, 105.5.1; see also vol. 77, 91.2.8. Earlier Tsongkhapa cited a shorter and incomplete version missing six lines, using a different translation; see p. 54. For the translation of *yi ge* in the first and fifth lines as "immutable" see the next note.
203. In Sanskrit a term for both "letter" and "immutable" is *akṣara* "immutable," since letters immutably indicate specific sounds. The Tibetan here and in the Tibetan translation of the above citation from the tantra is *yi ge* "letter"; however, Tsongkhapa suggests that we follow Buddhaguhya's commentary on the *Concentration Continuation Tantra* (pp. 135–36) where these two are taken as the moon and mantra series from among the four branches and where Tsongkhapa shows how the moon and mantra letters are immutable:

> It possesses the series of mantra letters (*yi ge, akṣara*); which are immutable (*mi 'gyur ba, akṣara*) since they do not deviate from vivid appearance due to thorough meditation; also, since the mind appearing as a moon and possessing the letters (*yi ge, akṣara*) does not change (*mi 'gyur ba, akṣara*) nor become separate from them, it possesses "immutability."

Similarly, Buddhaguhya's *Commentary on the "Vairochanābhisambodhi Tantra"* (P3490, vol. 77, 284.4.8–284.5.5) says:

> "Letter" (*yi ge*) is a word [meaning] "immutable" (*mi 'gyur ba*). Furthermore, what are they? Concerning that, letters are said to be two—"sounds and mind of enlightenment." Moreover, sounds are the forms of mantra letters. They are called "immutable" (*mi 'gyur ba*) because they do not change (*mi 'gyur ba*) from the nature of indicating the release of conventional and ultimate deities....The mind of enlightenment is to be taken as a moon disc; the mind of enlightenment that has the nature of thusness is blessed [to appear] as a moon disc because it is implanted with the seal (*phyag rgya, mudrā*) of the mind of enlightenment as a moon disc. The mind of enlightenment is called "immutable" (*mi 'gyur ba*) because since it is thoroughly established as non-erroneous, it does not change (*mi 'gyur ba*) from realization of the nature of emptiness as without the aspects of apprehended-object and apprehending-subject, and so forth. (*yi ge zhes pa rang bzhin mi 'gyur ba zhes pa'i tshig ste/ de la yi ge la yang rnam pa gnyis te/ sgra dang byang chub kyi sems so zhes pa'o// de la sgra ni sngags kyi yig 'bru ste des kun rdzob dang don dam pa'i lha rnams kyi rnam par grol ba ston pa las rang bzhin gzhan du mi 'gyur bas na mi 'gyur ba zhes bya ste...byang chub kyi sems ni zla ba'i dkyil 'khor la bya ste/ de bzhin nyid kyi rang bzhin byang chub kyi sems de zla ba'i dkyil 'khor du byin gyis brlabs pa ste/ zla ba'i dkyil 'khor du byang chub kyi sems kyi phyag rgyas btab pa'i phyir ro// byang chub kyi sems de la mi 'gyur ba zhes bya ste/ phyin ci ma log par yongs su grub pas stong pa nyid kyi rang bzhin la gzung ba dang 'dzin pa la sogs pa'i rnam par med par rtog pa can du mi 'gyur ba'i phyir ro.*)

From this passage in which the two types of *yi ge* are each described, with reasons, as being *mi 'gyur ba* ("immutable"), it is clear that *akṣara* is to be applied in its meaning as "immutable" both to the sounds and to the mind of enlightenment appearing as a moon disc. It is evident that the translators into Tibetan—the Tibetan Kawa Paltseg (*ska ba dpal brtsegs*) who, along with the Indian Sīlendrabodhi, translated the *Vairochanābhisambodhi Tantra,* and the reviser, the Tibetan Shonnupal (*gzhon nu dpal*)—used *yi ge* ("letter") as what they deemed to be the most cogent single translation for the general passage. Nevertheless, when it comes to the more suitable English translation, given that the term is being explained as meaning "immutable," these passages justify treating the English as the more directly meaningful "immutable" rather than "letters" here and in this citation from the tantra.

204. Chapter 5; P126, vol. 5, 252.1.7; Buddhaguhya's *Condensed Meaning of the "Vairochanābhisambodhi Tantra,"* P3486, vol. 77, 107.2.4.
205. P126, vol. 5, 256.2.7.
206. P3486, vol. 77, 106.1.6.
207. Losang Chökyi Gyaltshan, *Presentation of the General Teaching and the Four Tantra Sets, Collected Works,* vol. 4 (New Delhi, Gurudeva, 1973), 30b.6.
208. Losang Chökyi Gyaltshan, *Presentation of the General Teaching and the Four Tantra Sets,* 31a.1.
209. Chapter 5; P126, vol. 5, 252.1.8; Buddhaguhya's *Condensed Meaning of the "Vairochanābhisambodhi Tantra,"* P3486, vol. 77, 107.2.4.
210. Chapter 8; P126, vol. 5, 256.2.1; Buddhaguhya's *Condensed Meaning of the "Vairochanābhisambodhi Tantra,"* P3486, vol. 77, 109.5.7, and his *Commentary,* P3487, vol. 77, 233.2.5.
211. Chapter 6; P126, vol. 5, 253.1.5; Buddhaguhya's *Condensed Meaning of the "Vairochanābhisambodhi Tantra,"* P3486, vol. 77, 103.5.4.
212. P3486, vol. 77, 106.2.4.
213. Chapter 8; P126, vol. 5, 256.1.4; Buddhaguhya's *Condensed Meaning of the "Vairochanābhisambodhi Tantra,"* P3486, vol. 77, 104.1.8–2.6.
214. Chapter 8; P126, vol. 5, 256.2.1; Buddhaguhya's *Condensed Meaning of the "Vairochanābhisambodhi Tantra,"* P3486, vol. 77, 104.2.6–3.2.
215. P3486, vol. 77, 106.4.3–6. The first sentence of the text here differs slightly from that on p. 191 perhaps due to being a different translation or due to being remembered differently.
216. The Dharamsala edition reads *rims,* but the explanation reads *rigs,* as does the Delhi edition in both places.
217. The absence of production from self, inherently existent other, both, and neither.
218. See the Dalai Lama's evocative explanation of these three, p. 41.
219. Tsongkhapa (p. 64) lists these as:

    1. the topic of conferring initiation, thereby making a receptacle suitable for cultivating the path;
    2. the topic of keeping pledges and vows that are the basis for achieving feats;
    3. then the topic of approximation for the sake of generating ability;

4. the topic of achieving feats for the sake of effecting one's own and others' welfare once one has gained ability.

and slightly alters them when in the presentation of the two systems into (1) how to become a receptacle suitable for meditatively cultivating the path, (2) having become a receptacle, how to maintain purity of pledges and vows, (3) how to perform prior approximation while abiding in the pledges, and (4) how to achieve feats once the approximation is serviceable.

III: Supplement

1. The source for this is the late Khansur Ngagwang Legdan's oral teachings.
2. Ngagwang Paldan, *Presentation of the Grounds and Paths of the Four Great Secret Tantra Sets: Illumination of the Texts of Tantra* (rGyud smad par khang edition, no other data), 6b.7–7b.3; this work figures in all three supplements.
3. For an extended description of these in relation to the process of death see Lati Rinpoche and Jeffrey Hopkins, *Death, Intermediate State, and Rebirth in Tibetan Buddhism* (London, Rider and Co., 1979; rpt. Ithaca: Snow Lion Publications, 1980). The translation of the selections from Ngagwang Paldan avoids the author's rendering of these points in debate format.
4. Ngagwang Paldan, *Presentation of the Grounds and Paths of the Four Great Secret Tantra Sets,* 7b.4–8b.1.
5. Ngagwang Paldan, *Presentation of the Grounds and Paths of the Four Great Secret Tantra Sets,* 4b.4–5a.1. The citation begins in mid-sentence.
6. Tsonghapa indicated earlier that it is easier for beginners to meditate on the deity in front first and then oneself as a deity, since meditation on a deity in front requires many activities, whereas self-generation is aimed at developing *steady* concentration on oneself in divine form. Thus, the order of the first two of the branches could be reversed.
7. Alternatively, this step can include the appearance of a moon disc above which the tones of mantra resound.
8. Or, alternatively, the crown protrusion, hair-treasury (a single coiled hair in the middle of the brow), two eyes, two shoulders, neck, heart, and navel.
9. Duldzin Dragpa Gyaltshan (*Presentation of the General Rites of Action and Performance Tantra,* 549.4–550.3) structures the repetition of mantra within observing the form of the letters differently. Instead of per-

forming both whispered repetition and mental repetition first within observing the form of the letters at the heart of the deity in front and then both whispered repetition and mental repetition within observing the form of the letters at one's own heart, in his system one performs whispered repetition within observing the form of the letters at the heart of the deity in front and then within observing the form of the letters at one's own heart, after which one performs mental repetition within observing the form of the letters at the heart of the deity in front and then within observing the form of the letters at one's own heart. In his version, the steps of meditation are:

(1) Repeat mantra within observing the form of the letters
(a) Repeat mantra in whisper within observing the form of the letters
At the heart of the deity in front

Focusing on the three—the front deity, moon, and letters—repeat mantra in whisper, as if reading the letters, while exhaling.
While inhaling, switch to observing yourself as a deity without repetition.
Repeat the above.

At your own heart

Inhale—into your own heart from the heart of the deity in front—the moon disc together with the mantra letters standing at its edge.
Perform whispered repetition, focusing on the moon and letters.
At the end of exhaling, and emit the moon and letters back to the deity in front, focusing on moon and letters, without repetition.
Repeat the above.

(b) Repeat mantra mentally within observing the form of the letters

At the heart of the deity in front
Holding your breath after inhalation and focusing on the three—the front deity, moon, and letters—repeat mantra mentally as if listening to your own recitation.
While exhaling, switch to observing yourself as a deity without repetition.
Repeat the above.

At your own heart

Inhale—into your own heart from the heart of the deity in front—the moon disc together with the mantra letters standing at its edge without repetition.
Stop your breath and recite mantra mentally, focusing on moon

and letters, as if your mind is in the center of the moon disc and is reading the letters of the mantra standing on the edge of the moon disc facing inward.

When exhaling, stop repetition of mantra, and move the moon and letters with your breath to the deity's heart—focusing on the moon and letters.

With inhalation, repeat the above.

10. A far simpler alternative version of the concentration of abiding in sound replaces the first four steps with observing the written letters of the mantra around the edge of the moon disc at one's heart and then leaving the written letters and contemplating only the sounds.
11. Ngagwang Paldan, *Presentation of the Grounds and Paths of the Four Great Secret Tantra Sets,* 8b.3–9a.4.

Appendix 1: Lineages in Action and Performance Tantra

1. *rgyud sde spyi'i rnam par bzhag pa skal bzang gi yid 'phrog* (Dharmsala, Library of Tibetan Works and Archives, 1975), on Action Tantra, 16b.1–20a.2, and the short section on Performance Tantra, 25a.6–b.1. See also a translation of the entire book in Panchen Sonam Dragpa, *Overview of Buddhist Tantra,* trans. by Martin J. Boord and Losang Norbu Tsonawa (Dharmsala, India: Library of Tibetan Works and Archives, 1996). A longer presentation of the topic of lineage is given by Khaydrub Geleg Palsang (Lessing and Wayman, *Mkhas-Grub Rje's Fundamentals of the Buddhist Tantras,* 100–39); a debt to the translation and bibliographic prowess of Ferdinand Lessing and Alex Wayman is gratefully acknowledged.
2. Khaydrub Geleg Palsang (Lessing and Wayman, *Mkhas-Grub Rje's Fundamentals of the Buddhist Tantras,* 104.6).
3. Khaydrub Geleg Palsang (Lessing and Wayman, *Mkhas-Grub Rje's Fundamentals of the Buddhist Tantras,* 108.22).
4. Lessing and Wayman, *Mkhas-Grub Rje's Fundamentals of the Buddhist Tantras,* 108.18.
5. For their tantras see Khaydrub Geleg Palsang (Lessing and Wayman, *Mkhas-Grub Rje's Fundamentals of the Buddhist Tantras,* 113).
6. See Lessing and Wayman, *Mkhas-Grub Rje's Fundamentals of the Buddhist Tantras,* 113.
7. Khaydrub Geleg Palsang in Lessing and Wayman, *Mkhas-Grub Rje's Fundamentals of the Buddhist Tantras,* 115.

8. This is most likely number four in Lessing and Wayman, *Mkhas-Grub Rje's Fundamentals of the Buddhist Tantras,* 115.
9. Lessing and Wayman, *Mkhas-Grub Rje's Fundamentals of the Buddhist Tantras,* notes 16 and 17, p. 116.
10. See Khaydrub Geleg Palsang (Lessing and Wayman, *Mkhas-Grub Rje's Fundamentals of the Buddhist Tantras,* 125–6).
11. Ibid., 125–6.
12. Khaydrub Geleg Palsang (Lessing and Wayman, *Mkhas-Grub Rje's Fundamentals of the Buddhist Tantras,* 127) identifies the author's name as Suryagupta.
13. The Sanskrit name is taken from Lessing and Wayman, *Mkhas-Grub Rje's Fundamentals of the Buddhist Tantras,* 127.

Glossary

English	Tibetan
accumulation of merit	bsod nams kyi tshogs
accumulation of wisdom	ye shes kyi tshogs
Action Tantra	bya rgyud
activities	las
altruistic mind of enlightenment	byang chub kyi sems
analytical meditation	dpyad sgom
bliss of physical and mental pliancy	lus sems shin sbyangs kyi bde ba
burnt offering	sbyin sregs
calm abiding	zhi gnas
channels	rtsa
clear light	’od gsal
Complete Enjoyment Body	longs sku
concentration	bsam gtan
concentration bestowing liberation at the end of sound	sgra mthar thar pa ster ba’i bsam gtan
concentration of abiding in fire	me gnas kyi bsam gtan
concentration of abiding in sound	sgra gnas kyi bsam gtan

ENGLISH	TIBETAN
concentration with repetition	bzlas brjod dang bcas pa'i bsam gtan
concentration not relying on repetition	bzlas brjod la ma bltos pa'i bsam gtan
concentrations of the three principles	de nyid gsum gyi bsam gtan
deity yoga	lha'i rnal byor
divine approximation	lha'i bsnyen pa
divine pride	lha'i ngar rgyal
dualistic proliferations	gnyis snang gi spros pa
Emanation Body	sprul sku
emptiness	stong pa nyid
emptiness yoga	stong pa'i rnal byor
entry of a wisdom being	ye shes pa gzhug pa
excitement	rgod pa
exertion	rtsol ba
feat	dngos grub
ferocity	drag shul
fierce activities	drag po'i las
Form Body	gzugs sku
form deity	gzugs kyi lha
four-branched repetition	bzlas brjod yan lag bzhi ldan
generation in front	mdun bskyed

English	Tibetan
Highest Yoga Tantra	rnal 'byor bla med
illusory body	sgyu lus
imputedly existent person	btags yod kyi gang zag
increase	rgyas pa
initiation	dbang
introspection	shes bzhin
knowledge bearers	rig 'dzin
knowledge mantra	rig sngags
laxity	bying ba
lethargy	rmugs pa
letter deity	yi ge'i lha
maṇḍala	dkyil 'khor
mantra	sngags
meditative stabilization	ting nge 'dzin
mindfulness	dran pa
other-base	gzhan gyi gzhi
pacifying activities	zhi ba'i las
path of accumulation	tshogs lam
path of meditation	sgom lam
path of no-more-learning	mi slob lam
path of preparation	sbyor lam
path of seeing	mthong lam

English	Tibetan
Perfection Vehicle	phar phyin gyi theg pa
Performance Tantra	spyod rgyud
pledge	dam tshig
pledge-being	dam tshig pa
pliancy	shin sbyangs
pride of ordinariness	tha mal pa'i ngar rgyal
prior approximation	sngon du bsnyen pa byed pa
repetition	bzlas brjod
scattering	'phro ba
seal	phyag rgya
seal deity	phyag rgya'i lha
secret mantra	gsang sngags
self-base	bdag gi gzhi
self-generation	bdag bskyed
sign deity	mtshan ma'i lha
sound deity	sgra'i lha
special insight	lhag mthong
stabilizing meditation	'jog sgom
stage of completion	rdzogs rim
stage of generation	bskyed rim
suchness	de kho na nyid
tantra	rgyud

English	Tibetan
Truth Body	chos sku
ultimate deity	don dam pa'i lha
vitality	srog
vow	sdom pa
wind	rlung
wind yoga	rlung gi rnal 'byor
wisdom-being	ye shes pa
withdrawal	slar sdud pa
yoga of signlessness	mtshan med kyi rnal byor
Yoga Tantra	rnal 'byor rgyud
yoga with signs	mtshan bcas kyi rnal byor
yoga without signs	mtshan med kyi rnal 'byor

Bibliography

In the first section the titles are arranged alphabetically according to the English, followed by the Sanskrit and Tibetan; in the second section, by author. The English titles are usually abbreviated.

1. Sūtras and Tantras

Cloud of Jewels Sūtra
ratnameghasūtra
dkon mchog sprin gyi mdo
P897, vol. 35; sde dge 231, vol. *wa*

Compendium of Principles / Compendium of the Principles of All Ones-Gone-Thus (the root Yoga Tantra)
sarvatathāgatatattvasaṃgrahanāmamahāyānasūtra
de bzhin gshegs pa thams cad kyi de kho na nyid bsdus pa zhes bya ba theg pa chen po'i mdo
P112, vol. 4; sde dge 479, vol. *nya*
Sanskrit: *Sarva-tathāgata-tattva-saṃgraha,* reproduced by Lokesh Chandra and David L. Snellgrove. Śata-piṭaka Series, vol. 269 (New Delhi: International Academy of Indian Culture, 1981). Also: Isshi Yamada. *Sarva-tathāgata-tattva-saṅgraha.* Śata-piṭaka Series, vol. 262 (New Delhi: International Academy of Indian Culture, 1981)

Concentration Continuation Tantra (one of the four general Action Tantras)
dhyānottarapaṭalakramatantra
bsam gtan gyi phyi ma rim par phye ba
P430, vol. 9

Extensive Tantra of Vajravidāraṇā / Extensive Vidāraṇa Tantra
[not translated into Tibetan]

General Secret Tantra / General Tantra (one of four general Action Tantras)
sarvamaṇḍalasāmānayvidhiguhyatantra
dkyil 'khor thams cad kyi spyi'i cho ga gsang ba'i rgyud
P429, vol. 9

Guhyasamāja Tantra (a root Highest Yoga Tantra)
sarvatathāgatakāyavākcittarahasyaguhyasamājanāmamahākalparāja
de bzhin gshegs pa thams cad kyi sku gsung thugs kyi gsang chen gsang ba 'dus pa zhes bya ba brtag pa'i rgyal po chen po
Tibetan digital reprint edition: In *bka' 'gyur* (*sde dge par phud*, 442). TBRC W22084.81:181-297 (PDF of Delhi, India: Delhi Karmapae choedhey, Gyalwae sungrab partun khang, 1982–1985)
P81, vol. 3
Sanskrit text edited by S. Bagchi. *The Guhyasamāja Tantra* (Darbhanga, India: The Mithila Institute, 1965)

Hevajra Tantra
hevajratantrarāja
kye'i rdo rje zhes bya ba rgyud kyi rgyal po
Tibetan digital reprint edition: In *bka' 'gyur* (*sde dge par phud*, 417). TBRC W22084.80:3-28 (PDF in Delhi, India: Delhi Karmapae choedhey, Gyalwae sungrab partun khang, 1982–1985)
P10, vol. 1
English translation: D. L. Snellgrove. *Hevajra Tantra,* Parts 1 and 2. (London: Oxford University Press, 1959)
English translation together with Kṛṣṇāchārya's commentary: G. W. Farrow and I. Menon. *The Concealed Essence of the Hevajra Tantra with the Commentary of Yogaratnamālā* (Delhi: Motilal Banarsidass, 1992)

Kālachakra Tantra
paramādibuddhoddhṛtaśrīkālacakranāmatantrarāja
mchog gi dang po'i sang rgyas las byung ba rgyud kyi rgyal po dpal dus kyi 'khor lo
P4, vol. 1
English translation (chapter 1): John Newman. *The Outer Wheel of Time: Vajrayāna Buddhist Cosmology in the Kālacakra Tantra* (Ann Arbor, MI: University Microfilms International, 1987)
English translation and Mongolian text (chapter 2): Vesna Acimovic Wallace. *The Inner* Kālacakratantra: *A Buddhist Tantric View of the Individual.* 2 vols. PhD diss., University of California at Berkeley, 1995; and *Kālacakratantra: The Chapter on the Individual together with the Vimalaprabhā* (New York: American Institute of Buddhist Studies, 2004)

Mañjushrī Root Tantra
mañjuśrīmūlakalpa

'jam dpal gyi rtsa ba'i rgyud
P162, vol. 6
Questions of Subāhu Tantra (one of the four general Action Tantras)
subāhuparipṛcchānāmatantra
dpung bzang gis zhus pa zhes bya ba'i rgyud
P428, vol. 9
Saṃputa Tantra
saṃpuṭanāmamahātantra / saṃpuṭināmamahātantra
yang dag par sbyor ba zhes bya ba'i rgyud / yang dar par sbyor ba shes bya ba'i rgyud chen po
P26, vol. 2
Scriptural Division of the Knowledge Bearers
Rig 'dzin gyi sde snod
[?]
Susiddhi Tantra (one of the four general Action Tantras)
Susiddhikaramahātantrasādhanopāyikapaṭala
legs par grub par byed pa'i rgyud chen po las sgrub pa'i thabs rim par phye ba
P431, vol. 9; *sde dge,* 807, Dharma vol. 34
Sūtra on Skill in Means
upāyakauśalyanāmamahāyānasūtra
thabs mkhas pa zhes bya ba theg pa chen po'i mdo
P927, vol. 36
Ten Principles / Introduction to the Ten Principles
daśatattva / daśatattvāvatāra
de kho na nyid bcu pa
P2758
Vairochanābhisambodhi Tantra (a Performance Tantra)
mahāvairochanābhisambodhivikurvatiadhiṣhṭhā-navaipūlyasūtra-indrarājanāmadharmaparyāya
rnam par snang mdzad chen po mngon par rdzogs par byang chub pa rnam par sprul ba byin gyis rlob pa shin tu rgyas pa mdo sde'i dbang po rgyal po zhes bya ba'i chos kyi rnam grangs
P126, vol. 5
Vajrapāṇi Initiation Tantra
vajrapāṇyabhiṣekamahātantra
lag na rdo rje dbang bskur ba'i rgyud chen mo
P130, vol. 6

Vajroṣhṇīṣha Tantra
rdo rje gtsug tor gyi rgyud
[not translated into Tibetan]
Wisdom Vajra Compendium (an explanatory Highest Yoga Tantra, in the Guhyasamāja cycle)
jñānavajrasamucchayanāmatantra
ye shes rdo rje kun las btus pa
P84, vol. 3

2. Other Works

Ānandagarbha (*kun dga' snying po;* tenth century)
Illumination of the "Compendium of Principles"
sarvatathāgatatattvasaṃgrahamahāyānābhisamayanāmatantra-vyākhyātattvālokakarī
de bzhin gshegs pa thams cad kyi de kho na nyid bsdus pa theg pa chen po mngon par rtogs pa zhes bya ba'i rgyud kyi bshad pa de kho na nyid snang bar byed pa
P333, vols. 71–2; *sde dge* 2510, vol. *li*
Āryadeva (*'phags pa lha,* second to third century C.E.)
Lamp Compendium of Practice
caryāmelāpakapradīpa
spyod pa bsdus pa'i sgron ma
Tibetan digital reprint edition: In *bstan 'gyur* (*sde dge,* 1803). TBRC W23703.35:115–214 (PDF of Delhi, India: Delhi Karmapae choedhey, Gyalwae sungrab partun khang, 1982–1985)
P2668, vol. 61
Asaṅga (*thogs med,* fourth century)
Grounds of Bodhisattvas
bodhisattvabhūmi
byang chub sems dpa'i sa
Tibetan digital reprint edition: In *bstan 'gyur* (*sde dge,* 4037). TBRC W23703.129:4-427 (PDF of Delhi, India: Delhi Karmapae choedhey, Gyalwae sungrab partun khang, 1982–1985)
P5538, vol. 110
Sanskrit: Unrai Wogihara. *Bodhisattvabhūmi: A Statement of the Whole Course of the Bodhisattva (Being the Fifteenth Section of Yogācārabhūmi)* (Leipzig: 1908); (Tokyo: Seigo Kenyūkai, 1930–1936). Also: Nalinaksha Dutt. *Bodhisatt-*

vabhumi (Being the XVth Section of Asangapada's Yogacara-bhumi). Tibetan Sanskrit Works Series 7 (Patna, India: K. P. Jayaswal Research Institute, 1966)

English translation of the Chapter on Suchness, the fourth chapter of Part I, which is the fifteenth volume of the *Grounds of Yogic Practice:* Janice D. Willis. *On Knowing Reality: The Tattvārtha Chapter of Asaṅga's Bodhisattvabhūmi* (New York: Columbia University Press, 1979; reprint, Delhi: Motilal Banarsidass, 1982)

Atisha (982–1054)

Means of Achievement of Vimaloṣhṇīṣha

dri med gtsug tor gyi sgrub thabs

[?]

Bodong Choglay Namgyal (*bo dong phyogs las rnam rgyal,* 1376–1451)

Presentation of the General Tantra Sets

rgyud sde spyi'i rnam gzhag

Encyclopedia Tibetica: The Collected Works of Bo-do (Delhi: Motilal Banarsidass, New Delhi: Tibet House, 1969–1981)

Buddhaguhya (*sangs rgyas gsang ba*)

Commentary on the "Concentration Continuation Tantra"

dhyānottarapaṭalaṭīkā

bsam gtan phyi ma rim par phye ba rgya cher bshad pa

Tibetan digital reprint edition: In *bstan 'gyur* (*sde dge,* 2670). TBRC W23703.71:3-77 (PDF of Delhi, India: Delhi Karmapae choedhey, Gyalwae sungrab partun khang, 1982–1985)

P3495, vol. 78, 70.1.5

Commentary on the "Vajravidāraṇā Tantra"

vajravidāraṇī [*or* vidāraṇā]nāmadhāraṇīṭīkāratnābhāsvarā

rdo rje rnam par 'joms pa zhes bya ba'i bzungs kyi rgya cher 'grel pa rin po che gsal ba zhes bya ba

P3504, vol. 78

Commentary on the "Vairochanābhisambodhi Tantra"

vairocanābhisambodhivikurvitādhiṣṭhānamahātantravṛtti

rnam par snang mdzad mngon par rdzogs par byang chub pa rnam par sprul pa byin gyis rlob pa'i rgyud chen po'i 'grel pa

P3490, vol. 77, p. 229, *rgyud 'grel, cu* 1–230a.5; *sde dge* 2663, *rgyud, nyu* 261a.1–*tu* 116a.7

Also: vairocanābhisambodhivikurvitādhiṣṭhānamahātantra-bhāṣya rnam par snang mdzad mngon par byang chub pa rnam par sprul pa'i byin gyis brlabs kyi rgyud chen po'i bshad pa

P3487, vol.77, p. 110, *rgyud 'grel, ngu* 76b.8–337a.3; D2663, *rgyud, nyu* 65a.3–260b.7

Translation of chapters 1 and 2: Alex Wayman and R. Tajima. *The Enlightenment of Vairocana* (Delhi: Motilal Banarsidass, 1992)

Translation: Stephen Hodge. *The Mahā-Vairocana-Abhisaṃbodhi Tantra with Buddhaguhya's Commentary* (London & New York: RoutledgeCurzon, 2003)

Condensed Meaning of the "Vairochanābhisambodhi Tantra"

vairocanābhisambodhitantrapiṇḍārtha

rnam par snang mdzad mngon par rdzogs par byang chub pa'i rgyud kyi bsdus pa'i don

P3486, vol. 77

Translation: Stephen Hodge. *The Mahā-Vairocana-Abhisaṃbodhi Tantra with Buddhaguhya's Commentary* (London & New York: RoutledgeCurzon, 2003)

Butön Rinchendrub (*bu ston rin chen grub,* 1290–1364)

Extensive General Presentation of the Tantra Sets: Ornament Beautifying the Precious Tantra Sets

rgyud sde spyi'i rnam par gzhag pa rgyud sde rin po che'i mdzes rgyan

Collected Works, vol. 15, 1.1–609.7. Śata Piṭaka No. 55 (New Delhi: International Academy of Indian Culture, 1969); Toh. 5169.

Chandrakīrti (*zla ba grags pa,* seventh century)

Brilliant Lamp, Extensive Commentary [on the "Guhyasamāja Tantra"]

pradīpoddyotananāmaṭīkā

sgron ma gsal bar byed pa zhes bya ba'i rgya cher bshad pa

P2650, vol. 60

Dharmakīrti (*chos kyi grags pa,* seventh century)

Commentary on (Dignāga's) "Compendium of Prime Cognition"

pramāṇavarttikakārikā

tshad ma rnam 'grel gyi tshig le'ur byas pa

Tibetan digital reprint edition: In *bstan 'gyur* (*sde dge,* 4210). TBRC W23703.174:189–304 (PDF of Delhi, India: Delhi Karmapae choedhey, Gyalwae sungrab partun khang, 1982–1985)

P5709, vol. 130

Sanskrit: Dwarikadas Shastri. *Pramāṇavarttika of Āchārya Dharmakīrtti*. Varanasi, India: Bauddha Bharati, 1968. Also, Yūsho Miyasaka. "Pramāṇavarttika-Kārikā (Sanskrit and Tibetan)," *Acta Indologica* 2 (1971–1972): 1–206. Also, (chap. 1 and autocommentary) Raniero Gnoli. *The Pramāṇavarttikam of Dharmakīrti: The First Chapter with the Autocommentary* (Rome: Istituto Italiano per il Medio ed Estremo Oriente, 1960)

English translation (chap. 2): Masatoshi Nagatomi. "A Study of Dharmakīrti's Pramāṇavarttika: An English Translation and Annotation of the Pramāṇavarttika, Book I." Ph.D. diss., Harvard University, 1957.

English translation (chap. 4, stanzas 1–148): Tom J.F. Tillemans. *Dharmakīrti's Pramāṇavarttika: An Annotated Translation of the Fourth Chapter (parārthānumāna)*, vol. 1 (Vienna: Verlag der Osterreichischen Akademie der Wissenschaften, 2000)

Duldzin Dragpa Gyaltshan (*'dul 'dzin grags pa rgyal mtshan*)

Presentation of the General Rites of Action and Performance Tantra and Their Application to the Three Lineages, Set Down by Duldzin According to the Foremost [Tsongkhapa's] Practice

bya spyod kyi spyi'i cho ga'i rnam par bzhag pa rigs gsum la sbyor tshul rje'i phyag bzhes bzhin 'dul ba 'dzin pas bkod pa

Collected Works of Tsongkhapa, vol. na, 523–576 [from the library of His Holiness the Dalai Lama, no other data]

Hopkins, Jeffrey

Meditation on Emptiness

(London: Wisdom Publications, 1983); rev. ed. (Boston: Wisdom Publications, 1996)

Indrabhūti / Indrabodhi

Explanation of the "Condensation of the Saṃvara Tantra"

cakrasaṃvaratantrarājaśambarasamucchayanāmavṛtti

khor lo sdom pa'i rgyud kyi rgyal po bde mchog bsdus pa zhes bya ba'i rnam par bshad pa

P2129, vol. 49

Jetāri (*sgra las rnam rgyal*)

Means of Achievement of the Five Guards

pañcarakṣāvidhi

bsrung ba lnga'i cho ga

P3940–4, vol. 166

Jinadatta (*rgyal bas byin*)

Commentary on the Difficult Points of the "Guhyasamāja Tantra"

guhyasamājatantrapañjikā

dpal gsang ba 'dus pa'i rgyud kyi dka' 'grel

P2710, vol. 63

Kamalashīla (*pad ma'i ngang tshul;* ca. 740–795)

Stages of Meditation

bhāvanākrama

sgom pa'i rim pa; *sde dge* 3915–17, vol. *ki;* Dharma vol. 73, Tokyo *sde dge* vol. 15

P5310–12, vol. 102

Sanskrit: *First Bhāvanākrama.* G. Tucci, ed. *Minor Buddhist texts, II.* Serie Orientale Roma 9 (Rome: Istituto Italiano per il Medio ed Estremo Oriente, 1958). Pp.185–229. *Third Bhāvanākrama.* G. Tucci, ed. *Minor Buddhist texts, III.* Serie Orientale Roma 43 (Rome: Istituto Italiano per il Medio ed Estremo Oriente, 1971)

English translation (Second *Bhāvanākrama*): Geshe Lhundup Sopa, Elvin W. Jones, and John Newman. *The Stages of Meditation: Bhāvanākrama II* (Madison, WI: Deer Park Books, 1998). Also: Geshe Lobsang Jordhen, Lobsang Choephel Ganchenpa, and Jeremy Russell. *Stages of Meditation* (Ithaca, NY: Snow Lion Publications, 2001)

Contemporary commentary: Dalai Lama. *An Open Heart: Practicing Compassion in Everyday Life* (New York: Little Brown, 2001)

Khaydrub Geleg Palsang (*mkhas grub dge legs dpal bzang,* 1385–1438)

Extensive Explanation of the Format of the General Tantra Sets

rgyud sde spyi'i rnam par bzhag pa rgyas par bshad pa

Collected Works of the Lord Mkhas-grub rje dge-legs-dpal-bzaṅ-po, vol. 8, 443–630 (New Delhi: Guru Deva, 1980). Also: *Collected Works of Mkhas-grub dge-legs dpal,* vol. 11, 215–368 (New Delhi: Ngawang Gelek Demo, 1983)

English translation: Ferdinand D. Lessing and Alex Wayman. *Mkhas-Grub Rje's Fundamentals of the Buddhist Tantras* (The Hague: Mouton, 1968; reprint, Delhi: Motilal Banarsidass, 1978)

Lakṣhmi (*dpal mo*)

Means of Achievement of the Eleven-Faced Avalokiteshvara

bhaṭṭārakāryaikādaśamukhāvalokiteśvarasādhana
rje btsun 'phags pa spyan ras gzigs dbang phyug zhal bcu gcig pa'i sgrub thabs
P3557, vol. 79

Lodrö, Gedün
Calm Abiding and Special Insight
trans. and ed. by Jeffrey Hopkins
(Ithaca, NY: Snow Lion Publications, 1998)

Losang Chökyi Gyaltshan (*blo bzang chos kyi rgyal mtshan,* 1570–1662)
Presentation of the General Teaching and the Four Tantra Sets
bstan pa spyi dang rgyud sde bzhi'i rnam par gzhag pa'i zin bris
Collected Works, vol. 4 (New Delhi: Gurudeva, 1973)

Nāgārjuna (*klu sgrub,* first to second century, C.E.)
Means of Achievement of the Retention of the Thousand-Armed and Thousand-Eyed Avalokiteshvara
sahasrabhujāvalokiteśvarasādhana
spyan ras gzigs dbang phyug phyag stong sgrub thabs
P3555, vol. 79

Ngagwang Paldan (*ngag dbang dpal ldan,* b. 1797), also known as Paldan Chöjay (*dpal ldan chos rje*)
Presentation of the Grounds and Paths of Mantra / Illumination of the Texts of Tantra, Presentation of the Grounds and Paths of the Four Great Secret Tantra Sets
gsang chen rgyud sde bzhi'i sa lam gyi rnam bzhag rgyud gzhung gsal byed
rgyud smad par khang edition: no other data

Pabongkha Jampa Tandzin Trinlay Gyatsho (*pha bong kha pa byams pa bstan 'dzin 'phrin las rgya mtsho,* 1878–1941)
Miscellaneous Notes from Jo-nay Pandita's Explanation of the "Great Exposition of Secret Mantra"
rje btsun bla ma co ne paṇḍi ta rin po che'i zhal snga nas sngags rim chen mo'i bshad lung nos skabs kyi gsung bshad zin bris thor tsam du bkod pa
Collected Works, vol. 2 (New Delhi: Chophel Legdan, 1972).

Padmasambhava (*padma 'byung gnas*)
Means of Achievement of Mahākaruṇika
thugs rje chen po'i sgrub thabs
n.d.

Paṇchen Sönam Dragpa (*paṇ chen bsod nams grags pa,* 1478–1554)
General Presentation of the Tantra Sets: Captivating the Minds of the Fortunate
rgyud sde spyi'i rnam par bzhag pa skal bzang gi yid 'phrog
Dharamsala, Library of Tibetan Works and Archives, 1975.
English translation: *Overview of Buddhist Tantra,* trans. by Martin J. Boord and Losang Norbu Tsonawa (Dharmsala, India: Library of Tibetan Works and Archives, 1996)

Ratnākarashānti (*shāntipa / rin chen 'byung gnas zhi ba*)
Means of Achievement of the Five Guards
pañcarakṣāviddhi
bsrung ba lnga'i cho ga
P3947, vol. 80
Precious Lamp, Commentary on the Difficult Points of the "Kṛṣhṇayamāri Tantra"
kṛṣṇayamārimahātantrarājapañjikāratnapradīpa
gshin rje'i dgra nag po'i rgyud kyi rgyal po chen po'i dka' 'grel rin po che'i sgron ma
P2782, vol. 66

Shāntideva (*zhi ba lha,* eighth century)
Engaging in the Bodhisattva Deeds
bodhisattvacaryāvatāra
byang chub sems dpa'i spyod pa la 'jug pa
P5272, vol. 99; *sde dge* 3871, *dbu ma,* vol. *la*

Shrīdhara (*dpal 'dzin*)
Innate Illumination, Commentary on the Difficult Points of the "Yamāri Tantra"
yamāritantrapañjikāsahajāloka
gshin rje gshed kyi rgyud kyi dka' 'grel lhan cig skyes pa'i snang ba
P2781, vol. 66; *sde dge* 1918

Subhagavajra (*skal pa bzang po'i rdo rje*)
Stages of the Great Vehicle Path
mahāyānapathakrama
theg pa chen po'i lam gyi rim pa
P4540, vol. 81

Tsongkhapa Losang Dragpa (*tsong kha pa blo bzang grags pa,* 1357–1419)
Explanation of the Ethics Chapter
byang chub sems dpa'i sdom pa byung nas tshul khrims kyi

phung po yongs su dag par bya ba'i tshul rnam par bshad pa byang chub gzhung lam zhes bya ba

P6145, vol. 154

English translation: Mark Tatz. *Asaṅga's Chapter on Ethics, With the Commentary of Tsong-Kha-pa, the Basic Path to Awakening, the Complete Bodhisattva* (Lewiston/Queenston: The Edwin Mellen Press, 1986)

Explanation of the Root Infractions

rtsa ltung gi rnam bshad / gsang sngags kyi tshul khrims kyi rnam bshad dngos grub kyi snye ma

P6188, vol. 160

English translation: Gareth Sparham. *Tantric Ethics: An Explanation of the Precepts for Buddhist Vajrayāna Practice* (Boston: Wisdom, 2005)

Great Exposition of Secret Mantra / The Stages of the Path to a Victor and Pervasive Master, a Great Vajradhara: Revealing All Secret Essentials

rgyal ba khyab bdag rdo rje 'chang chen po'i lam gyi rim pa gsang ba kun gyi gnad rnam par phye ba / sngags rim chen mo

P6210, vol. 161

Basic edition for the 1977 publication of the translation of the first volume: (Dharamsala, Shes rig par khang, 1969)

Tibetan digital reprint edition: TBRC W2CZ7854. 1 vols. (PDF of Lhasa: dpal ldan, date unknown)

Peking 6210, vol. 161. Also: (Delhi: Ngawang Gelek, 1975). Also: (Delhi: Guru Deva, 1979)

English translation (chap. 1): H.H. the Dalai Lama, Tsong-kha-pa, and Jeffrey Hopkins. *Tantra in Tibet* (London: George Allen and Unwin, 1977; reprint with minor corrections, Ithaca, NY: Snow Lion Publications, 1987). Revised edition: Tsongkhapa, with a commentary by the Dalai Lama. Translation, editing, and explanatory material by Jeffrey Hopkins. *The Great Exposition of Secret Mantra, Volume One: Tantra in Tibet*. (Boulder: Snow Lion, 2016)

English translation (chaps. 2-3): H.H. the Dalai Lama, Tsong-kha-pa, and Jeffrey Hopkins. *The Yoga of Tibet* (London: George Allen and Unwin, 1981; reprinted as *Deity Yoga* (Ithaca, NY: Snow Lion Publications, 1987). Revised edition: Tsong-khapa, with a commentary by the Dalai Lama.Translation, editing, and explanatory material by Jeffrey Hopkins. *The Great Exposition of Secret Mantra, Volume Two: Deity Yoga* (Boulder: Snow Lion, 2017)

English translation (chap. 4): H.H. the Dalai Lama, Dzong-ka-ba, and Jeffrey Hopkins. *Yoga Tantra: Paths to Magical Feats* (Ithaca, NY: Snow Lion Publications, 2005). Revised edition: Tsongkhapa, with a commentary by the Dalai Lama. Translation, editing, and explanatory material by Jeffrey Hopkins. *The Great Exposition of Secret Mantra, Volume Three: Yoga Tantra* (Boulder: Snow Lion, 2017)

English translation (chaps. 11 and 12): Thomas F. Yarnall. *Great Treatise on the Stages of Mantra (sngags rim chen mo) : (Critical Elucidation of the Key Instructions in all the Secret Stages of the Path of the Victorious Universal Lord, Great Vajradhara) : Chapters XI-XII, The Creation Stage* (New York: American Institute of Buddhist Studies, 2013)

Great Exposition of the Stages of the Path / Stages of the Path to Enlightenment Thoroughly Teaching All the Stages of Practice of the Three Types of Beings / Great Exposition of the Stages of the Path Common to the Vehicles

lam rim chen mo / skyes bu gsum gyi nyams su blang ba'i rim pa thams cad tshang bar ston pa'i byang chub lam gyi rim pa

Tibetan digital reprint edition: In *gsung 'bum (tsong kha pa, bla brang par ma)*. TBRC W22273.13:51026 (PDF of bla brang: bla brang bkra shis 'khyil, [199?])

(Delhi: Ngawang Gelek, 1975). Also: (Delhi: Guru Deva, 1979)

P6001, vol. 152

Edited Tibetan: Tsultrim Kelsang Khangkar. *The Great Treatise on the Stages of the Path to Enlightenment (Lam Rim Chen Mo).* Japanese and Tibetan Buddhist Culture Series, 6 (Kyoto: Tibetan Buddhist Culture Association, 2001)

English translation: Lamrim Chenmo Translation Committee. *The Great Treatise on the Stages of the Path to Enlightenment.* 3 vols. Joshua W.C. Cutler, editor-in-chief, Guy Newland, editor (Ithaca, NY: Snow Lion Publications, 2000–2004)

English translation of the part on the excessively broad object of negation: Elizabeth Napper. *Dependent-Arising and Emptiness,* 153–215 (London: Wisdom Publications, 1989)

English translation of the part on the excessively narrow object of negation: William Magee. *The Nature of Things: Emptiness and Essence in the Geluk World,* 179–192 (Ithaca, NY: Snow Lion Publications, 1999)

English translation of the parts on calm abiding and special insight: Alex Wayman. *Calming the Mind and Discerning the Real,* 81–431 (New York: Columbia University Press, 1978; reprint, New Delhi, Motilal Banarsidass, 1979)

Small Exposition of the Stages of the Path / Medium-Length Exposition of the Stages of the Path to Enlightenment to be Practiced by Beings of the Three Capacities

lam rim chung ba / skyes bu gsum gyis nyams su blang ba'i byang chub lam gyi rim / lam rim 'bring

Tibetan digital reprint edition: In *gsung 'bum* (*tsong kha pa, bla brang par ma*). TBRC W22273.14:5–474 (PDF of bla brang: bla brang bkra shis 'khyil, [199?])

(Dharmsala, India: Tibetan Cultural Printing Press, 1968); (Delhi: Ngawang Gelek, 1975). Also: (Delhi: Guru Deva, 1979)

English translation of the section on special insight:

Jeffrey Hopkins. In *Tsong-kha-pa's Final Exposition of Wisdom* (Ithaca, NY: Snow Lion Publications, 2008)

Robert Thurman. "The Middle Transcendent Insight." *Life and Teachings of Tsong Khapa,* 108–185 (Dharmsala, India: Library of Tibetan Works and Archives, 1982)

Edited Tibetan text and Japanese translation of the section on special insight: Tsultrim Kelsang Khangkar and Takada Yorihito. *A Study of Tsong khapa's Mādhyamika Philosophy 1: Annotated Japanese translation of the Vipaśyanā Section of Medium Exposition of the Stages of the Path (Lam rim).* Tsong kha pa chuugan tetsugaku no kenkyuu 1, Bodaidousidairon chuuhen, kan no shou: wayaku, Tsultrim Kelsang Khangkar and Takada Yorihito (Kyoto: Buneido, 1996)

Japanese translation: Tsultrim Kelsang Khangkar and Takashi Rujinaka. *The Treatise on the Stages of the Path to Enlightenment by rJe Tsong kha pa: An Annotated Japanese Translation of Byang chub Lam rim chung ba* (Kyoto: Unio Corporation, 2005)

P6002, vol. 152

Varabodhi (*byang chub mchog;* also, *ye shes mchog*)
Clear Realization of Susiddhi
susiddhikarasādhanasaṃgraha
legs par grub par byed pa'i sgrub pa'i thabs bsdus pa
P3890, vol. 79
Yeshay Gyaltshan (*ye shes rgyal mtshan,* 1713–1793)
Illumination of the Meaning of Action Tantra
bya rgyud don gsal
Collected Works, vol. 9 (New Delhi: Tibet House, 1976)

Index

Shambhala Publications
2129 13th Street
US-CO, 80302
US
https://www.shambhala.com
617-424-0030

The authorized representative in the EU for product safety and compliance is

eucomply OÜ
Pärnu mnt 139b-14
ECZ, 11317
EE
https://www.eucompliancepartner.com
hello@eucompliancepartner.com
+372 536 865 02

ISBN: 9781611803587
Release ID: 157594684

www.ingramcontent.com/pod-product-compliance
Lightning Source LLC
LaVergne TN
LVHW101345280826
846697LV00028B/159
* 9 7 8 1 6 1 1 8 0 3 5 8 7 *